The Capture of
the USS *Pueblo*

The Capture of the USS *Pueblo*

The Incident, the Aftermath and the Motives of North Korea

JAMES DUERMEYER

McFarland & Company, Inc., Publishers
Jefferson, North Carolina

LIBRARY OF CONGRESS CATALOGUING-IN-PUBLICATION DATA

Names: Duermeyer, James, 1946–
Title: The capture of the USS Pueblo : the incident, the aftermath and the motives of North Korea / James Duermeyer.
Description: Jefferson, North Carolina : McFarland & Company, Inc., Publishers, 2019 | Includes bibliographical references and index.
Identifiers: LCCN 2018057316 | ISBN 9781476675404 (softcover : acid free paper) ∞
Subjects: LCSH: Pueblo Incident, 1968. | Korea (North)—Foreign relations—United States. | United States—Foreign relations—Korea (North)
Classification: LCC VB230 .D84 2019 | DDC 359.3/4320973—dc23
LC record available at https://lccn.loc.gov/2018057316

BRITISH LIBRARY CATALOGUING DATA ARE AVAILABLE

ISBN (print) 978-1-4766-7540-4
ISBN (ebook) 978-1-4766-3555-2

© 2019 James Duermeyer. All rights reserved

No part of this book may be reproduced or transmitted in any form or by any means, electronic or mechanical, including photocopying or recording, or by any information storage and retrieval system, without permission in writing from the publisher.

Front cover images *from top:* Crewmen of USS *Pueblo* (AGER-2) leave a U.S. Army bus at the United Nations Advance Camp, following their release by the North Korean government at the Korean Demilitarized Zone on 23 December 1968 • Representatives of the United States and North Korean governments meet at Panmunjom, Korea, to sign the agreement for the release of the *Pueblo* crew, 22 December 1968. Major General Gilbert H. Woodward, U.S. Army, Senior Member, United Nations Command Military Armistice Commission, is in the left foreground, with his back to the camera • USS *Pueblo* (AGER-2), off San Diego, California, 19 October 1967 (official U.S. Navy photographs)

Printed in the United States of America

McFarland & Company, Inc., Publishers
 Box 611, Jefferson, North Carolina 28640
 www.mcfarlandpub.com

To the brave officers and enlisted men of the
USS *Pueblo* who suffered months of cruel torture
and mistreatment at the hands of their North Korean
captors. In spite of the physical and psychological
damage inflicted on the crew, their faith and hope
sustained them in their darkest hours. I salute them all.

Acknowledgments

A special thank you to my wife, Janet, who encouraged me in my goal to take a different and fresh look at the fate of the USS *Pueblo* and its crew.

I also wish to thank Dr. Joyce Goldberg, professor of history at the University of Texas at Arlington, who kindly encouraged me, and offered sage advice while I wrote the book.

Table of Contents

Acknowledgments vi

Abbreviations ix

Preface 1

Introduction 4

ONE—The Ships 7
    Destroyers and Liberty Ships 7
    USS Liberty 8
    Clickbeetle—The Spy Ships 16
    The Pueblo 19
    Orders 24
    Rule of the Sea 26

TWO—Leadership and Risk Analysis 28
    Leadership 28
    Risk Analysis 31

THREE—Reactions 50
    On the Pueblo 50
    Within the Military Chain of Command 59
    Within the Intelligence Community 61
    In South Korea 63
    In the Situation Room, Washington 65
    At the White House 67
    Reaction of Congress 87
    Reaction of the Public 90

FOUR—*Juche***—Why North Korea Seized the *Pueblo*** 99
    The Washington Viewpoint 99
    The North Korean Perspective 100
    Juche 103

Table of Contents

Elements of Juche   104
The Propaganda of North Korea   106
The Effect of Juche *and Kim's Propaganda on the Treatment of the* Pueblo *Prisoners*   109

Five—Negotiations for Freedom   132

Six—The Navy Court of Inquiry   151

Epilogue   163

Chapter Notes   173

Sources Consulted   189

Index   195

Abbreviations

AGTR Auxiliary General Technical Research
AKL Auxiliary Cargo, Light
CandC Command and Control
CIA Central Intelligence Agency
CINCPAC Commander in Chief Pacific
CINCPACFLT Commander in Chief Pacific Fleet
AGER Auxiliary General Environmental Research
CDR Commander
COMINT Communications Intelligence
CNO Chief of Naval Operations
CNFJ Commander Naval Forces Japan
CO Commanding Officer
COMSEVENTHFLT Commander Seventh Fleet
CT Communications Technician
DIA Defense Intelligence Agency
DMZ Demilitarized Zone
DPRK Democratic People's Republic of Korea (North Korea)
DTG Date Time Group
ELINT Electronic Intelligence
HUMINT Human Intelligence
IFF Identification Friend or Foe
JCS Joint Chiefs of Staff
JRC Joint Reconnaissance Center
KORCOM Korean Communist
KPA Korean People's Army (North Korea)
KWP Korean Worker's Party (North Korea)
KGB Committee for State Security in the Soviet Union
LBJL Lyndon Baines Johnson Library

Abbreviations

LCDR Lieutenant Commander
LT Lieutenant
LTJG Lieutenant Junior Grade
MAC Military Armistice Commission
MIG Mikoyan-Gurevich (Former Russian Aircraft Builder)
MND Ministry of National Defense (North Korea)
NAVSECGRU Naval Security Group
NKN North Korean Navy
NMCC National Military Command Center
NSA National Security Agency
NSC National Security Council
ROK Republic of Korea (South Korea)
ROKJCS Republic of Korea Joint Chiefs of Staff
ONI Office of Naval Intelligence
ONIP Office of Naval Intelligence Publications
PFIAB President's Foreign Intelligence Advisory Board
SDS Students for a Democratic Society
SECDEF Secretary of Defense
SIGINT Signal Intelligence
SITREP Situation Report
U.N. United Nations
UNC United Nations Command
USS United States Ship
USSR Union of Soviet Socialist Republics

Preface

The attack and seizure of the USS *Pueblo* by the North Korean Navy on a frigid day in January 1968 captured world attention and angered the American public during one of the most tumultuous decades in U.S. history. Further fanning national furor was the death of one crew member and the imprisonment of the *Pueblo's* crew of eighty-three American sailors. The *Pueblo* incident was another of many distracting issues that sidetracked the presidency of Lyndon Johnson. Historians Warren Cohen and Nancy Bernkopf Tucker opined that, "In many ways the *Pueblo* affair proved a fitting capstone for a troubled presidency."[1] Of course, the *Pueblo* incident assumed a low priority in comparison to the Vietnam War, the overarching geopolitical obsession of the Johnson presidency.

Within the command structure of the U.S. Navy, which I was part of for twenty years, never-ending debates swirled about where to place the blame for the loss of the ship and crew. Historical, hide-bound Navy tradition dictates that the commanding officer of a U.S. Navy ship is ultimately responsible for whatever happens to a ship under his/her command. This tenet serves well, unless the Navy has overloaded the command with numerous restrictive directives. Questionable leadership within the National Security Agency (NSA) and the Navy placed the *Pueblo* in an indefensible situation. Using the ultimate responsibility axiom, myopic Navy leadership took steps to punish Commander Lloyd Bucher and other crew members for what the Navy perceived as their lack of action against the North Korean attackers. In its narrow focus, the Navy fell short of identifying other points of failed responsibility within the Naval chain of command. The Navy's quick-to-judge tactic of blaming Commander Lloyd Bucher resulted in overwhelming public support for Bucher and his crew, and an embarrassment for the Navy. The action of the Navy's assigning Commander Bucher to be its stalking horse fooled

Preface

no one. The American public learned that a series of blunders on the part of the Navy and the Johnson administration had placed the *Pueblo* in a perilous situation, which was not Bucher's doing. Lieutenant Commander William Armbruster, a Naval Intelligence Officer, writing for the *Naval War College Review* in 1971, examined the effect of public opinion on the Navy's decision following the *Pueblo* Court of Inquiry and wrote, "Public opinion has historically been a potent force to be reckoned with in American political history." He went on to write, "The apparent public hostility during the Court of Inquiry was possibly a factor in determining final disposition by the Navy." He continued, "Many, frustrated by the system, found it easy to identify with Commander Bucher—a helpless victim of an insensitive, unresponsive, military bureaucracy."[2]

Foreign policy blunders were not confined to the Navy. The White House and Johnson cabinet, the National Security Agency (NSA), and Central Intelligence Agency (CIA) all held the same short-sighted, misfocused view of international relations, that is, a belief that smaller communist nations could not act autonomously, but were instead, influenced by either the Soviet Union or China. This global misjudgment reflected a lack of cross-agency intelligence communication and poor leadership, thereby exacerbating an already embarrassing situation played out on the world stage. Following the Second World War and into the early part of the Cold War, the United States was the world's most powerful nation. Yet, America, by the action of the North Koreans, learned a discomfiting lesson from an isolationist, autocratic country of lesser global significance. Members of the Johnson administration and the Navy were left wringing their hands as they weighed answers and responses to the *Pueblo* situation.

My research examines post-incident primary and secondary works, including papers of President Lyndon Johnson, cabinet members of the Johnson administration, CIA, NSA, Congressional hearing records, Congressional Records, firsthand accounts of USS *Pueblo* officers and crew members, as well as authors who have examined isolated leadership deficiencies regarding the *Pueblo* incident.

Today, North Korea remains an isolated, guarded, and dangerous country. Insight into the political actions of the country is not always evident. What is evident is that North Korea continues to be in the world news as a country with a hidden sense of inferiority, desperately wishing to be recognized as a formidable, if not superior, world power by its near-constant saber rattling and outright threats voiced toward those nations that it perceives as enemies, most specifically, the United States.

The capture of the *Pueblo* by North Korea raised a plethora of questions. One that continues to be debated today: Why did North Korea hijack the *Pueblo* and hold the ship and crew? Second, why does North Korea continue to make world threats and demands? Korean political and historical written sources provide perspective to the North Korean actions and answer these questions. An examination of American leadership found that the involved government agencies floundered in formulating answers, ultimately attributing the action to covert instructions from one or both of the major communist powers, China or the Soviet Union. To the contrary, my research would indicate that North Korea acted independently, with its leader at the time, Kim Il-sung, strictly following a blind fidelity to the ideology called *Juche*, a philosophy that demands "independence in politics, self-sufficiency in the economy, and self-reliance in national defense."[3] The capture of the USS *Pueblo* can be attributed to the inadequacy of American leadership and the lack of cross-agency coordination, coupled with Kim Il-sung's allegiance to the ideology of *Juche*. This blind adherence to *Juche* has been passed on to Kim's son, Kim Jong-il, and his grandson Kim Jong-un, the present autocratic leader of North Korea, and remains the bedrock foundation of North Korea today.

Several excellent works have been written regarding the *Pueblo* incident, and some of the ideas of those authors are echoed herein. In addition, a review of the available literature on North Korean foreign policy and political thought reveals a distinct pattern in that country's international relations, propaganda, and overt political actions, all of which demonstrate and confirm the adherence of North Korea's succession of leaders to the ideology of *Juche*.

Introduction

On May 1, 1960, a young Cuban political journalist, Antonio Prohias, learned that he was on the verge of being arrested as a spy, accused of working for the CIA. In fact, he was an award-winning satirical political cartoonist who worked for the Havana daily newspaper *El Mundo*. His views, however, ran contrary to the Castro political machine and fearing incarceration, he fled to the United States. Three months later, he was hired by *MAD Magazine*, where for years, he drew a satirical cartoon called "Spy vs. Spy," which depicted two spies at constant odds, attempting to outwit and assassinate one another.[1] While the cartoon drawn by Prohias was political, tongue-in-cheek satire demonstrating the deadly and costly methods superpowers would use to dominate an adversary, the satire mirrored the real-world political climate that flourished during the Cold War (1947–1991). In reality, the U.S. government was in an all-out covert war of espionage with the Soviet Union and China, with each nation attempting to learn tightly held political and military secrets and gather intelligence from their adversaries. The United States was also not above spying on its allies.

Following the First World War, the U.S. government ventured deeply into espionage, attempting to pry into the confidential affairs of other nations. Officials viewed government sanctioned espionage acts with ambivalence, some favoring them as valuable, while others were critical of such "ungentlemanly practices." The central office conducting these operations was a clandestine branch of the State Department that functioned until 1929 when Henry L. Stimson became Secretary of State and promptly closed down the section. Stimson needed no prompting to take such action. In a later interview, he stated that his reason for eliminating the cryptanalytic section was, "Gentlemen do not read each other's mail."[2] Secretary Stimson would most likely be astonished at the evolution of covert data gathering in the 1960s and beyond.

Introduction

"Intelligence is an institution as old as politics and war. It consists of knowing as much as possible about the opponent, his habits, resources and intentions, a reasonable aim in war, politics, business or personal affairs."[3] Without a doubt, the United States engaged in the clandestine and deadly spy business during the Cold War, and the two major agencies tasked with intelligence gathering were the Central Intelligence Agency (CIA) and the National Security Agency (NSA). They were not alone, as individual agencies often formed one or more of their own intelligence branches. For example, military branches had their own data gatherers. The U.S. Navy's intelligence arm was the Office of Naval Intelligence (ONI), charged with gathering intelligence for use primarily within the Navy.

Just how far has the spy business progressed since the days of Henry Stimson? Code writing ability expanded with the growth of the computer to the point that variations on encryption methodology could be nearly limitless. To break the encryption codes, a computer is required, having the necessary speed and capacity to test every possible solution, and NSA has such a computer with massive capabilities. NSA was established "by presidential directive in 1952 as a separately organized agency within the Department of Defense." Its primary function is "monitoring secure United States communications and an intelligence information mission that involves manning listening posts the world over for monitoring the communications of other nations and processing this usable intelligence...."[4] Because building and decrypting code is the primary function of NSA, today "NSA's headquarters at Fort Meade, Maryland, is the computer capital of the world," and occupies five and a half acres of computer machinery.[5] In 1972, Patrick McGarvey, who worked in the U.S. intelligence community, estimated that NSA processed in excess of over one hundred tons of "paper per day [to] record the radio and Morse codes of other nations' communications intercepted by the National Security Agency."[6] The largest part of NSA's mission is collecting and analyzing communications intelligence (COMINT), signal intelligence (SIGINT), and electronic intelligence (ELINT), data that is gathered using multiple methods.[7] Human intelligence gathering (HUMINT) produces "spy versus spy" scenarios, where individuals are dispatched to foreign sites to mingle with the populace as on-ground eyes and ears. Airborne SIGINT and ELINT platforms include planes, balloons, dirigibles, and gliders used for aerial photography and to monitor ground activities as they collect messages of interest to the Navy's intelligence staff. Adding another layer of bureaucracy in the tasking of spy ships, safety for the ships became the responsibility of the Joint Reconnaissance Center (JRC), an arm of the JCS.[4] The JRC was responsible for coordinating all reconnaissance operations in the air, at sea, and undersea. Proper command and control of spy ships suffered from this multi-layered relationship between NSA, JCS, JRC, and the Navy. The situation, by its nature, contained too many levels of administrative and operational control, resulting in operational inefficiencies in timeliness and command. Peter Blau and Marshall Meyer in *Bureaucracy in Modern Society* wrote that too many layers of bureaucracy only serve to promote inefficiency: "The increasing subdivision of decisions intensifies problems of coordination...."[5] The consequences of this lack of single-source command and control became glaringly apparent in both the USS *Liberty* and *Pueblo* incidents. The attack against the *Liberty* provides historical perspective for the later attack and seizure of the *Pueblo*. Of equal importance is that the calamity of errors precipitating the attack on the USS *Liberty* should have been a watershed moment in time for the U.S. Navy and the NSA, providing a list of practices to be avoided in the future. The fact that it did not drive necessary safety changes for the next class of spy ships is glaring proof of the two agencies' shortsighted leadership.

USS Liberty (AGTR 5)

The USS *Liberty* (AGTR 5) was a converted World War II ship rigged by NSA to be a waterborne listening post. The key word is "rigged." The *Liberty* was not built with the intent of being anything other than a ship to haul cargo. The original name of the *Liberty* was *Simmons Victory*, and the vessel was "designated as a Fleet Issue Ship," in other words, a cargo ship. *Liberty*'s keel was laid on February 23, 1945, in Portland, Oregon, at the Oregon Shipbuilding Corporation as World War II was nearing its conclusion. In less than three months (February 23–May 4, 1945), the completed ship was delivered to the Maritime Commission's War Shipping Administration, but saw no action during the waning days of World War II. The ship was later sold to private companies, changing hands twice before being placed in the reserve fleet in 1948. The *Simmons Victory* was called back into service during the Korean War and made numerous voy-

USS Liberty (AGTR 5)

USS *Liberty* AGTR 5. One of the first converted liberty ship hulls to be used as a spy ship. The *Liberty* was attacked by the Israeli Navy and Air Force at the start of the Six-Day War, 1967 (U.S. Navy photograph).

ages as assigned by the Military Sea Transportation Service in support of allied forces in Korea. On June 11, 1958, *Simmons Victory* entered the National Defense Reserve Fleet in Olympia, Washington.[6] But on March 25, 1963, the ship was transferred to the Navy. *Simmons Victory* was renamed *Liberty* and was refitted to become an Auxiliary General Technical Research Ship and reclassified as AGTR-5 on April 1, 1964.[7] *Simmons Victory*, an aging cargo ship, had been transformed into the USS *Liberty*, an electronics spy ship working for the Navy and NSA. The *Liberty* carried a complement of 294 men, including three marines for security duties and three NSA civilians. In late May 1967, it left its home port of Norfolk, Virginia, and headed for deployment off the coast of Africa. In an attempt to monitor the escalating hostilities that had begun in the Middle East among Egypt, Syria, and Israel, and lacking real-time intelligence information on the conflict, the "National Security Agency requested [concurrence from] the Joint Chiefs of Staff to move the *Liberty*" to the coast of Egypt. On June 2, 1967, the *Liberty* steamed to its assigned listening area

One—The Ships

thirteen miles off the coast of Egyptian-controlled Sinai and thirty-eight miles from the Israeli coast.[8] On June 4, 1967, Israel declared war against Egypt. The *Liberty* was then in the middle of a regional war.[9] Upon realizing the error in placement of the ship, the Navy sent five successive radio messages to the *Liberty*, all of which ordered the ship to depart the area and remain one hundred miles from the war zone. Through ineffectual management, leadership's lack of attention to detail, bloated chains of command/communication, and lack of proper onboard radio equipment, the messages never reached the *Liberty*, and the ship continued to sit in the midst of a war. One of the last messages warning the ship to pull back from the danger area required a confirmation message in order for it to be sent. That confirmation message was misrouted to Hawaii, thereby delaying the message for "an incredible sixteen and a half hours," far too late to save the spy ship and its crew.[10] On the afternoon of June 8, the

USS *Liberty* showing the damage inflicted by the Israelis. The ship is listing to starboard after sustaining severe damage as a result of gunfire, and an Israeli torpedo that struck the ship amidships, killing 34 crew members and wounding 173 (photograph by CT1 Rich Carlson from USS *Pueblo*.org web site).

USS Liberty (AGTR 5)

ship was attacked by the Israeli Air Force and Navy for reasons that are still debated. The ship was not in a position to adequately defend itself against a full-fledged air attack, which resulted in the body of the ship suffering thousands of holes caused by the armor-piercing shells, along with damage to vital equipment. As if that was not severe enough, the attack was continued by Israeli torpedo boats, "which launched torpedoes and fired artillery at the ship. Under the command of its wounded captain, William McGonagle, the *Liberty* managed to avert four torpedoes, but one struck the ship at the waterline."[11] The ship lifted momentarily as a result of the impact and settled back into the water. "The torpedo struck dead center in the NSA spaces, killing nearly everyone inside, some by the initial blast and others by drowning."[12] Captain McGonagle launched three lifeboats, thinking that the ship would probably go down. But even the lifeboats were attacked by the Israeli raiders. The lifeboats that remained on board the *Liberty* were also destroyed by gunfire. Such action is a blatant violation of international law. The *Liberty* did not sink, though the ship listed heavily from its damage. After a two hour attack, the Israelis broke off. The attack resulted in thirty-four U.S. Navy crewmen killed and one hundred seventy-three wounded. With over 800 holes in her hull, miraculously, the *Liberty* was able to leave the area under its own power on June 9, and was met that day by three U.S. Navy warships that escorted the disabled ship to Malta for medical aid for crew members and dry dock for the ship. For his brave action in saving the ship and members of its crew, McGonagle was later awarded the Medal of Honor.

Off the coast of Egypt and Israel, the United States had been caught off guard. "Friendly forces" had failed to keep their friends informed of their operations and locations, resulting in tragedy. Historian Richard K. Smith offered a succinct summary when he stated that a lesson learned from the *Liberty* incident is that "nations do not have 'friends.' They have only interests...."[13] The true interests behind the attack may never be known, but rather than addressing responsibility head-on, the U.S. government initially denied having any U.S. ships in the war zone area.[14] Was this deliberate lie intended for the world community or the American public? What would have been lost if the truth had been revealed immediately? I contend that it is a leadership flaw to deceive rather than to tell the truth when there would be no negative consequences to the security or safety of the audience or the listening asset. The leadership shortcoming of carrying out an act of deceit only serves to exemplify incompetence

One—The Ships

and results in the American public left wondering whether their government is being forthright in keeping Americans safe and informed.

Shortly after the attack on the *Liberty*, Clark Clifford, then Chairman of President Johnson's Foreign Intelligence Advisory Board, conducted an investigation of the incident and concluded that it was "not an intentional attack" by the Israelis.[15] Clifford, however, concluded that "there were gross and inexcusable failures in the command and control of subordinate Israeli naval and air elements." He added that "the unprovoked attack on the *Liberty* constitutes a flagrant act of gross negligence."[16] But there was a great deal of doubt in the credibility of the Israeli account of the attack. For example, the Israelis claimed that following the air attack on the *Liberty*, the Israelis signaled by flashing light, sending "A-A," which means, what is your identity? The Israelis claim that the *Liberty* answered with an identical "A-A," which they claim was proof that the *Liberty* was being evasive. Therefore, they began a torpedo attack on the *Liberty*. However, as Clifford points out in his report, the signal lights on the *Liberty* had been destroyed in the air attack. There were also other inconsistencies in the justification presented by Israel.

Both the Navy and the CIA conducted their own investigations into the incident with findings that echoed Clifford's report. Thereafter, the Johnson administration adhered to the Clifford finding, as have the eight presidential administrations that followed.[17] Perhaps attributing the attack to gross negligence was convenient in light of the fact that "Johnson was probably the best friend Israel ever had in the White House." But Johnson never "lost sight of the fact that Israeli and American interests were not [always] identical." Even so, as the two countries were friends, the United States was providing considerable material and diplomatic support to the Israelis." What was of mutual interest to the two countries was "to settle the matter quickly and quietly, which they did."[18]

Yet, according to historian Robert Dallek, within the Johnson administration there may have been dissenters to Johnson's treatment of the matter. Dallek writes, "Behind the scenes, the highest officials of the U.S. government, including the president, believed it 'inconceivable' that Israel's 'skilled' defensive forces could have committed such a gross error."[19] But was it gross error? Later investigation revealed that an airborne Israeli naval observer had sent a report to the Israeli Chief of Naval Operations. In that report he stated that "the ship cruising slowly off El Arish was an 'electromagnetic audio-surveillance ship of the U.S. Navy, named *Liberty* whose marking was GTR-5.'"[20] If this report is true, then at least a portion of the Israeli military chain of command knew that the *Liberty* was an American vessel. But, perhaps within the Johnson administration it was politically expedient to declare the attack a case of Israeli negligence. After all, there is some evidence that points to an unfortunate lack of due diligence on the part of the Israeli Navy and Air Force. Yet, to the contrary, there is evidence today that the Johnson administration intentionally, above all, "wanted to protect Israel from embarrassment" rather than telling the American public the details of the attack on the *Liberty*.[21] To that end, Navy and NSA officials even threatened members of the *Liberty* crew with "court martials and jail time" if they ever told anyone what had truly happened to the spy ship.[22] An attempt to cover up the event seems to have been put in place.

Even today, conspiracy theorists contend that Israel and the United States colluded in an attack on the spy ship in an effort to blame Egypt and thereby bring the United States into the war on the side of the Israelis.[23] While that speculative opinion seems unlikely, the Soviets also attempted to seize a propaganda moment in history. Yevgeny Primakov, who at the time was working as a journalist for *Pravda*, wrote that it was a case of collusion between the United States and Israel.[24] Now, nearly fifty years after the incident, controversy still swirls as to whether or not the Israelis intentionally attacked the *Liberty* and what could have been the possible motive for doing so. On June 8, 2007, the *San Diego Union Tribune* carried an article written by retired Navy Captain Ward Boston, Jr., who served as legal counsel during the Navy Court of Inquiry into the *Liberty* attack. In his article and in a written declaration, he contended that the attack was certainly intentional.[25]

An interesting corollary to Boston's opinion is voiced by James Bamford in his book, *Body of Secrets.* He wrote that the Israelis built their war strategy against Egypt and concealed the plan behind "a carefully constructed curtain of lies. Lies about the Egyptian threat, lies about who started the war, lies to the American president, lies to the U.N. Security council, lies to the press, lies to the public."[26] Bamford quotes historian Richard K. Smith, who "noted in an article on the *Liberty* for *United States Naval Institute Proceedings,* 'any instrument which sought to penetrate this smoke so carefully thrown around the normal fog of war would have to be frustrated.'"[27] If this was indeed the case, it was in Israel's best interest to eliminate a spy ship that could intercept vital communi-

One—The Ships

cations that might ultimately part the veil of lies that Israel relied upon to commence the attack on Egypt. But, just like other theories regarding the cause of the Israeli attack on the *Liberty,* without concrete proof, they remain theories. Why does the controversy continue? In the words of McGeorge Bundy, President Johnson's chairman of a special committee in charge of the Middle East crisis, "The American people love conspiracy."[28]

Whether or not the attack on the *Liberty* was unintentional or for some other unknown reason is immaterial fifty years after the incident. Our focus, instead, is on the point of reference that the ship was sent to an escalating war theater through faulty leadership decisions on the part of the Navy and NSA, thereby causing death and injury to American sailors. Adding to the situation was the fact that the ship was not properly prepared with the best equipment (the ship had faulty communication capabilities) to receive instructions to vacate the area. It seems inconceivable that the Navy would send one of its ships to sea without adequate radio equipment and the most expeditious message routing protocol locked into place for radio traffic. Yet, as we will see, the USS *Pueblo* travelled under the same leaky communication umbrella.

The *Liberty* Incident is discussed in some detail for a purpose. It is useful to study the *Liberty* incident because there is a striking similarity between factors that placed both the *Liberty* and the *Pueblo* in harm's way, as the *Liberty* event was on June 8, 1967, and the *Pueblo* incident occurred seven months later on January 23, 1968. Lessons learned from the *Liberty* debacle should have been applied to future spy ship missions, yet both incidents raise questions about poor leadership oversight and attention to detail, coupled with inadequate communication capabilities that led both ships to disaster. As with the *Pueblo* incident, the Navy conducted a Court of Inquiry to investigate the circumstances that led to the attack on the *Liberty.*[29] Rear Admiral Isaac Kidd, Jr., served as president of the board, whose findings on the *Liberty* incident included:

1. Command and Control of the *Liberty* was exercised by senior echelons in the chain of command, not at the ship level. Directing and planning of the ship's actions and movements were discussed at higher command levels without including the ship and/or informing it by using immediate communication.[30]
2. Radio traffic relay stations tasked with sending messages to the

Liberty were inadequately staffed and were not briefed on the priority and mission of the spy ship. Nor did these stations send messages according to precedence order, meaning that *Liberty* did not receive its message traffic in a timely manner. If precedence protocol had been followed, *Liberty* may have been able to move from the area and avert the subsequent disaster.[31]
3. The *Liberty* had outdated radio equipment and lacked back-up signaling devices on board to communicate with the Israeli attackers.
4. Due to inadequate communication, senior echelon commands did not know where the *Liberty* was physically located as late as the fifth of June, only three days before the ship was attacked. Without that information, it may have been more difficult to immediately send aid to the disabled ship.[32]

Admiral John S. McCain, Jr., Commander of the U.S. Atlantic fleet, sent a summary message to the Chief of Naval Operations regarding the Court of Inquiry findings. In that message he stated, "Communications limitations continue with us. Improvements in equipment never seem quite able to fully offset load increases and the ever present personnel error. Where such combine with staffing delays and completely unexpected actions through mistake by another state, the results cannot be other than explosive in international potential."[33]

The failure to provide proper communication systems was not lost on Congress. At a congressional hearing before the Subcommittee on Department of Defense held on April 8, 1968, Democratic Congressman Robert Lee Fulton Sikes of Florida had already discerned the leadership shortcomings, especially the failure to provide proper communication equipment for the *Liberty*, when he stated, "A general conclusion could be drawn from the staff reports that the use and operational capabilities of the Defense Communications system is nothing less than pathetic, and that the management of the system needs to be completely overhauled."[34] Republican Congressman John Jacob Rhodes of Arizona echoed this sentiment at the hearing when he stated that the handling of messages meant to be sent to the *Liberty* was "a comedy of errors."[35] And finally, as recorded in the *Congressional Record* on July 12, 1968, Republican Congressman Seymour Halpern of New York stated, "I was shocked to learn that a Navy communications 'foul-up' led to the presence of the U.S.S. *Liberty* off the

Sinai coast in June 1967, where it was mistaken for an Egyptian vessel and attacked by Israeli torpedo boats and planes."[36]

The Navy and NSA placed the *Liberty* in harm's way. The ship was sent into an unstable and escalating war zone, unable to properly communicate with its chain of command or adequately identify itself to observers and subsequent attackers. Admiral McCain's response to the Court of Inquiry seems to show little regard for the loss of thirty-four sailors and injury to one hundred seventy-three others. In addition, the Court of Inquiry found no American individuals responsible for this tragedy. This seems to be a case of senior NSA and Navy officers covering for their counterparts or failing to focus on essential details of the ship's mission and subsequently pinpoint and take responsibility for these errors. Unfortunately, failure to accept responsibility and nearly-identical leadership foibles reoccurred in the *Pueblo* incident.

The findings of the *Liberty* Court of Inquiry revealed several issues regarding spy ships that needed to be addressed and corrected in order to prevent such incidents in the future. While communication failure was one issue, management's poor attention to detail was never mentioned. Glaringly significant, the fact that the capture of the USS *Pueblo* occurred only a matter of months after the attack on the *Liberty* demonstrates that American leadership, whether military or governmental, failed to examine its own practices of command and control in addition to not providing adequate protection to the ships and men placed in harm's way. Were the findings and recommendations just so much lip service? An examination of the *Pueblo* Incident may help to answer that question.

Clickbeetle—The Spy Ships

Even prior to the *Liberty* incident, Navy officials had become "disenchanted with the entire NSA ocean-going program," seeing themselves as nothing more than "seagoing chauffeurs and hired hands for NSA."[37] The loss of the USS *Liberty* demonstrated the immense danger inherent in operating a spy ship, yet the Navy wanted its own surveillance ships, separate and apart from NSA intervention. NSA, of course, wished to retain control of the spy ships. At the Navy's insistence, compromise was reached between the two agencies. Both the Navy and NSA would submit their mission requests to the JCS for consideration. Because the space and per-

Clickbeetle—The Spy Ships

sonnel on board the ships was limited, "most intercepted communications were therefore forwarded to NSA for "more detailed analysis."[38] But there was still the matter of the Navy's wish for its own ships to carry out those missions. The project to obtain and outfit spy ships was given to a pentagon research team led by Dr. Eugene Fubini, a physicist and member of the Pentagon research staff.

Fubini, an Italian immigrant, worked on Pentagon initiatives in the early 1960s.[39] His spy ship project was code-named "Operation Clickbeetle" and involved the reactivation and refitting of three small, moth-balled Navy cargo ships that were designated by the Navy as Auxiliary General Environmental Research (AGER) vessels in a veiled attempt to classify the spy ships as ocean research ships instead of ELINT collectors. But in fact,

USS *Banner* AGER 1. The first of the smaller intelligence ships that followed the liberty class ships. *Banner* experienced similar problems as *Pueblo* with faulty communication gear and harassment by the Soviets and Chinese (U.S. Navy photograph).

One—The Ships

they were "electronic and radio intelligence gathering, small non-combatant naval ships that" would operate "close to potential enemies."[40] The first built was the USS *Banner* (AGER 1), followed by the *Pueblo* (AGER 2) and the *Palm Beach* (AGER 3).[41] At 176 feet in length, these ships were much smaller than their predecessor *Liberty* class spy ships, which were over 400 feet in length.[42] Their mission would be to collect ELINT, electronic intelligence, for analysis by the Navy and NSA. While the ships were to be under the command of the Navy, the ship's missions could be either a Navy mission, or an NSA mission. The agencies alternated their tasking of the ships. Navy directed missions were called Mode 1, and NSA taskings were Mode 2. "At the time of the *Pueblo's* [capture], the ship was in Mode 1."[43]

The data to be collected included "radar frequencies, pulse repetition rates, IFF (Identification Friend or Foe) signals, and the location of radar sights," as well as open communication.[44] While expectations for the ships may have been high, in an attempt to outfit the ships for the least cost, shortcuts were taken and budgets were cut, resulting in "appalling complacency and shortsightedness in the planning and execution of the *Pueblo's* mission."[45]

The USS *Banner* was the first AGER to set sail. Her mission sent her to the Far East off the northern borders of the Soviet Union, where weather extremes coated the little ship with so much ice that the skipper, Lieutenant (LT) Robert Bishop, worried that the ship was so top heavy there was danger of it rolling over. Budget cutting measures in refitting the ships became more evident on the *Banner* as the crew experienced communication problems and mechanical woes, such as at "least one total breakdown of both her engines."[46] That danger was less significant than others experienced by the *Banner*, as the ship was harassed by the Soviets, who bumped the ship, buzzed it with MIGs[47] and helicopters, and threatened it with cannon fire. According to Sam Tooma, who was a civilian oceanographer on the *Banner*, the crew was told never to talk about their altercations with the Soviets.[48] At one point the *Banner* was surrounded by "Communist Chinese trawlers" in the Yellow Sea and aggressively rammed by a "Russian patrol vessel," facts that were revealed in a conversation between Bishop, *Banner's* commanding officer, and Lieutenant Commander (LCDR) Lloyd Bucher just prior to Bucher taking command of the USS *Pueblo*.[49] This life-threatening harassment should have served the Navy and NSA as lessons learned; perhaps these spy ship missions were more dangerous than perceived by agency officials, facts that should have been considered in mission risk analysis. Operation Clickbeetle, as implemented by the Navy and NSA, sent small, lightly-armed, hastily reconfigured ships into harm's way, into missions fraught with danger. But the missions of the *Banner* were wildly successful. Literally reams of "intercepts [were] sent back to Washington exceed[ing] expectations."[50] NSA and the Navy wanted still more. *Banner's* missions were expanded to include incursions near China and North Korea, and the conversion of a second spy ship was hastened. In 1967, the USS *Pueblo* was the second AGER to sail, and her mission would prove catastrophic.

The Pueblo

Commander (CDR) Lloyd M. Bucher was ordered to the USS *Pueblo* and took command of the spy ship in 1967 as it was being refitted in the shipyard at Bremerton, Washington. The transition from its previous role as an inter-island, auxiliary cargo carrier to its new mission as a spy ship required nearly a year, with the ship finally commissioned in ceremonies on May 13, 1967. In *Bucher: My Story,* the commander described the multitude of problems associated with converting and bringing the *Pueblo* online. Many of the budget-cutting measures became apparent during refitting, as the ship received scant attention from Washington Navy officials. Unnecessary and bulky equipment remained on the ship from its previous cargo-carrying role. The lifeboat was in the wrong place, the galley was too small, and the ship was lacking a proper interior communication system. Improper armament had been ordered, and the external communication equipment was balky. Lieutenant Junior Grade (LTJG) Carl "Skip" Schumacher, the operations officer on the *Pueblo* in charge of the ship's communication gear, summarized communication capabilities when he stated, "Communications had been a problem on the *Pueblo* ever since she had been commissioned." He went on to write that, "The *Banner* had [encountered] great difficulty" [in communication] in the same geographic area off the coast of Korea.[51]

One of the most telling examples of lack of attention to detail by the Navy was the absence of proper oversight of classified material, equipment, and documents assigned to the *Pueblo* during the fitting out of the ship. Not only did the Navy send all classified equipment and publications

One—The Ships

The *Pueblo* was an Army ship before it was converted to a Navy freighter. This photograph is of the Army FP 344, later to become the *Pueblo* (U.S. Navy photograph).

they believed were needed for *Pueblo* to carry out its mission, they also sent all classified material that would normally be assigned to a small Navy cargo ship. Apparently, in the Navy chain of command, not everyone knew that the former Navy cargo ship was now a spy ship and not a cargo carrier. Therefore, *Pueblo* received a double allotment of classified material, plus all secret material required by the on-board crypto personnel. In some cases there were as many as ten copies of superfluous publications sent to the ship. While the *Pueblo* security officer had been able to return some of the shipments, the sheer volume was overwhelming. So uncoordinated was the agencies' assignment of classified material to the small ship, that the ship even received an additional shipment of classified material the morning it set sail on its first mission. The ship had no choice but to carry an over-allowance of classified material. In addition, the ship did not have

The Pueblo

the equipment or the means to properly destroy classified material, and the commanding officer and the security officer were well aware that they did not have enough weighted bags on the ship to properly jettison the material if an emergency situation occurred.[52] Apparently the Navy did not see this as a problem, even though Commander Bucher had asked his chain of command for proper self-destruction capabilities while the ship was being fitted out.

The Navy simply did not want to hear about problems associated with the refitting of the small spy ship. The ship was a low priority item in the Navy's much bigger Vietnam War efforts. As a result, inefficiencies and problems received little attention in Washington. Navy officials did take note, however, when it was discovered during the refitting that all electronic intelligence gear on the *Pueblo* had been installed upside down

USS *Pueblo* AGER 2 (photograph from U.S. Naval History and Heritage Command).

One—The Ships

in the communication spaces. Even so, when Bucher continued to demand that deficiencies be corrected before sea trials, Navy and shipyard authorities showed an impatience "that stemmed from their intense desire to be rid of a mess diverting their attention from servicing units urgently needed in the escalating Vietnam War."[53]

Problems persisted with the *Pueblo* during sea trials as the steering mechanism malfunctioned each of the first two days of testing, leaving the ship unable to steer itself and necessitating a tow back to its Bremerton, Washington, berth. *Pueblo* left Bremerton in September 1967 and moved to San Diego to undergo refresher and predeployment training. At the end of this training, the ship was inspected by the Commander, Service Group One to ensure that the ship was ready for sea. LTJG Schumacher, *Pueblo's* operations officer summed up that inspection. "The inspecting team that came aboard found that many questions on their list did not

The USS *Palm Beach* AGER 3. The *Palm Beach* saw little action as the Clickbeetle project came to a close, and the spy ships were decommissioned shortly after the *Palm Beach* came on line (U.S. Navy photograph).

apply or could not be answered by *Pueblo* officers for security reasons. Frustrated, they gave up and declared us ready—for something."[54]

Steering problems continued to be experienced as the ship was transiting to Pearl Harbor after leaving San Diego, breaking down at least "twice a watch," (twice every four hours).[55] The same thing occurred when *Pueblo* reached its home port in Yokosuka, Japan. The steering mechanism again had malfunctioned, and the ship had to be berthed in Japan by a yard tug.[56]

The Navy and NSA wanted sea-borne spy platforms. Mining electronic data was the priority, not the hazardous conditions inherent in the mission, the safety of the ship and crew, or in what mechanical condition the platforms arrived on site. The cobbled together spy ships would remain a low priority of the Navy, and this lack of attention by appropriate officials would reap a calamitous result. "The *Pueblo* would sail into the Sea of Japan for operations off the North Korean east coast poorly prepared for its mission and subsequent actions by the North Koreans."[57]

After reaching Pearl Harbor on November 14, 1967, Commander Bucher paid a visit to Commander in Chief Pacific Fleet (CINCPACFLT) headquarters. While there, he spoke with an intelligence officer and later to Captain George L. Cassell, Chief of Staff of Operations for CINCPACFLT. Bucher learned that his first mission would be off the coast of North Korea. Perhaps Bucher was clairvoyant. He wrote, "I was moved to ask ... what happens if they [North Koreans] attack us when on station outside their claimed twelve-mile territorial limit?" The answer he received from Captain Cassell was ironic. Bucher was told, "actual violence is considered highly unlikely to occur." Cassell added, "In the unexpected event of a serious attack against *Pueblo*, it would probably happen beyond the range of immediate assistance. We've got plans written. But you can count on everything being done as quickly as possible to come to your assistance and that in any case a retaliation would be mounted within twenty-four hours. Contingency Plans for such an occurrence are written and approved. *We consider the risk to be nominal if not nonexistent.*"[58] Bucher left that meeting feeling optimistic because he had been told that in case of trouble, "there was some definite plan to take care of contingencies."[59]

Because we know the outcome of the *Pueblo* mission, we can adduce a pattern in the Navy's approach to operational control of the spy ships. Responses to issues of operational importance border on arrogant and cavalier. The Navy's "can do" attitude is admired when results are favorable. When results are unfavorable, or detrimental, there is a follow-up pattern of senior officials searching for scapegoats instead of accepting responsibility. What other possible reason would Captain Cassell have had in first advising Bucher that all manner of military assistance would come to the *Pueblo* in the unlikely event that the ship found itself in trouble with the North Koreans, but later at the post-capture court of inquiry, denying that he had ever made such a statement. Such a denial has only one plausible explanation, and that would be to absolve Cassell from any wrongdoing in making such a promise in the first place.

Orders

On December 1, 1967, *Pueblo* reached Yokosuka, Japan, which was to be its home port. Bucher and the *Pueblo* would be under the operational control of the Commander Naval Forces Japan (CNFJ), led by Rear Admiral Frank L. Johnson. Johnson's decision-making and operational directions would play a significant role in *Pueblo's* fate.

On December 31, 1967, *Pueblo* received its operating orders from CNFJ (Admiral Johnson), orders that described the overall mission of *Pueblo's* first foray as a spy ship. The orders stated that *Pueblo* would operate in the Sea of Japan to monitor naval activity off the coasts of four North Korean ports while "sample[ing] the electronic environment" and "conducting surveillance of Soviet Naval Units."[60] *Pueblo* was to remain thirteen nautical miles from the coast of North Korea, and while cruising off North Korea's coast, the spy ship was to monitor and determine the nature and extent of North Korean naval activity around the ports of "Chongjin, Songjin, Mayang Do, and Wonsan." This information could give NSA analysts clues as to the size and scope of any military installations or operations in those areas. In those same operating orders, there were three other directives that deserve analysis.

First, the *Pueblo* was directed to intercept and conduct surveillance of Soviet naval units. In other words, Bucher and his ship were ordered to place themselves in harm's way even as Navy and NSA officials were well aware that the Soviets had previously harassed, bumped, and threatened the USS *Banner* when it had conducted surveillance of Soviet naval units. Second, the orders stated that *Pueblo* was to "Determine KORCOM (Korean Communist) and Soviet reaction, respectively, to an overt intel-

Orders

ligence collector operating near KORCOM periphery and actively conducting surveillance of USSR naval units." In other words, the directions were to go cruise in the Soviets' back yard to test their reaction to the spy ship's intrusion. Finally, the *Pueblo* was to be alert and report any deployment of Korcom/Soviet (military) units that may be "indicative of pending hostilities or offensive actions against U.S. forces."[61] It would appear to be flawed leadership to deliberately direct a lightly armed U.S. ship and crew into the crosshairs of the Soviet Navy and North Korean military without measuring the risk involved and thoroughly preparing for the safety of the ship and its crew in all possible contingencies. NSA and Navy experts were well aware of the difficulties encountered by the USS *Banner* at the hands of the Soviets during the spy ship's foray into Soviet waters. The *Pueblo* and its crew were secondary to the results in the overall quest for intelligence data.

The *Pueblo* received sailing orders on December 18, 1967, directing the ship to sail on January 8, 1968, for the Tsushima Straits and move to an area off the northern coast of North Korea. From there it was to move slowly south along the North Korean coast.[62] Directive H in those orders is interesting. It stated that "Injolled (definition unknown, perhaps a typo for 'inhold') defensive armament should be stowed or covered in such a manner as to not elicit unusual interest from surveying/surveyed units(s). Employ only in cases where threat to survival is obvious."[63] Admiral Johnson, who oversaw the writing of the sailing orders, remained convinced that the .50-caliber machine guns, the only real armament that *Pueblo* carried, should be stowed below decks, out of sight. He repeated this to Commander Bucher in a meeting on January 3, saying, "I am against arming your ship. It could lead to trouble for you which you are not prepared for." He continued, "I suggest you keep your guns covered and pointed down, or better yet, stow them below decks."[64] On the following day, Johnson inspected the *Pueblo* and told Bucher as he noticed the .50-caliber guns on their mounts, "Remember you are not going out there to start a war." Referring to the guns, he said, "keep them covered and don't use them in any provocative way at all. It doesn't take much to set those damned Communists off and start an international incident. That's the last thing we want."[65]

Perhaps Admiral Johnson was offering what he believed to be sound advice, but either directly or indirectly, he was telling Bucher that the display and/or use of the only defense armament on the *Pueblo* was to remain

One—The Ships

visually off-limits, an odd admonishment to give to the commanding officer of a U.S. Navy ship, especially in light of the blatant threats and aggressive activities lately demonstrated by North Korea. It is flawed leadership, indeed, that directs a subordinate to sail into known danger where it is relatively certain that the adversary will be waiting and also directs him to leave any defensive armament stowed. While we certainly cannot know the underlying motive in Johnson's admonition, could it have been an attempt to ensure that his subordinate would not take an action that might reflect poorly on his own leadership? If so, Johnson might have been better served to simply advise Bucher that in the first indication of any altercation with the North Koreans, to turn his ship seaward (east) and order flank speed to remove himself from harms way.

It is flawed leadership to ignore attention to detail, proper equipping, and defense of a ship with eighty-three men aboard. It is also flawed leadership to send a lightly armed ship and crew into a situation fraught with a multitude of possible catastrophic actions, any one of which could include sinking the ship and killing its crew. Hidebound Navy tradition, multi-layered disjointed bureaucracy, and shortsighted decision-making put the USS *Pueblo* in harm's way. One of the final statements in the operating orders message underscores this blindered thinking. It stated that the estimate of risk to the *Pueblo* for the mission was "minimal, since *Pueblo* will be operating in international waters for the entire deployment."[66] More than anything else, this false assumption proved to be the undoing of the *Pueblo*. This minimal risk assessment derived from the Navy's blind faith in the rule of the sea and faulty Navy and NSA leadership resulted in only a perfunctory attempt to properly analyze the risk associated with the mission of the USS *Pueblo*.

Rule of the Sea

Throughout history, wars of words and swords have been fought over the extent of nations' rights within their individual coastal waters. In the 1960s, a primary tenet employed in the logic of the Navy and NSA when they formed the spy ship fleet and sent the ships on their missions was based upon articles of the 1958 Geneva Convention on the High Seas. Each signatory ratified article 8, which stipulated that "Warships on the high seas have complete immunity from the jurisdiction of any State other

Rule of the Sea

than the flag State," and international law recognized the territorial waters of each country to extend twelve miles from a nation's coast.[67] The faith the Navy and NSA placed in this tenet cannot be overemphasized, because the two agencies, and indeed the entire U.S. government, fully relied on this facet of international law. The United States believed that in accordance with the Geneva Convention of 1958, all nations would comply with the coastal boundary rule. Thus, ships passing by coastal nations could transit unmolested as long as they remained twelve miles or more from that nation's coast. So tightly did the U.S. government and the Navy cling to this point of law that it seemed inconceivable that any nation would flagrantly defy it to the extreme of attacking or capturing a U.S. warship. The fallacy in this reasoning was that there were some nations, including North Korea, that had not signed the document.[68] North Korea paid little attention to world opinion. These facts, apparently, were immaterial to the U.S. leadership that sent the *Pueblo* on its deployment, yet certainly should have entered into the risk analysis preparatory to the spy ship mission, especially in light of the *Liberty* tragedy only seven months earlier. Navy and NSA leadership made only a perfunctory attempt to properly analyze the risk associated with the mission of the USS *Pueblo*. Couple this feeble analysis with multi-layered bureaucratic, fragmented responsibility, and it was a wonder that *Pueblo* ever left port. Clearly, poor risk analysis practiced in the leadership chain of command above *Pueblo's* level proved to be the primary cause of the capture of the *Pueblo*. The deficient risk analysis used for the *Pueblo* mission warrants further examination.

Two

Leadership and Risk Analysis

Leadership

To define flawed leadership, we must first understand the meaning of leadership. An all-encompassing, finite definition of leadership may exist in numerous dictionary sources, but if we sampled a myriad of definitions, we would find that there is not one single hard and fast definition for the term leadership. Multiple definitions prove that the ingredients of leadership may be rife with ambiguities and subject to sociological and political filters. Yet, hundreds of books, articles, and classroom courses are taught under the guise of defining leadership principles. Professor and former Air Force officer Phillip J. Hutchison has written in the *Journal of Leadership Studies,* that the term "leadership" is so broad that it may be an example of an "ideograph." He wrote that an ideograph is, "a single highly recognizable word that acts as a repository for key values that reflect deeply ingrained cultural politics."[1] Common values such as setting goals, leading the way to a goal, nurturing followers, perseverance, skill, respect for subordinates, and other commonly used leadership characteristics easily come to mind and can apply to the leadership ideograph. But there are other less obvious leadership values that bear examination and that were neglected by Navy and administration officials in the events surrounding the capture of the USS *Pueblo.*

A leader must be able to see "the big picture," to see all aspects of the path to goal achievement. The responsible leader must examine the costs of reaching the goal in terms of risk to personnel and materiel. At what point does the risk of damage to personnel, materiel, or political image cancel the project or goal? The risk assessment in the case of the *Pueblo* was perfunctory at best. A rating of minimal risk was rubber stamped by "pedestrian functionaries" at all levels of *Pueblo's* chain of command. Admiral James B. Stockdale, now deceased, wrote extensively on leadership. Stockdale was a prisoner of war for over seven years during the Vietnam War, received the Medal of Honor, was past president of the Naval War College, and was a Vice Presidential candidate in 1992. Stockdale used the term "pedestrian functionaries" to describe individuals who reside within a "business as usual" environment in which "bureaucratic procedure" is "the order of the day." He continued, "In the military, for example, the fortunes of war have a way of throwing commanders into new decision-making territory where there is no one to issue philosophic survival kits."[2] Paraphrasing Admiral Stockdale, in order to meet the demands of a fluctuating wartime scenario, a leader must be open to changing tactics, i.e. to be flexible. But Navy and NSA saw no need for flexibility. Such was the case with the *Pueblo*. Pedestrian functionaries in the NSA and Navy chains of command did not carry out a proper risk assessment of the spy ship mission, instead choosing to rubber stamp the initially assigned minimal risk rating. The big picture was not analyzed by NSA and Navy leadership with flexibility, especially in light of current world situations and warnings, and lessons from previous spy ship experiences were not taken into account in mission planning.

A leader must continue to search for variables by reading and studying the potential issues that could affect the progress toward reaching the goal in order to obtain all aspects of the big picture. The question must be asked, what new and unforeseen aspects might affect our progress? In *Pueblo's* mission, a number of variables arose, most evident of which were the many warnings. A leader must be a student who strives to continually learn of and analyze all variables. But just as important, the leader then must be flexible enough to change the plan as the variables are weighed. The Navy, NSA, and Johnson administration officials neglected to carefully study geopolitical currents and classified material related to North Korea, and to ask probing questions prior to *Pueblo's* sailing. The flexibility to change Pueblo's mission did not seem to be in their decision-making process.

Next, leaders must always assume responsibility for their orders and actions. Stockdale raises the question, "Is the leader willing to commit him[/her]self to the full consequences implicit in his [/her] policies? There is always the temptation to better your own position by thinking only about yourself." Navy leaders in the *Pueblo* chain of command and officials in the Johnson administration were unwilling to take responsibility and admit their mistakes following the capture of the spy ship. Instead, they frantically searched for scapegoats. Stockdale wrote, "You cannot use your profession as a shield from responsibility for your actions," and the good leader needs "the ability to meet personal defeat without succumbing to emotional paralysis and withdrawal, and without lashing out at scapegoats or inventing escapist solutions." In the case of the *Pueblo*, individuals within the Navy chain of command, up to the White House, searched for scapegoats to avoid accepting responsibility. In many cases, the resultant object of their search was the captain of the ship, CDR Lloyd Bucher.

So intent was the Navy to pin the blame for the capture of the *Pueblo* on Commander Bucher that they set in motion a virtual witch hunt in Yokosuka. The Naval Investigative Support Office (NISO) in that city began rounding up all of Bucher's friends and interrogating them. When questioning Bucher's friends, they first played a tape of Bucher's confession and followed that with questions. Surprisingly, "most of their questions concerned Pete's sex life," said one of Bucher's friends. (Bucher was called "Pete" by his closest friends.) "They were really scraping the bottom of the barrel." They asked if Bucher had slept with a number of different bar girls. One can only speculate as to the purpose of this line of questioning, but perhaps they were trying to find out if Bucher had revealed any details to outsiders in a moment of passion. One of the officers being interrogated became so incensed that he took a swing at one of the NISO interrogators. Bucher's friends were then asked if they felt that Bucher was a traitor. There is no indication that any of them answered affirmatively. One NISO official half-heartedly apologized to the interrogation subjects by saying that they "had been given this job to do by Washington, to look into this area. And everyone we've talked to has high regard for this man."[3] It is almost pathetic to see the lack of sane Navy leadership and to learn the lengths that the Navy would go in trying to find or manufacture a scapegoat. The search for a scapegoat was not confined to Yokosuka. The same desperation to point blame was rampant in Washington, as well.

Leaders must be cognizant of history. Stockdale wrote that "to ignore this fund of wisdom is the epitome of vanity." American officials knew the previous hostile actions of the North Korean government, which had frequently attacked South Korean fishing boats and launched numerous raids across the demilitarized zone (DMZ). They also knew the circumstances surrounding the attack on the USS *Liberty* only months before the *Pueblo* mission. And finally, they knew the dangerous difficulties encountered by the *Banner* while on similar missions. If we follow Stockdale's logic, it would seem that Navy and NSA leaders believed that their planning process was somehow superior to previously learned lessons. History was ignored, and the *Pueblo* was sent into a known hostile environment.

Finally, there is another often-heard adage that states that a good leader will not send his followers into a situation that he/she would not be willing to personally undertake. A leader is his/her brother's keeper. The Navy knowingly sent a mechanically marginal, poorly armed ship with eighty-three crew members into harm's way, seemingly daring the Soviets and the North Koreans to confront the *Pueblo*. Knowing the inherent danger, yet throwing caution to the wind, NSA and the Navy ignored the carelessness of such an order in light of the danger, whereas a good leader looks out for the followers and sees to the responsibility for ensuring their safety.

Risk Analysis

Over-confident Navy and NSA reasoning (which Stockdale referred to as "vanity"), on the point of international maritime law governing free passage to ships at sea to be twelve nautical miles from an adversary's coast line, was the bedrock that the Navy and NSA used as the basis for declaring the *Pueblo* mission to be one of minimal risk. While a dangerous, but not calamitous, action off an adversary's coast had occurred during the *Banner* missions, its significance should not have been excluded from consideration. The same flawed reasoning served as the first step in the equally slipshod risk analysis of the subsequent *Pueblo* mission. Assigning a risk label to a spy ship mission was not done unilaterally. Admiral Frank Johnson, in his role as CNFJ and administrative supervisor of the *Pueblo*, initially assigned the rating. His rating then moved up his chain of command. Concurrence with the assigned rating would be obtained from multiple levels of military leadership, the NSA, JCS, and sometimes ended with the Secretary of Defense for approval. That chain of command consisted of CNFJ, CINCPACFLT, Commander in Chief Pacific (CINCPAC), JCS, and the super secret 303 Committee, an arm of the National Security Council in Washington, D.C.[4] The 303 Committee included representatives from the State and Defense Departments, Central Intelligence Agency (CIA), and the White House. They were represented by Richard Helms, Director of Central Intelligence; Nicholas Katzenbach, Under Secretary of State; Paul Nitze, Deputy Secretary of Defense; and Walt Rostow, National Security Advisor to the President. After the capture of the *Pueblo*, Helms testified before congress and stated that the 303 Committee knew this to be a risky mission. They based this on the experiences encountered by the USS *Banner* on a similar mission.[5] But in spite of their concerns, the 303 Committee approved the mission.

With multiple layers of military bureaucracy, opportunities for inattentive leadership and/or a dangerously routine rubber-stamping process could occur. In the case of the *Pueblo* mission, a documented, thorough analysis of risk was simply not completed. To be a proper analysis, the Navy and NSA should have first formed their own explicit definition of risk. Having done so would have enabled them to explore all of the various consequences of a successful or unsuccessful mission. Knowing the possible consequences of mission failure, the Navy and NSA should have investigated and evaluated the effect of those factors and their bearing on the risk. "Yet, history has shown that the politicians [and military] ... regularly undertake commitments incompatible with resources, and ... put forward propositions which are at times dangerous as well as irresponsible."[6]

During the House Armed Services Subcommittee hearings that began on March 4, 1969, Admiral Johnson took responsibility for his actions by stating, "I personally made the initial determination of the risk evaluation." Johnson further stated that he considered such factors as geographical location, political climate, nature and scope of the task, a study of previous missions, whether friendly support forces were available, and if the mission would take place in international waters.[7] While Johnson alleges that he took the foregoing factors into account, it is more believable that he relied most heavily on the fact that the *Pueblo* would be operating in what the United States leaders believed to be international waters. Thus, believing that his risk analysis was complete and thorough, Johnson assigned a rating of minimal risk to the *Pueblo* mission.

Statistician Ralph Strauch, writing for the Rand Corporation, disagreed with Johnson's assessment. He concluded that the *Pueblo* risk assessment proved to be "...significantly deficient."[8] And while Strauch's study was written two years after the capture of the *Pueblo,* his analytical

Risk Analysis

study forms an excellent guide to what should have taken place in evaluating the risk involved in the spy ship mission.

Examining Johnson's criteria, it is possible to see that the geographical location would indicate a hostile, frigid winter scenario, one in which *Pueblo* had never operated, and one where ice build-up on the ship would be a concern. Regarding the political and diplomatic climate, civilian and military officials knew that North Korea exhibited an overt hatred of the United States, a fact that should have served to caution U.S. officials considering spy ship missions off the North Korean coast. Additionally, no support and military aid plan was available, and Naval assets were clearly too far away for assistance.[9] In addition, there had been multiple warnings of a political and military nature that Johnson seemingly ignored. If Johnson, in fact, considered these criteria, it appears that he gave little weight to any of them.

When pressed further, Admiral Johnson later admitted that he initiated the requests for missions for the *Banner* and *Pueblo* and assigned a minimal risk classification to *Pueblo's* mission primarily because *Pueblo* would be operating in international waters, there had been no "North Korean naval activity at sea in January and February" (*Pueblo* was seized at the end of January), and North Korea had not reacted to previous USS *Banner* missions off its coast.[10] In hearings, Admiral Johnson admitted that when assigning the risk factor, no specific criteria were used. This is contrary to what he had earlier testified. Upon learning that no criteria were used to assign the risk to a mission, Michigan Representative Lucien Nedzi, a hearing committee member, asked Johnson, "There is no formal definition of terminology here, you just rely on [the] Webster [dictionary] to help you develop it?" Johnson replied, "In effect," thus answering Nedzi's question affirmatively.[11] It can easily be seen that contrary to recommendations outlined in Strauch's post-incident report, the Navy did not have a grasp of the meaning or definition of the term "risk." It seems incongruous that a risk classification could be assigned to a mission when the true meaning of the word "risk" was not defined. In further testimony, Johnson went on to say:

> Minimal risk means to me that because the ship had the safety which was afforded to it by the right to operate on the high seas in international waters, there was minimal risk overall. However, in certain areas there was a greater degree of minimal risk, if you want to use that kind of a grading, and I tried to make this clear to the committee....[12]

Two—Leadership and Risk Analysis

In his reasoning, and the reasoning of those in the chain of command above him, Admiral Johnson remained fixed to the rule of the sea and admitted that this tenet formed the basis for his risk analysis and assignment of a risk classification. There seems to be little evidence that proper consideration was given to potential consequences and, more importantly, to the effect of external and internal factors bearing on the possible risk. Apparently, the bulk, if not all, of the mission requests originating from Johnson were assigned a minimal risk classification. In Johnson's defense, he was not alone in his lack of attention to detail. As his mission requests moved up the chain of command, the request and assignment of risk was generally rubber stamped by his seniors. For example, when Admiral Ulysses S. Grant Sharp, who was CINCPAC during the time of the *Pueblo* mission (and two levels above Johnson) was asked during later hearings if it was true that all mission requests that came to his desk were classified as minimal risk, he replied, "I would say as a general statement that is probably right." He went on to say that he could not recall any mission being classified other than minimal risk.[13] In addition, there is no indication in Sharp's testimony that he ever changed any risk classification that came to his desk. Admiral Thomas Moorer, CNO and member of the JCS at the time of the *Pueblo* incident and four levels above the Commanding Officer of the *Pueblo*, testified at the hearings that the risk assigned to the spy ship mission was minimal because the *Pueblo* would be operating "totally in international waters." When asked who originally assigned the minimal risk classification to the *Pueblo* mission, Moorer could not name the person responsible. This answer seems astonishing, yet also demonstrates the lack of attention to detail and low priority given the spy ship missions by the CNO and others in his chain of command. But in his defense, it should be remembered that the number one priority with the Johnson administration, and thus, Moorer, was the execution of the war in Southeast Asia. In the *Pueblo* hearing, Moorer went on to say that because it was a minimal risk assignment, "there were no dedicated forces" assigned to come to the aid of the *Pueblo* if the ship got into trouble.[14] Of course, this is contrary to what Commander Bucher had been told by Captain Cassell, Chief of Staff Operations, Commander in Chief Pacific Fleet (CINCPACFLT) in Hawaii prior to the *Pueblo's* sailing.

During the hearings, Admiral Moorer was pressed further by New York Representative Otis Pike and subcommittee Assistant Chief Counsel Frank Slatinshek. They continued to ask the CNO about the mechanics of assigning the risk factor to the *Pueblo* mission. Moorer knew that the risk assignment was faulty and when pressed by questioning, he attempted to have the hearings closed in an effort to keep the inadequate process from becoming public knowledge.[15] Yet, the damage had been done, and cracks in the risk assignment process revealed by Moorer would become wider after the subsequent testimony of Admiral Johnson.[16]

From testimony at the hearings, it is apparent that the risk classification was never questioned after it was assigned by Johnson and forwarded up the chain of command. It is also apparent that possible consequences of failure were not considered nor were internal and external factors bearing on the risk considered. The Navy was blinded by its primary reliance on the international rule of the sea, which it used to set the risk classification, a reliance so strong that it was held from the lowest to the highest echelon in the Navy, as well as NSA and the Johnson administration. These same officials naively believed that all nations would adhere to that rule of the sea governing coastal waters. As a result, possible consequences of a U.S. ship's electronic incursion into North Korean offshore waters were not considered. If consequences of an attack by an adversary had been considered, contingency plans could have been developed to protect the ship and crew, but, as attested to by Admiral Moorer, a well-developed contingency plan was not formulated. "Neither the U.S. Air Force nor the U.S. Navy had set aside any air cover or seaborne assets to assist the spy ship, and their understrength local units could not scramble enough of the right type of planes in time to drive off the *Pueblo's* tormentors."[17] As former political reporter and author Jack Cheevers wrote in *Act of War*, when under attack from the North Koreans, Bucher learned that, "The comforting mantra that international law would shield him on the high seas, so often repeated by Navy brass, had been exposed as a foolish illusion."[18]

A second standard listed by Strauch in the Rand report stated that, "The effect of factors bearing on risk should be carefully evaluated and alternative explanations considered."[19] At the time of the sailing of the *Pueblo*, it was ironic that there were numerous external factors, or indicators, that warranted serious examination for their relationship to the *Pueblo's* mission. None of these indicators was covert, and aside from brutal weather conditions, all can be categorized as chronologically, ever-escalating belligerence on the part of the North Koreans, incidents that should have been used in the risk analysis prior to assigning a risk classi-

Two—Leadership and Risk Analysis

fication to the mission. If a simple "what if" scenario had been bandied about by the Navy and NSA, could a plan B have been formulated? No such alternate plan has been revealed in my research, which on the surface at least, seems very short sighted.

In October 1966, if more attention had been devoted to the North Korean risk indicators, a bedrock fundamental voiced by Kim Il-sung, the autocratic North Korean leader, might have been heeded. In a speech broadcast at the second Workers Party of Korea Conference, Kim repeated a goal that he had held since early in the decade. It was his intent to neutralize the United States in Korea, subvert and liberate the Republic of Korea (ROK), and unify North and South Korea by any means possible, advocating the use of unconventional methods. In Kim's words, "Comrades, the greatest national task confronting the Korean Workers Party (KWP) and the Korean people at the present stage is to accomplish the country's unification and the victory of the revolution on a nationwide scale." Kim continued, "It is also wrong merely to shout against U.S. imperialism without taking concrete action to stop its aggression." To back up his own admonitions to his army and populace, Kim fired ranking officials within the KWP Liaison Department, the Guerilla Guidance Section, and the Propaganda and Instigation Bureau, and sent them to penal camps. He replaced all of these officials with hard-line military officers. He wanted "quick, dramatic results."[20] Clearly, South Korea and its American ally were on notice from Kim.

The verbally hostile North Korean leader put his words into action throughout the period 1966 to 1969. Historians and military scholars have given a name to this period, calling it the Second Korean Conflict, a period of sporadic and intense armed warfare between the Democratic People's Republic of Korea (DPRK) and the ROK, which then, directly or indirectly, involved the United States. During this time, raids across the Demilitarized Zone (DMZ) skyrocketed, with 444 incidents in 1967 versus only 37 in 1966.[21] Mostly unpublicized, fighting between North and South Korean troops in the period 1966 to 1969 took place regularly in skirmishes along the border. "The fighting, originally seen as a nuisance rather than a serious danger, eventually threatened to explode into a crisis of the first magnitude," and "[o]n several occasions, the peninsula teetered on the edge of war."[22] During a visit to South Korea in November 1966, President Johnson and Secretary of State Dean Rusk awoke on November 2, and learned that seven American soldiers in an eight man patrol had been killed during the night by North Korean infiltrators. One American soldier, Private First Class David L. Bibee survived by playing dead, after being severely wounded by grenade fragments.[23] The attack on the American patrol made headlines across the nation, with the *Washington Post* being so bold as to write, "another warning that no reliance can be put on any arrangements with Asian Communism that are not self-enforcing or buttressed by power."[24]

Major General Richard G. Ciccolella, at the next scheduled meeting of the Armistice Commission on November 5, gave a stern verbal warning to the North Koreans across the table, stating:

> Make no mistake. The path of self-destruction that you have [taken] is leading toward more bloodshed. The responsibility for whatever course may develop from continued acts of hostility will rest clearly on your side. The United Nations command will not shirk its duties under whatever conditions exist. Your side is now traveling on a collision course. My mission is to stay at this table until you understand the gravity of the present situation.[25]

The quote from General Ciccolella is included not only to show the seriousness of the situation at the time, but also as an aside to reveal that now, fifty plus years later, the United States is sending essentially the same message to the North Koreans in response to North Korea's goading on the world stage. It is indeed ironic, that North Korea continues a practice started years ago to push itself to the brink of war and self-destruction, with the *Pueblo* incident fitting neatly within that pattern.

The following year, in January 1967, North Korean aircraft crossed into South Korean air space, and North Korean shore batteries fired on and sank a South Korean ship. The North continued to test the defenses of the South by making several amphibious assaults. During one raid, the North Korean military attempted to reach a munitions depot where nuclear weapons were stored by the U.S. and South Korean military. There were at least two ship-to-shore firefights, one in the South and one in the North. In another incident, North Korean artillery fired on and destroyed a South Korean barracks. The U.S. Army responded by building up its defenses and declaring certain areas in and around the demilitarized zone (DMZ) to be hostile fire zones. "Korea had become a combat zone."[26]

Infiltration raids across the DMZ rose steadily. The number of North Korean espionage agents captured or killed rose from 205 in 1966 to 787 in 1967. The South Koreans were naturally concerned about large-scale North Korean military and espionage intrusions. In early November 1967,

Two—Leadership and Risk Analysis

ROK Foreign Minister Choe Kyu-ha met with Secretary of State Dean Rusk, relating to Rusk and warning him that the North Korean intent was to slow down the South Korean economy and "stimulate tension within the country." He also stated that the North Koreans were building new airfields and were being equipped militarily by the Soviets. Because of the increasing threat, the South Korean delegation then asked for more military equipment, including patrol boats and destroyers.[27] This plea to our state department should also have served as a warning of growing North Korean aggression. But perhaps, the warning was blunted by the South Koreans then asking Rusk and his Deputy Assistant Secretary for East Asia, Samuel Berger, to increase South Korean manufacturing firms' participation in providing war materials to the Vietnam front. Choe gave the example of Korean troops in Vietnam "wearing underwear manufactured in the United States." Choe wanted his country to have a chance "to participate in bidding on contracts for delivery of goods and services in Vietnam."[28] While the North Korean incursions were very serious, apparently the ROK delegation could not pass up an opportunity to chase a dollar. After all, as some unknown wag said in the past, "war is good business."

The number of South Korean and American military personnel killed by North Korean incursion patrols rose from 35 in 1966 to 131 in 1967. North Korean aggression was so serious that on November 2, 1967, Arthur J. Goldberg, U.S. Ambassador to the United Nations (U.N.), wrote a six-page letter to the U.N. Security Council to "draw to the attention of the Council and all members of the United Nations the recent sharp increase in the scope and intensity of the North Korean military attacks and other armed activity in Korea in violation of the Military Armistice Agreement signed July 27, 1953." Goldberg's report was very specific, citing infiltration raids by North Korea into South Korea and the DMZ. He wrote that there had been 543 such incidents just in 1967, and included "setting ambushes, laying mines [in the roads near the DMZ that were used by the U.N. forces] … performing raids near the Demilitarized Zone, and … other subversive activities in the interior of the Republic of Korea." He also cited the "over twenty" instances of armed bands landing and coming ashore in the South, causing havoc and attempting to set up organized guerilla activities.[29]

The low intensity war continued and ramped up into 1968. The firefights between the North and South were so plentiful that Major General Gilbert Woodward, who would eventually sign the negotiated settlement agreement freeing the *Pueblo* crew, made this statement: "Communist

Risk Analysis

North Korea has made 1968 the bloodiest year in Korea since 1953."[30] Indications of risk to a lone U.S. spy ship sailing off the coast of North Korea could not have been more clear. Following the capture of the *Pueblo*, "Some 120 North Korean commando agents landed on the east coast of the Republic of Korea (ROK) between October 31 and November 2, 1968, the largest intrusion into the Republic since the end of the war."[31]

There are at least two theories to account for the increased militaristic activities of the North Koreans. One theory, held by Vandon Jenerette, a former U.S. Army officer, as well as others, rests on the contention that the North Koreans were attempting to establish a second war front for the United States, thereby drawing American resources from Vietnam. According to Jenerette, Kim Il-sung made this very clear when he said in a speech that he was appealing to other communist countries to send troops to aid Vietnam in its struggle against the United States.[32] The second theory, held by the South Korean government at the time, was that the North Korean raids were intended to foment unrest and eventual insurrection to bring down the South Korean government, much like what had occurred in Vietnam. Nicholas Sarantakes agrees with this theory, based upon "what little documentation is available," and other scholarly interpretations.[33] If that was the intent of the North Koreans, they greatly underestimated the resolve and dedication of the South Koreans to their own form of government. A fine example of this commitment to their government by the South Koreans is the citizens' participation in the capture of the North Korean guerrillas who made a raid on the South Korean Blue House in an attempt to assassinate South Korean President Park Chung-hee (narrative follows). Was there yet a third theory regarding the North Korean increased militancy? At least one official in the Johnson administration believed there might be, when he/she stated, "The theory goes that the communists are determined to keep the U.S. humiliated as long as we stay in the Far East, and Korea is as good a place as any to keep up the humiliation."[34]

Warnings to top officials continued. On December 7, 1967, John S. Foster, Jr., Director of Defense Research and Engineering, submitted a memorandum to his boss, Secretary of Defense Robert S. McNamara:

> Kim Il-sung has embarked on a course of drastically increased conflict ... [Kim hopes to] cripple the ROK economy, cause the United States to withdraw, and eventually communize the country. A force of special agents is already operating in ROK. [In addition to other actions, Kim] might open the option of conventional air

Two—Leadership and Risk Analysis

> strike and ground attack ... assuming we would not use nuclear weapons This is expected to heat up considerably....[35]

With American involvement in the Vietnam War continuing to escalate in 1967, it is likely that McNamara paid scant attention to linking his research director's memo to spy ship missions.[36]

During 1966–68, North Korean officials became ever more confrontational, warning U.S. officials that espionage at sea and in the air would not be tolerated and that they would take defensive action. Specifically, on January 6, 1968, Radio Pyongyang warned the United States that it was aware of an increase in "provocative acts" by the United States in North Korea's coastal waters. While not stating so directly, the North Koreans most likely were referring to U.S. spy ships sitting off their coast. This was clear warning that parking U.S. ships in North Korean coastal waters would not be tolerated.

Another strong warning that stands as a glaring example of flawed leadership and the consequences of multi-layered bureaucracy took place on December 29, 1967, approximately a week before *Pueblo* left on her ill-fated mission. This warning came from the director of the NSA and was sent to the CNO, cautioning him that the *Pueblo* mission might need to be reevaluated as to its risk.[37] Perhaps because the message was crossing agency boundaries (NSA to Navy), the originator did not want to infringe on another agency's responsibility. Senior levels within NSA felt that their agency should not get involved in a "Navy operational matter," which could lead to the agency's being "open to criticism."[38] As a result, the carefully worded caution did not carry the impact needed. The word "warning" never appeared in the message. Essentially, NSA's message represented a "warning opportunity missed."[39] If the warning had been processed correctly and heeded, it could have prevented the *Pueblo* debacle. Compounding the problem, through human errors at multi-layered communication stations, the message was lost in the communication labyrinth and never seen by CNO, but was seen by the staff at CINCPAC. The message advised that both the North Korean Air Force and Navy were taking more aggressive actions against foreign military incursions into their territory. NSA also cautioned that North Korea was not following generally recognized international protocol pertaining to boundaries.[40] With managerial inattention to detail, the inefficient Navy communication system mishandled the message. The *Pueblo* mission and priority were not changed. In the Navy communication system, the message was not only mishandled, but

Risk Analysis

incorrectly prioritized, misrouted, and never forwarded to JCS, CINC-PACFLT, or *Pueblo*. This was a warning from NSA that was bungled by both the NSA and the Navy, with the Navy later attempting to obfuscate knowledge of the message's existence, a fact that was not lost on the house committee on armed services. In the summary report of the hearings, dated July 28, 1969, committee members wrote the following terse text:

> The handling of the NSA warning message by the Joint Reconnaissance Center, the Joint Chiefs of Staff, the Office of the Defense Intelligence Agency, the Office of the Commander in Chief Pacific, and the office of the Chief of Naval Operations is hardly reassuring. At best, it suggests an unfortunate coincidence of omission; at worst, it suggests the highest order of incompetence.

The committee added:

> The incredible handling of the NSA warning message on the *Pueblo* mission is hardly looked upon with pride by responsible authorities in the Pentagon. It obviously is a proper source of considerable embarrassment. However, the subcommittee is as much concerned with the demonstrated lack of candor of witnesses on this subject as it is with the actual incident itself.[41]

Clearly, the house committee was well aware of the Navy's attempt to obscure the facts surrounding the mishandled NSA message. The bureaucratic layers over the *Pueblo* nearly ensured that messages and communication might be missent, and that was the case with the NSA message. Those operational units that might have been able to come to the aid of the *Pueblo* as it operated off the coast of Korea were CNFJ in Japan, Commander of the Seventh Fleet in the Gulf of Tonkin off Vietnam, CINCPACFLT in Honolulu, CINCPAC in Honolulu, the National Military Command Center in Washington, and the JCS in Washington. In other words, the communication net stretched nearly half way around the world, a distance that "restricted easy and rapid military response to the *Pueblo's* needs."[42] This message, if it had reached the proper recipient, at the very least might have prompted a more detailed examination of the risk to *Pueblo* before the ship sailed. Of interest is the fact that when Navy officials were questioned by a special panel of the House Armed Services Committee headed by U.S. Representative Otis Pike, the Navy never mentioned "the existence of the NSA message." The subcommittee characterized the collective silence (of the Navy officials who testified before them) as "a deliberate effort to bury the warning."[43] Not only did the Navy attempt to bury the message, but so did NSA. According to author James Bamford, in a meeting at NSA's headquarters the morning of January 23, Lieutenant

Two—Leadership and Risk Analysis

General Marshall Carter, head of NSA, was handed a copy of the earlier warning message. After reading it, Carter said, "I don't want anybody in this room to call or to bring to anybody's attention the existence of this message." He further stated that he would be keeping the message in order to "save our ass," if and when the message was ever revealed.[44] His remarks would seem conspiratorial and short sighted on his part.

The seemingly clear warnings from North Korea continued into January 1968. On January 11, Radio Pyongyang issued another warning, stating that as long as the "U.S. Imperialist aggressor troops conduct reconnaissance by sending spy boats, our naval ships will continue to take determined countermeasures."[45] The warning could not have been more clear, and yet the Navy continued to believe that Kim's rhetoric meant little. After all, the spy ship missions were protected by the sovereignty afforded by sailing in international waters, were they not?

During the week of January 13, five days after the *Pueblo* had set sail from Yokosuka, a North Korean statement was reprinted in a Japanese Newspaper, *Sankei Shimbun*. It stated that North Korea would take action against the USS *Pueblo* if it remained in North Korean waters.[46] North Korea had actually named the *Pueblo* in its warning, yet American officials and the Navy took little notice, making no changes in *Pueblo's* mission. Because Japan was a strong military ally of the United States, it would seem that the statement would be quickly forwarded through diplomatic and military channels to the appropriate Washington decision-makers. It is not known if this was done. Nevertheless, *Pueblo's* mission would proceed as planned.

On January 17, 1968, Kim Il-sung attempted his most audacious act to that point. A 31-man North Korean Army detachment dressed in South Korean Army uniforms crossed the DMZ after cutting entry holes in the defensive fencing in the American guarded sector.[47] Their mission was to reach the Blue House, the South Korean president's residence, and "cut off the head of [South Korean President] Park Chung-hee."[48] All the men in the detachment were officers in their mid-twenties, and they had trained for this mission for two years. The North Koreans were well armed with "grenades, automatic weapons, and explosives." But they also had a secondary target, the U.S. embassy in Seoul.[49] They moved slowly, and on January 19, they came upon a group of South Korean woodcutters. Instead of moving away from the woodcutters and proceeding with their mission, the soldiers took the opportunity to attempt to turn the South Koreans

Risk Analysis

against their government by detaining them and undertaking to indoctrinate them by preaching the glories of communism. Here, they made a mistake. They had no way of knowing that when they released the South Koreans and went on with their assassination mission, the South Korean men immediately reported them to the police. It was simply unfathomable to the guerillas that South Koreans would not be enamored with the communist indoctrination issued by the guerillas, and that they would not wish to join in Kim Il-sung's grand plan of reunification of Korea. The key to the guerillas' failure was the strong and full support of the South Korean populace. Some months later, General Charles Bonesteel, Commanding General of the U.S. Eighth Army and commander of the U.N. forces in Korea, was referring to yet another failed attempt at infiltration from the

The Blue House, presidential residence of the President of South Korea. North Korean commandos came within hundreds of meters of the building in a quest to kill South Korean President Park Chung-hee two days before the *Pueblo* was captured (https://stripes.com/news/s-korea-calls-north-s-mock-attack-on-blue-house-childish-1.443995, photograph by Sung Il-Choi/U.S. Army).

Two—Leadership and Risk Analysis

North when he said ... "it was a losing game to begin with for the North because of [their] miscomprehension of the situation in the South."[50]

Not knowing that authorities had been warned, the guerillas continued toward the Blue House in their faux ROK uniforms and came within 800 meters before being stopped at gunpoint. After an intense gun battle, the attackers scattered, but were tracked down near Seoul and captured or killed. The attackers had come to within "eight hundred meters of Park's residence, stopped more by luck and individual initiative than by grand design."[51] All of them were killed except one, who revealed the extent of their training and mission.[52]

This clandestine, insurgency, guerilla manner of fighting with its response by the allies was given a term by the U.S. Army: low-intensity conflict (LIC).[53] Fought with far fewer American troop numbers (hence the term low), LIC guerilla warfare by the North Koreans recorded missions that were sometimes just as deadly as missions with larger troop numbers. As serious as the attempted Blue House attack had been, the event captured only moderate world attention, for example, pushed to page 12 in the *New York Times*.[54] But the attack, followed only two days later by the capture of the USS *Pueblo*, caused great unease in South Korea, infuriating the ROK military, which quietly began making preparations for war against the North.[55] South Korean President Park Chung-hee condoned these preparations for war against North Korea. But as with so many other world issues at the time, President Johnson and Joint Chiefs' Chairman, General Earle Wheeler, saw the warning and the resultant dissatisfaction of the South Koreans only through the prism of the

Park Chung-hee, president of South Korea at the time of the Blue House raid and capture of the *Pueblo*. It was all the Americans could do to keep him from sending the South Korean Army to war against the North (https://commons.wikimedia.org/wiki/File:Park_Chung-hee_1963%27s.png, original source Republic of Korea).

Risk Analysis

Vietnam War. Giving little thought to the Blue House attack, they were more concerned that Park would pull his ROK divisions out of Vietnam unless the United States took retaliatory action against North Korea.[56] Park "vehemently insisted on action" and retaliation.[57] Park had been a former ROK army division commander on the DMZ, and from his experience, he firmly believed that the only way to respond to the North Korean raids was to retaliate in kind, but with greater force than that carried out by the North. Park, of course, was not alone in his thinking as the South Korean populace backed him. "Massive street demonstrations were staged by students and citizens of Seoul. They were demanding that Americans support [South] Korea by standing fast," meaning to retaliate for the North Korean attacks.[58] It took great American pressure from U.S. Army General Charles Bonesteel and William Porter, U.S. Ambassador to South Korea, to dissuade the ROK leader from his planned attack.[59] According to Secretary of State Dean Rusk, President Johnson had a great deal of respect for Park, but certainly did not want to advance a new war in Korea. Johnson's respect for Park was due to Park's great progress in South Korea, "economically and socially and politically." Johnson admired that Park "was tough in defense of the interests of South Korea, but was reasonable and balanced and was not provocative or militant in his general attitude toward North Korea."[60] Helping to calm Park, President Johnson's envoy, Cyrus Vance, offered President Park $100 million in military aid, including a few new F-4 fighter planes, but Park had to agree not to initiate a new war with the north.[61] Park agreed to the deal, toned down his criticism, and South Korean fighters (2–3 divisions, 30–50 thousand men) remained in Viet-

General Charles Bonesteel, who was primarily responsible for preventing all-out war between South and North Korea following the Blue House raid and capture of the *Pueblo* (U.S. Army photograph).

nam where they had earned the respect of U.S. General William Westmoreland, who addressed the ROK fighters, stating, "You have earned a reputation among communist forces as men to fear, respect ... and avoid."[62] With such a reputation, Washington certainly did not want to jeopardize the participation of those troops.

While Park backed down from a full scale attack on North Korea, he quietly allowed a South Korean raid into North Korea in the eastern sector of the DMZ "that resulted in thirty North Korean casualties."[63] But, in all likelihood, if Park's plans for a full-scale retaliatory attack had been allowed to move forward, it would surely have reopened the Korean war front.

Vance related his meeting(s) with Park to President Johnson after returning from Seoul, telling Johnson that Park had been upset that the United States had not retaliated for the Blue House raid and the capture of the *Pueblo*. Park had also told Vance that if retaliatory action would have been taken that the Soviets and Chinese would "stand aside." Apparently Park was of the opinion that North Korea had acted unilaterally in both incidents. Vance also related that Park had told him that North Korea's political plan was "to destroy morale and to harm us and the South Koreans."[64]

One can only imagine the intense pressure that General Charles Bonesteel was experiencing as commander of the U.N. and U.S. military forces. The South Korean government and the South Korean citizenry wanted war with North Korea in retaliation for the Blue House raid. And to top it off, on January 23 the *Pueblo* was captured, and South Korea became a powder keg ready to explode. South Korea would likely have only needed a few words of encouragement from their American allies and the entire South Korean military would march north, and the United States would be embroiled in another world conflict. Perhaps it was this intense pressure on Bonesteel, but at that point, he stated regarding *Pueblo's* capture; "It was a most inexcusable and infuriating thing." In addition, he suggested the strongest course of action he had ever voiced. He "argued for a blunt nuclear ultimatum against Kim Il-sung: release the *Pueblo* or else."[65] Bonesteel was not alone in his thoughts. There were others in Washington who agreed with him. The United States public had little idea that the nation had been pushed by the North Koreans to the brink of war, and they certainly had little idea that the use of nuclear weapons to punish the North Koreans was being seriously considered in many quarters. This drastic course of action was not carried out, of course, but the American public never knew how close to a nuclear confrontation our military came when the capture of the *Pueblo* was stirred into the low intensity conflict.

Following the Blue House raid, it was now apparent to Washington and South Korea that Kim Il-sung had no qualms about reopening the war with the South and with the Americans. The Blue House incident was a flagrant North Korean military threat and should have concerned officials overseeing the *Pueblo* operation. But it did not. Instead it was examined only from its possible debilitating effect on troop strength in the Vietnam War.

Perhaps the strongest and clearest warning occurred on January 20, 1968, when the North Korean representative at the 260th meeting of the Military Armistice Commission bluntly warned that America's continued use of spy boats under the cover of naval craft, "will only result in disrupting the armistice and inducing another war." This warning could not have been misinterpreted. It was issued only three days before the North Koreans seized the *Pueblo*.[66]

The warnings from North Korea were clear. North Korea would not tolerate imperialist aggression in its coastal waters. Yet, throughout the Navy chain of command above the *Pueblo*, not one Navy official voiced concern or opined that the mission should be cancelled, as attested to by Admiral Moorer in the *Pueblo* hearings.[67] "Admiral Johnson regarded the hostility of North Korea as a fact of the Cold War."[68] Even Secretary of Defense McNamara, testifying before the Appropriations Committee on the *Pueblo* incident, admitted that he was aware that cross-border attacks by the North Koreans in 1967 had increased over ten times the number during prior years. Yet, he and Navy leaders saw no reason to cancel the spy ship mission.[69] In fact, aside from the bungled NSA message, no one associated with the *Pueblo* cast of officials capable of voicing concern for the ship and crew's safety came forward with a specific recommendation to revise or cancel the mission.

It is apparent that Navy and NSA officials, while aware of the North Korean warnings and indications of hostile intent, chose to classify them as insignificant, dismissing them as typical Kim Il-sung rhetoric. Prudent leadership should have weighed the anticipated mission results against the consequences of *Pueblo's* possible loss. In addition, American officials did not consider the potential for negative aspects of the mission, "such as harassment, attack or seizure of the ship, involvement of additional

Two—Leadership and Risk Analysis

U.S. military forces[for protection]..." and made no "attempt to rate these consequences...."[70] Finally, U.S. officials did not clearly define the risk and gave little thought to factors bearing on the risk. Those factors included clear warnings from North Korea, the nation that was obviously unafraid of reopening all-out war against the South and the United States, and a late warning to the Navy from the NSA. The Navy and the Johnson administration missed all indicators and warnings that such a fate could befall the *Pueblo*, even after recognizing that the Pyongyang regime had violated the DMZ more than fifty times, ambushed U.S. and allied ground forces, attempted to assassinate the president of the ROK (with a possible secondary target, the American embassy), and in the preceding months, seized twenty South Korean fishing vessels for "entering North Korean territorial waters."[71] The Rand report, written by Ralph Strauch two years after the seizure of the *Pueblo*, includes findings that are fundamental to planning for a spy ship mission. For example, Strauch contended that at each successive command echelon, a further assessment of risk to *Pueblo* should have taken place.[72] As revealed in the hearings, it did not. Instead, like a snowball rolling down a hill, the *Pueblo* mission gained speed and mass. Ex-intelligence agent Patrick McGarvey referred to this phenomenon as "bureaucratic inertia, the military's [Navy's] penchant for 'positive thinking'" and "the failure of the entire intelligence community to organize itself to meet the needs of technical collection...."[73] Enlightened, receptive leadership willing to properly weigh mission risks was found lacking at all levels within the *Pueblo's* Navy chain of command and within the Department of Defense. Former British Foreign Secretary David Owen, in *The Politics of Defence*, wrote, "The details of the *Pueblo* mission and its authorization ... reveal the weakness of the whole intelligence procedure in the planning and conduct of a highly sensitive mission."[74]

The demonstration of flawed leadership within the military in general and the Navy specifically was not lost on members of Congress. On January 24, 1968, a day after the capture of the *Pueblo*, Democratic Representative Robert Sikes of Florida stood and addressed the House, stating, "It is inconceivable that an American intelligence vessel, loaded with highly classified equipment and documents would be sent into dangerous waters without nearby support of American forces." Sikes continued, "The might of America's power must be available wherever and whenever it is needed to protect American interests, but it should be obvious that studied and careful preparation can help to avoid dangerous incidents like this one,

Risk Analysis

where a spark could ignite a war."[75] It was obvious to Representative Sikes that the Navy and the intelligence community had not demonstrated due diligence in their preparation for *Pueblo's* mission.

Lessons learned were, of course, too late for the *Pueblo*. But only two months later, in response to a pointed set of questions in a March 7, 1968, memorandum from Deputy Secretary of Defense Paul Nitze to JCS Chairman, General Earle Wheeler, the Chairman responded on March 29, 1968, that he believed spy ship missions should be continued. He couched his answers by saying that protection should be provided "for operations in high risk areas." He went on to say that an analysis should be made regarding the need for the intelligence data "versus the risk involved."[76] Wheeler also wrote that "The capability of the U.S. to retaliate would tend to deter anyone from deliberately [attacking] a U.S. ship."[77] Yet, that same military capability was certainly not a deterrent to the North Koreans who brazenly hijacked the *Pueblo*. In his defense, Wheeler may have had little knowledge of just how irrational North Korea could be. As to his belief that the spy ship missions should continue, how ironic then that the USS *Banner* was decommissioned a short time later, and the spy ship program was scrapped. Contrary to what General Wheeler believed, somewhere, someone in authority finally recognized that the risk was just too great for benefits received.

Three

Reactions

On the Pueblo

It would be difficult to generalize about the thoughts of the eighty-three *Pueblo* crew members as they experienced possibly the most terror-filled event of their lives, the North Korean attack on their ship. However, firsthand accounts by CDR Lloyd Bucher and his operations officer, LTJG Carl "Skip" Schumacher, present a clear picture of their thoughts in those tense moments. Schumacher described January 23, 1968, as "My Longest Day." When he was awakened at 0315 to dress and assume the 4–8 a.m. watch on the bridge, he thought that the day would be routine. The ship had been at sea for thirteen days, collecting very little intelligence data and experiencing no intervention from adversaries. The thought occurred to Schumacher that it was so cold that the "Koreans were smart enough" not to chase the *Pueblo* around in the Sea of Japan in the dead of winter. The frigid temperatures had forced the crew to chip ice from the deck and the superstructure to ensure that the ship did not become top heavy in its transit to North Korea.[1] When Schumacher assumed the watch, he learned that due to inadequate electronic communications capabilities, the ship had been unable to report to CNFJ that the *Pueblo* had been observed by North Korean trawlers, a message that the ship had been attempting to transmit since the previous day. Because of prior experiences, the abilities of the *Pueblo* remained a concern to the crew. Still, on this frigid January morning, Schumacher and the crew believed that they "had the military backing of the United States ... and the protection afforded by the internationally recognized right to sail on the high seas."

While eating lunch on January 23rd, a day with freezing temperatures and "wintry clouds," Bucher had been called to the bridge in time to see "a Russian-built, modified SO-1 class sub chaser" headed toward the

On the Pueblo

Pueblo at full speed. This was not the first time that the *Pueblo* had encountered a sub chaser. While the ship was lying off the northern coast of North Korea on January 20, a sub chaser passed them at 4,000 yards, but had shown no interest in *Pueblo* and had gone away. The following day, *Pueblo* transited south to take up a listening location closer to Wonsan. On January 22, while lying off Wonsan, two North Korean ships approached the *Pueblo*. The ships came to within 1,500 yards and one of the ships broke off and passed the *Pueblo* one hundred yards off the starboard beam. It is believed that the ships were intelligence collecting trawlers. Neither of the North Korean ships flew an ensign or flag. Later, the ships closed to within thirty yards and passed down *Pueblo's* port side. At approximately 4 p.m. both ships left the area.[2] The *Pueblo* was now alone until the 23rd.

On January 23, Bucher had left his lunch and gone to the bridge, where he watched as the SO-1 sub chaser approached. Compared to the 12–13 knot top speed of the *Pueblo*, it is estimated that the SO-1 is capable of at least 20 knots.[3] Bucher stated that he was more annoyed than alarmed. The sub chaser circled the *Pueblo* and after a short interval, circled again while showing a flag signal asking for the nationality of the *Pueblo*, even though it is probable that the North Korean ship knew the identity of the American ship, as the *Pueblo* had been mentioned by name in the North Korean statement that had been republished in Japan during the week of January 13. The North Korean ship may have been simply stalling for time, awaiting additional naval units and instructions from its naval chain of command. In answer to the North Korean ship's flag hoist request, *Pueblo* raised a new U.S. Flag, and the North Koreans then knew for certain that they had an American Navy ship to deal with. The North Korean sub chaser hoisted a flag message, "Heave to or I will open fire."[4] Shortly thereafter, three DPRK high-speed torpedo boats arrived on the scene, and all four DPRK ships began circling the *Pueblo*, all with their guns pointed at the ship, and with armed personnel standing at their rails. If these smaller craft were the Soviet-built P4 boats, they were capable of nearly 50 knots in speed. *Pueblo* did not stand a chance at outdistancing them in an attempt to quickly leave the area.

Bucher now believed that a "full-fledged harassment operation appeared to be imminent."[5] He recalled that the same harassment tactics had occurred with the USS *Banner*, and he wrote that he now was "bracing for a test of nerves, not battle." Bucher's reaction became more acute as

Three—Reactions

he recalled the inadequacy of the classified material destruction capabilities of the ship, and he asked Chief Warrant Officer Gene Lacy, his engineering officer, if the ship could be scuttled "quickly if we had to." He was told that it would take an inordinate amount of time to sink the *Pueblo*. Still, Bucher began the destruction process to rid the ship of classified material. While doing so, he held to the thought that "the situation was not that critical and was unlikely to become so." While the DPRK ships circled, Bucher exclaimed for the benefit of his crew, "We're not going to let these sons-o'-bitches bullshit us!" According to Bucher, no sooner had he made that statement, when another torpedo boat and sub chaser joined the harassment. The *Pueblo* was now surrounded by six North Korean war ships and two MIGs flying overhead. One of the lead North Korean ships was flying signal flags that spelled out, "Heave to or I will fire." Bucher answered by flag, "I am in international waters." The North Koreans persisted, moving closer to the *Pueblo*. Seeing that the North Koreans were preparing to come alongside in an attempt to board the *Pueblo*, Bucher swore, "I'll be Goddamned if they are going to get away with it."[6] He then turned the *Pueblo* east to depart the area of conflict, ordered the ship to full speed (12–13 knots), and signaled the North Koreans that he was "departing the area." Bucher considered ordering the ship to general quarters, but realized that placing crew members on the open deck in an attempt to uncover, man, load, and fire the .50 caliber machine guns would be certain death for the men. They would have been cut down by North Korean machine guns before they could man the *Pueblo* gun mounts. This decision by Bucher would later haunt him in the months and years ahead, and it would serve as the bedrock of the Navy's later investigations and accusations against the captain of the spy ship.

While the North Korean Navy (NKN) had not yet fired on the *Pueblo*, it may have been that they were waiting for permission from their chain of command. "New evidence suggests that the [North Korean] Ministry of National Defense (MND) participated in the seizure. NSA judged that the MND might have been involved in the tracking and seizure, given references in NKN voice communications to 'the comrade ... from the top' just prior to the seizure." The North Korean sub chaser also received "orders from the top" to go "farther in toward Wons[a]n before boarding *Pueblo*, which was still in international waters."[7] Shortly thereafter, the North Koreans began a sustained burst of cannon fire from the sub chasers, joined by machine guns on the torpedo boats. Several *Pueblo* crew members were injured, and Bucher was wounded by flying particles from the shattered windscreen and was then struck by shrapnel. Bucher's initial reactions had been annoyance, then resignation at being subject to harassment. This was soon followed by defiance and an attempt to move out of the area, only to have his ship and crew subjected to deadly gunfire.

Meanwhile, communication was finally reestablished with CNFJ, and Schumacher rushed to send an SOS message to Japan asking for assistance, alerting CNFJ that the *Pueblo* was surrounded by two North Korean sub chasers, four torpedo boats, and two circling MIGs. Shortly after the situation report had been sent to Japan, it became apparent that the North Koreans were going to attempt to board the ship. One of the torpedo boats approached "*Pueblo's* starboard quarter with eight to ten armed men positioned and ready to board the *Pueblo*."[8] Bucher ordered the ship ahead at one-third speed (other sources say that it may have been an order for full speed) on a course of 080 to depart the area. Bucher was attempting to put distance between the *Pueblo* and its pursuers. Of course, this was futile as the speed of the North Korean ships made that impossible. As Schumacher described his feelings, "a cold dread was building up inside me." He also described the reaction of those within the crypto spaces as being full of fear. As the ship moved eastward, one of the sub chasers again began a barrage of firing upon the *Pueblo.* With its limited speed, the *Pueblo* could never outrun her pursuers. But even as the ship was being fired upon by the North Koreans' 57 mm cannon, Schumacher wondered if there was something more that he could do to speed the destruction of classified material before the ship was sunk, "or we were all killed." Shortly thereafter, when he saw his commanding officer preparing to surrender the ship, Schumacher stated he could not speak to him. He wrote that if he had tried to speak to Bucher, "I would have burst into tears. *Rigor mortis* set in in my spirit. My ship, my Navy, my captain, my crew, my life—all gone."[9]

While the North Koreans fired upon the *Pueblo,* Bucher continued with the destruction of classified documents and equipment. Because the means of destruction was inadequate, the crew even brought wastepaper cans to the classified area and lit fires in them to destroy documents. Members of the crew wielded axes and sledge hammers in a futile effort to destroy classified equipment, but they had little success in destroying the machines. "It was truly a chaotic emergency destruction effort, and the

Three—Reactions

result was that only a small percentage of the "classified material aboard the ship was destroyed. A massive amount of classified material was left untouched."[10]

Bucher's attempt to take the ship and crew away from North Korea and to safety failed. In addition to the 57 mm cannon fire from the sub chaser, the smaller gun boats were raking the *Pueblo* with machine gun fire. By flag hoist, the *Pueblo* was again ordered by the North Koreans to heave to or suffer further gunfire. Realizing the situation was hopeless, Bucher stopped the *Pueblo,* and the ship was subsequently boarded by eight to ten North Koreans brandishing automatic weapons with fixed bayonets and led by two DPRK officers.[11] The last radio message sent by the *Pueblo* to the communication station in Kami Seya, Japan read, "Have been directed to come to all stop and being boarded. Four men injured and one critically. Going off the air now and destroying this gear."[12]

The time was 1:45 p.m. on January 23, 1968. Control of the *Pueblo* had been seized by the North Korean Navy. The North Koreans went to the *Pueblo's* pilot house and ordered the helmsman to follow the North Korean sub chaser into Wonsan harbor. Shortly after, a second boarding party came aboard and a pilot was among them. He went to the pilot house and took over the helm, rang up "all ahead flank," and the spy ship headed into Wonsan at 12.5 knots. At approximately 7:00 p.m., "the ship was brought to 'full stop,' and moored to a concrete pier in Wonsan."[13] The *Pueblo* crew would now begin their harrowing and tortured prison confinement at the hands of the North Koreans.

As a career Navy officer, Bucher knew that his choice not to send his men to the gun mounts was contrary to the Navy tradition of not giving up the ship without a fight. As commanding officer of the *Pueblo,* he was the only man who could make that decision. But in reality, Bucher did not have sufficient time to properly arm his ship for defense. He had previously been told to keep his guns below deck, been told that he would be protected by his being in international waters, and knew that hitherto the North Koreans had been complacent when American ships had neared their coast. He had been firmly warned that he was not to go into the North Korean waters "to start a war." This advice and assurance contributed to the *Pueblo's* inability to defend itself when the North Korean Navy arrived.

Bucher chose to protect the welfare of his crew instead of attempting to have his under-armed ship fight, and thereby risk additional injury or

On the Pueblo

death to his sailors. He came to the conclusion that further resistance would only "result in our being shot to pieces and a lot of good men killed to no avail." He later recalled, "The feeling of utter loneliness and complete severance from any reliable support became suddenly so overwhelming that I wanted to cry out for help from anybody with a sensible suggestion about what to do! Four of my officers were on the bridge with me, but none of them came forward with a single word of advice."[14] Instead, Bucher devoted his energy to destroying as much of the classified material onboard as possible before the North Koreans boarded, his last attempt at defiance before being subjugated by the North Koreans. Bucher and his crew were helpless and forced to pilot the ship into Wonsan harbor. In Wonsan, Bucher and his crew were forced from the ship and would soon be transferred to a North Korean prison.

From the *Pueblo's* mooring site, the men were marched to two waiting North Korean buses. As they moved along, they were "showered with kicks and punches" by their captors who also poked the men with bayonets. "Rifle butts smashed into the prisoners' heads with such force that some men almost lost consciousness," while other soldiers inflicted karate blows to the Americans, "much to the delight of the cheering onlookers." A crowd, perhaps hastily assembled by Kim Il-sung's propaganda officials, had gathered to watch the Americans being led to prison, with many of the North Koreans spitting on the Americans and shouting, "Kill Yankee, Kill Yankee."[15] The Americans were bused to a rail depot where they boarded a waiting train. They were blindfolded, and many of the windows on the train had been covered. As several hours passed riding on the dilapidated train, the North Korean soldiers continued to beat the Americans. As the train transported the American sailors to prison to suffer a nearly year-long incarceration, Schumacher came to the conclusion in his mind that he "...had to kill myself. Then I would win. The Democratic People's Republic of Korea would lose." Schumacher held on to this course of action for a time while being repeatedly beaten in prison, making half-hearted attempts to end his life, but later abandoned the idea. Schumacher wrote of his feelings as he rode to his fate in the North Korean prison bus: "Each of us was an island. Each of us was on his own. I had never felt so cut off, so alone, in my life. I was no longer a member of the huge American military establishment. I had been amputated from it by the Koreans."[16]

If that was the reaction of the *Pueblo's* operations officer, imagine the feelings of the commanding officer, CDR Bucher. In the training of a naval

Three—Reactions

officer, it is ingrained into each young ensign that the commanding officer of a Navy ship is ultimately responsible for everything that occurs onboard that ship. Yet, on January 4, 1968, before leaving on his mission, Bucher had spoken to the previous commanding officer of the *Banner*, Commander Charles Clark.[17] They talked about contingencies and whether the North Koreans might attempt to board the *Pueblo*. Clark remembered Bucher saying, "...if those bastards come out after me, well, they're not going to get me."[18] On January 23, 1968, in order to save the lives of his crew, CDR Bucher gave up the ship, for which he was ultimately responsible, to the North Koreans without firing a single defensive shot.

The train on which the crew had been riding came to a stop, and the guards on the train untied the hands of the crew. They were made to walk on the train platform amid lights and popping flashbulbs. Once again they boarded buses and were taken to what seemed to be a military compound, where the buses stopped outside a "rectangular, four story building with a tile roof." The crew surmised that they were in Pyongyang. Bucher and the crew were forced at the point of a bayonet into the building where they climbed the stairs to the third floor. The crew nicknamed this prison,

Google Earth photo of "The Barn" prison where the *Pueblo* crew spent the first six weeks of their imprisonment by the North Koreans (photograph from USS *Pueblo*.org web site).

On the Pueblo

"The Barn."[19] Bucher was pushed into a room and the door was closed. Bucher described the room;

> [The room had a radiator that did not work, hence the] room was very cold. A blackout curtain covered the window, which had been nailed shut. A naked light bulb hung from the ceiling on a thin cord tufted with dust. There was a small table and a straight-backed chair and, against the wall, a cot with a course muslin sheet, a brown wool blanket, and a pillow filled with rice husks.[20]

No sooner had Bucher been pushed into his cell than the guards returned and took him to interrogation. During most of the interrogations there was an interpreter, whom the crew named "Max." After asking Bucher a few perfunctory questions, they took him back to his room. But shortly thereafter the North Korean guards came for Bucher again. This time, he met with a North Korean major that the crew nicknamed "Squint." The major asked more questions, but this time, Bucher's service record was laying open on the table in front of the major. The service records of the entire crew had been taken from the *Pueblo,* and using them, the North Koreans could determine whether or not the Americans were lying in their answers to an interrogator's questions. It was not long after this that

Google Earth photo of "The Farm," the second prison site where the crew was taken after six weeks at "The Barn." The crew would spend the duration of their confinement at this site (photograph from USS *Pueblo*.org web site).

Three—Reactions

Bucher and his officers were escorted into a room and faced a North Korean general, who informed the men that they were to be shot as spies, a threat that was often repeated in subsequent days.

Only two days after the *Pueblo's* capture, on January 25, the North Koreans broadcast an alleged confession by Bucher, in which *Pueblo's* CO admitted to "criminal espionage activities."[21] Closer examination of the broadcast revealed many discrepancies and blatant untruths that Bucher likely inserted in order to indicate that he was being pressured by the North Koreans to write such a document. The confession was subsequently printed in the *Pyongyang Times* in February 1968.[22] A second confession written by Bucher on September 21, 1968, is also interspersed with untruths and nonsensical phrases that show the commander was attempting to demonstrate defiance at being forced to write the confession(s). For instance, he made the statement, "The absolute truth of this bowel wrenching confession is attested to by my fervent desire to paean the Korean people's Army, Navy, and their government and to beseech the Korean people to forgive our dastardly deeds unmatched since Attila. I swear the following account to be true on the sacred honor of the Great Speckled Bird."[23] The North Koreans did not, of course, understand Bucher's subtle, insincere humor.

Ironically, with the Johnson administration lamenting and casting aspersions on the Bucher confession, it turned out that Bucher was not the only officer making a bogus confession. After brutal beatings and interrogations, the North Koreans extracted confessions from several members of the *Pueblo* crew. On succeeding days, the North Koreans broadcast the orchestrated propaganda confessions of Lieutenant Stephen Harris, the officer in charge of the on-board SIGINT section, who was told that if he did not sign a confession, his SIGINT detachment crew members would be further harmed. His confession was followed by similar coerced confessions from Lieutenant Edward Murphy, the executive officer; Lieutenant Carl "Skip" Schumacher, the operations officer; Dunnie Tuck Jr., oceanographer; and Marine Sergeant Robert Hammond, Korean linguist and intercept operator. These men reported that in each case, the confession was written by the North Koreans, and subsequently, the men were forced to write the same confession in their own writing and sign it. Then they were to read the confession aloud while being filmed. Examples of the treatment of these men to coerce their signing were starvation, threat of execution, beating and torture, and sleep deprivation. In addition, they were made to walk around the floor on their knees, sit at attention in straight chairs for long periods of time, "exploiting the element of fear by creating noises in an adjoining room which sounded as though other crew members were being killed, and informing the crew that they would be shot as spies if they did not confess."[24] In the case of Robert Hammond, the beatings continued for six straight hours because he would not admit that he spoke Korean. All of the confessions contained a central theme. The crew members were to admit that they had "deliberately penetrated deep into North Korean coastal waters for espionage purposes."[25]

Bucher and the *Pueblo* crew were interrogated and physically beaten routinely during their eleven months in captivity. Both Bucher and Schumacher wrote of the beatings of the crew by their North Korean captors. The initial routine beatings were endured by the crew, but when the North Koreans learned that they had been humiliated by the *Pueblo* sailors by appearing in pictures and North Korean news conferences defiantly extending their middle fingers, the beatings became more severe. Being bloodied routinely by the DPRK guards led to several medical complications for the crew. Hospital Corpsman First Class Herman Baldridge was the *Pueblo's* corpsman, but he too was a prisoner and was not equipped to administer proper medical aid in prison. The North Korean prison physician only aided the most seriously injured of the crew, and not always with favorable results. The crew's injuries were the result of North Korean gunfire during the *Pueblo's* capture, malnutrition while in prison, and the severe beatings inflicted by the prison guards.

Within the Military Chain of Command

At approximately 7:20 p.m. in Honolulu on January 22, (2:20 p.m. January 23 in Korea) Admiral John Hyland, CINCPACFLT, learned of the attack and boarding of the *Pueblo*. This was after the following events had already transpired:

1. A message from *Pueblo* reporting that they had been ordered to heave to or be fired upon had been received at CNFJ. CNFJ staff took no action, rather waiting to see any further developments.
2. After *Pueblo's* message regarding being boarded was received by CNFJ, they phoned 5th Air Force (General Seth McKee) in

Three—Reactions

Fuchu, Japan, and asked for assistance from the Air Force. The air force plotted *Pueblo's* position and reviewed the status of aircraft that might be able to assist *Pueblo*, but no action was taken.

3. CNFJ phoned Admiral Johnson in Tokyo, where he was attending a conference. Johnson started for Yokosuka immediately. He asked if 5th Air Force had been notified.
4. Another phone call to 5th Air Force was made by CNFJ to determine what action was taking place. Yokosuka was informed that no aircraft were available, and that it would take two to three hours to ready aircraft. However, General McKee also placed a call to Okinawa to check availability of aircraft there to respond to the *Pueblo* distress messages.
5. General McKee placed a call to Pacific Air Force Command in Hawaii, who agreed with McKee's actions thus far.
6. Through communication channels, Admiral Horace Epes, flag officer of carrier division one on the USS *Enterprise* also learned of *Pueblo's* plight and after study, determined that due to time and distance limits, his forces on the *Enterprise* could not reach and assist the *Pueblo* before it was inside the North Korean three mile limit.
7. Finally, the war room at Pacific Headquarters in Honolulu and the Pacific Fleet Intelligence Center received calls from CNFJ and the Pacific Indications Center regarding *Pueblo*, and the information was quickly given to Commander in Chief Pacific Fleet, Admiral John Hyland.

Hyland and his aide, Captain Cassell, subsequently made their way to CINCPACFLT headquarters where they reviewed all available information regarding the *Pueblo* capture. The reaction of the U.S. Navy was predictable. "Naval officers were generally shocked that the *Pueblo* had been captured by the enemy without a serious fight and that she had been taken into Wonsan harbor apparently without any attempt by her crew to sink her."[26] The attack and capture of a U.S. Navy ship had happened only once before, in 1807, when Commodore James Barron surrendered the USS *Chesapeake* to the British.[27] Aside from the fact that questionable leadership had played a role in the capture of the *Pueblo*, the predictable Navy reaction was that military retaliation must be strongly and swiftly administered.

Within the Intelligence Community

From his headquarters, Admiral Hyland phoned Admiral Johnson, CNFJ, in Yokosuka, Japan, and learned that at 1:06 a.m. the Commander Seventh Fleet, Admiral William Bringle, ordered the positioning of the USS *Enterprise* closer to the Korean coast and was planning to move other Navy assets to the area in preparation for retaliation.[28] Hyland then conferred with the CNO, Admiral Moorer, and sent a message to Bringle ordering him to place a destroyer in international waters off the port of Wonsan, in preparation for the destroyer to enter Wonsan Harbor, physically take back the *Pueblo* by force, and tow the ship back to sea. Hyland also discussed the idea of pin-point bombing the *Pueblo* to destroy the ship and its trove of classified material, keeping it from the Soviets. Air strikes on Wonsan and other North Korean targets were also discussed. But even the highest ranking officer in the Navy could not approve this daring rescue and coordinated air strikes against North Korea without authorization from the JCS and President Johnson. By 11 a.m. Washington time, the president had made his initial decision and passed it along to the JCS. With the orders of the JCS in hand, Hyland notified Bringle by message. "It is desired that no show of force be deployed in area of *Pueblo* incident."[29] There would be no immediate retaliatory military action. U.S. Naval forces that had been steaming toward North Korea were ordered to proceed no farther north than the coast of South Korea. "The unprepared posture of the U.S. armed forces in the area had precluded prevention of the *Pueblo's* capture, and any immediate counterblow had been ruled out."[30] While the military reacted by requesting retaliatory action, its request was not granted. For now, the *Pueblo* and crew would remain in the hands of the North Koreans.

Within the Intelligence Community

Never before in the NSA or Navy's history had such a treasure trove of classified material been forcibly taken from the United States. Thus, the risk of such an event happening would seem to have been extremely low at the time. But even if an emergency should occur, the Navy naively believed that a complete destruction of classified material on the *Pueblo* could be carried out satisfactorily. This parochial thinking did not account for the huge volume of classified material which the spy ship had been forced to carry on board. Admiral Thomas Moorer, Chief of Naval Oper-

Three—Reactions

ations (CNO), in his testimony at congressional hearings following the release of the *Pueblo* crew stated, "the ship [*Pueblo*] was provided with weighted canvas bags for use at sea, two paper shredders, and an incinerator. Gasoline was also available."[31] Apparently, the CNO had no grasp of the sheer volume of classified material on the *Pueblo* nor the gravity of the risk involved in not having a proper means of destruction on the spy ship. This is not surprising considering the custom of delegation of authority within the Navy. And within the military, officers at the top of management pyramids exercised their influence "using relatively fewer rather than relatively more direct mechanisms of control...."[32] When asked if he felt certain that all echelons in *Pueblo's* chain of command were aware of the "lack of self-destruct capability for both the vessel itself and intelligence gathering equipment," Moorer answered, "I am confident that they were."[33] If the top leader of the Navy and all of his subordinates were aware that the *Pueblo* did not have the capability to destroy the ship and its classified material, did anyone realize the consequences of this risk? Was any thought given to cancelling the mission until the self-destruction inadequacies could be remedied?

Without proper risk analysis, the consequences were a gold mine of classified American military documents and equipment later confiscated by the North Koreans when they captured the *Pueblo*. Retired Navy Commander and government Intelligence Analyst Richard A. Mobley, writing for *Studies in Intelligence*, a CIA publication, quoted Admiral John Hyland, Commander in Chief of the Pacific Fleet (CINCPACFLT), who said, "Compromise of sensitive information can very well be turned against the United States and ultimately cause the loss of untold lives in other confrontations." Hyland also called the incident a "tragedy." At the time he made these remarks, the full extent of the loss of classified material on the *Pueblo* had not been fully assessed. Specifically, officials did not know that the "cryptographic hardware captured aboard the *Pueblo* might be married up with keying material being provided to the Soviet Union by the Walker spy ring...."[34]

The Soviets hastened to investigate the intelligence bonanza contained on the U.S. ship. On January 28, 1969, "the CIA reported that a Soviet Pacific Fleet aircraft had made a highly unusual flight into North Korea. The agency believed that the aircraft might have carried Soviet personnel to examine *Pueblo* and its surviving equipment."[35]

In an article for *Military History*, historian Mitchell Lerner wrote:

Shortly after the [*Pueblo*] seizure, a North Korean aircraft flew to Moscow carrying almost 1,000 pounds of cargo salvaged from *Pueblo*. Among the many items lost were a detailed account of top-secret American intelligence objectives for the Pacific; classified U.S. communications manuals, a number of vital NSA machines and the manuals that detailed their operation and repair, the NSA's Electronic Order of Battle for the Far East; information on American electronic countermeasures; radar classification instructions; and various secret codes and Navy transmission procedures. Little wonder, then, that an NSA report described the loss as a "major intelligence coup without parallel in modern history."[36]

Robert E. Newton, writing for the NSA Center for Cryptologic History, summarized the loss of classified material in the capture of the *Pueblo*: "the loss that resulted from the subsequent compromise of classified material aboard the ship would dwarf anything in previous U.S. cryptologic history. It also gave the North Koreans and the Soviets a rare view of the complex technology behind U.S. cryptographic systems. Over the long term, the compromise would severely affect the U.S. SIGINT capability to exploit several major target areas for years to come."[37]

According to a report prepared by a joint team composed of members of the CIA, Defense Intelligence Agency (DIA), and Navy, Air Force, and Army intelligence personnel to assess the damage to U.S. intelligence programs caused by the loss of the *Pueblo*, the magnitude of the damage was immense. The data compromise divulged "U.S. intelligence capability to collect from multiple sources, process and evaluate, and disseminate large volumes of information on a near real time basis to military forces in the field and Naval forces afloat in time of war." Additionally, U.S. SIGINT capabilities and technical operational data were revealed, including the existence, location, technical capabilities, manning, and coverage of "many SIGINT sites and detachments...."[38] As grave as those compromises were, NSA and Navy leadership did not consider the consequences of these losses in the risk analysis during preparations for the *Pueblo* mission.

In South Korea

While the attack on the Blue House had stirred the people of South Korea to advocate immediate military retaliation, the capture of the *Pueblo* further amplified that fervor. General Charles Bonesteel, U.S./U.N. commander in South Korea heard of the plight of the *Pueblo* from Yokosuka at approximately 2:25 p.m. He immediately alerted his component com-

Three—Reactions

manders to heighten readiness. Later, on the morning of January 27th, Bonesteel met with the South Korean Joint Chiefs of Staff. General Bonesteel was the right man to meet with and smooth the ruffled feathers of the South Koreans. Bonesteel was a tall, unimposing, thin, gray-haired man who wore an eye patch later in his career due to a detached retina. He was educated at Oxford as a Rhodes Scholar. In appearance and mannerisms, he lacked the charismatic leadership characteristics of a Patton, for example, but he possessed other intellectual talents far more important to the task at hand. First, he could "process an immense amount of information in a short time." Next, he could "discern subtle connections" between items of data. He also "demonstrated impressive political acumen" and the "difference between the possible and the ideal." Understanding that difference, he was able "to do more with less." Fourth, "Bonesteel embraced the unorthodox," allowing him to develop his own unique solutions. And finally, Bonesteel could make his own decisions and "made them without hesitation."[39] In addition, Bonesteel knew that he had limited resources, as the majority of America's fighting potential was tied up in Vietnam, and he knew that a second large military front would not be tolerated by the American public. He had to work with the resources at hand. The military refers to this situation as "economy of force," using the resources available at the moment.[40] Armed with intellectual prowess and a knowledge of his finite troop strength, Bonesteel was the man to meet with the South Koreans and convince them that starting an all-out war with the North Koreans was not in the interests of South Korea or the United States. But it would not be easy.

The South Koreans, at all levels, were incensed that the United States had made no statements nor taken any action following the Blue House attack. Now, North Korean aggression in taking the *Pueblo*, further angered the South Koreans. As Bonesteel said later, "The damned *Pueblo* occurred two days later [following the Blue House raid] and that really put the fat in the fire."[41] On January 27, four days after the capture of the *Pueblo*, General Bonesteel met with the South Korean JCS. He related his experiences in a message he sent to the U.S. JCS that same day. He wrote that in their meeting, the ROK JCS stated that they wanted to be "adequately and timely informed of U.S. intentions because [those plans would] affect their mobilization planning, national emergency planning, martial law plans and numerous other vital plans conducted by the ROK government." The ROK wanted to press the Americans to alert them before retaliatory action was going to occur against North Korea. More bluntly, and even more alarming to Bonesteel was that ROK demanded that they and their U.S. allies take "clear, punitive action to teach Kim Il-sung a lesson."[42] The South Koreans were ready to go to war with the North. It fell to Bonesteel to ensure that would not occur. He deserves a great deal of credit for keeping a lid on "the quiet war," not allowing these low intensity campaigns from the North to roil into another full-out war on the Korean peninsula. It took a great deal of negotiating, promising, and smoothing of ruffled feathers on the part of Bonesteel and Ambassador William Porter. But they were successful, as all-out war was prevented. In addition, Bonesteel subsequently initiated and placed into operation a great many innovative defense procedures, all of which served to stymie the North Koreans from further attempts to infiltrate, attack, and subvert South Korea. The ROK troops were trained in the new defense procedures and with the help of the Americans, further enemy incursions were, in essence, stopped at the DMZ. It was General Bonesteel who had analyzed Kim's grand insurgency plan, and he deserves credit for stopping it before it could succeed.

In the Situation Room, Washington

Walt W. Rostow, Special Assistant for National Security to President Lyndon Johnson, received a 12:15 a.m. phone call on January 23, 1968.[43] The urgency of the call caused him to dress hurriedly and be taken to the White House where he went directly to the Situation Room. Before alerting the president, he checked all known data regarding the attack, boarding, and seizure of the USS *Pueblo*. One of his first calls was to General Marshall Carter, the head of NSA. He inquired about Command and Control of the *Pueblo*. Carter informed Rostow that "there was a clear division of responsibility between NSA and the JCS concerning" the operational control of the spy ships. While NSA gave technical guidance in the ship's program, operational control belonged to the Navy. In other words, what had happened to the *Pueblo* was now the responsibility of the Navy and JCS. NSA would not be getting involved in any attempt to rescue the ship. Rostow subsequently called Hawaii to get any late reports that they might have, and then spoke with Secretary of State Rusk and Secretary of Defense McNamara. Assured that he knew as much as possible about the situation,

Three—Reactions

he called the president at approximately 2:25 a.m. On the phone, Johnson replied, "Thank you," and hung up.[44]

Following Rostow's phone calls, events in Washington quickly commenced. Secretary of State Dean Rusk cabled U.S. Ambassador William Porter in Seoul with orders to begin negotiations with the North Koreans for the release of the ship and its crew. The initial negotiator for the United States would be Rear Admiral John V. Smith, chief spokesman for the Military Armistice Commission.[45]

By 9:00 a.m. on the 23rd, an administration crisis team had formed and held the first of many meetings. Later, the number of attendees at *Pueblo*/North Korea meetings varied, but generally included General Earle Wheeler, Chairman of the Joint Chiefs; Walt Rostow, Special Assistant for National Security Affairs; Dean Rusk, Secretary of State; Nicholas Katzenbach, Under Secretary of State; Samuel Berger, Assistant Secretary of State; Robert McNamara, Secretary of Defense; Paul Nitze, Deputy Secretary of Defense; Arthur Goldberg, U.N. Ambassador; Richard Helms, CIA Director; General Maxwell Taylor, Foreign Intelligence Advisory Board Chairman; Bromley Smith, National Security Council Executive Secretary; and Clark Clifford. Clifford had served on President Kennedy's President's Foreign Intelligence Advisory Board (PFIAB) and transitioned onto President Johnson's PFIAB, where he served as chairman prior to being named Secretary of Defense. Clifford was a trusted member of Johnson's "kitchen cabinet." On January 19, 1968, Johnson would name him Secretary of Defense to succeed Robert McNamara, only four days before the *Pueblo* incident.[46] Because Clifford was not sworn in as Secretary of Defense until March 1, 1968, both he and McNamara attended the *Pueblo* strategy meetings. As a confidant of the president, Clifford's influence with the committee was held in high regard.[47] It was this select group of advisors who would ultimately present President Johnson with an array of possible actions that the United States could take in response to the capture of the *Pueblo*. First reactions of committee members centered on military retaliation. Ideas were discussed that included bombing the *Pueblo*, sending retaliatory raids on Wonsan or Pyongyang, knocking out a key military installation in North Korea, naval shore bombardment from outside the twelve mile limit, or enlisting the South Koreans to stage a large invasion into North Korea.[48]

At the first crisis team meeting in the Situation Room on January 23, the president joined the group at 10 a.m. and quite possibly at his insistence, a 10:25 a.m. call was made to Admiral Hyland in Hawaii, advising him to stand down and ordering that no immediate military action be taken. This was followed by a radio message to CINCPAC (Admiral Sharp) from the Chairman of the Joint Chiefs, General Wheeler, which stated that "The Administration is currently focusing on diplomatic actions to obtain return of the *Pueblo* and her crew."[49] In the same message, Wheeler also informed Sharp that a large number of military assets, including the aircraft carriers *Kitty Hawk* and *Enterprise*, would be moved closer to the Korean peninsula as a precautionary measure and to make them more readily available if military action ramped up. An additional "10,000 tons of air munitions" would be sent to South Korea. In the same message, it was revealed that a number of missiles would be sent, along with "nine surveillance and attack submarines." So, while President Johnson preferred, and would follow, a diplomatic course of action, planning was simultaneously taking place in the event a military response became necessary.

At the White House

Examining the reaction of President Johnson and his closest advisors requires a situational perspective. In the wake of the assassination of President Kennedy, Johnson saw the immediate opportunity to enact what he believed to be "economic and social justice," in the form of drastic social programs. "In 1964–5, before Vietnam drained his influence and infested his outlook, Johnson had the liberty and flexibility to concentrate on his social legislative agenda." As Johnson had once mused, "I never thought I'd have the power. I wanted the power to use it. And I'm going to use it."[50] But Johnson's plans, while partially legislated, became less reachable, as other issues began to drive the Johnson agenda, foremost of which was the war in Vietnam.

It can be argued that 1968 was the most frustrating and complex year of the Johnson administration. "The *Pueblo* incident formed the first link in a chain of events—of crisis, tragedy, and disappointment—that added up to one of the most agonizing years any president has ever spent in the White House."[51] Multiple factors leading up to 1968 derailed some of President Johnson's intended social programs with most of those distracting factors centered around the Vietnam War. The United States had begun

Three—Reactions

intensive bombing of selected North Vietnamese targets in 1965. At almost the same time, anti-war protests grew from college campuses to "national prominence in 1965. Anti-war marches and other protests, such as the ones organized by Students for a Democratic Society (SDS), attracted a widening base ... peaking in early 1968...."[52]

Johnson's detractors were not limited to civil disturbances. Voters agreed and the November elections saw the Democrats lose "forty-seven House seats, three Senate seats, and eight governorships.[53] Those results confirmed Johnson's decision on a question that he had been wrestling. At the end of March, he announced that he would not seek reelection. His announcement prompted pols from both sides of the aisle to begin issuing barbed speeches aimed at assisting their respective party into the oval office in the fall. GOP politicians, of course, used the *Pueblo* as an example

On October 21, Hundreds of young protestors converged on Washington, D.C. (1967), to protest the war in Vietnam. They are shown holding protest signs near the reflecting pool at the National Mall. Washington was just one of many cities where protests were held (White House photographer Frank Wolfe photo; https://catalog.archives.gov/id/192603).

of the Democrats' indecision in the face of communism. California representative Bob Wilson spouted, "Our State Department (Johnson's cabinet) has settled down into a rut of defeatism, puny protest, and wishy-washy talk-a-thons with the North Koreans."[54] In addition, Johnson was also subjected to growing anti-war arguments from his own party in Congress, led by the powerful voice of Senate Majority Leader, Mike Mansfield. Mansfield had been an opponent of the Vietnam War as early as 1962, when the United States was providing military advisors and lending financial support to South Vietnam, and later "became an implacable critic of the American position [concerning Vietnam]."[55] By 1968, the media had also drifted away from their previous backing of the president's war efforts. This was especially true after some reporters "went to Vietnam as supporters of U.S. policy and then, after witnessing the war, grew skeptical."[56] The television nightly news was broadcasting film footage of the war along with the daily American casualty numbers, giving rise to further public dissatisfaction in the manner in which the war was being conducted.

But it may not have been just the war in Vietnam, or the *Pueblo* incident or other political incidents that prompted the American publics' view on President Johnson. While the war in Vietnam remained constantly in the minds of the American public, the same public was simply tired of Lyndon Johnson. Historian Robert Dallek wrote:

> Though Johnson found it difficult, if not impossible, to admit, his behavior was largely responsible for the complaint about his offensive personal style. It wasn't simply that he was overbearing or that people didn't like him, as he complained in moments of self-pity, but his grandiosity, explosiveness, and deviousness raised question about his fitness to be President. [His personal flaws were] as much a part of the man as his passion to help the disadvantaged and serve the national well-being.[57]

By November 1967, nearly 500,000 American troops were in Vietnam, and U.S. commanders were asking for more personnel. With spending on the war at nearly $25 billion per year, military deaths over 15,000, casualties over 100,000, and nightly television broadcasts carrying the spiraling war costs, disillusionment with the war grew across the United States. "The mounting number of American casualties in South Vietnam [was] having a profound effect upon American opinion."[58] Fully 50 percent of Americans disapproved of Johnson's handling of the Vietnam War.[59] The administration's lack of transparency concerning the war resulted in 65 percent of the American public complaining "that [Johnson] was not

Three—Reactions

fully informing the country about" the true details and figures of the war effort.[60] The dissatisfaction peaked in January 1968 with the capture of the *Pueblo* on January 23, and the psychologically disastrous Tet offensive carried out by the North Vietnamese on January 30, 1968. The countrywide scope of the attacks within Vietnam caused upheaval in the American public, sapping "much of the remaining grassroots support for continuing the war." Walter Cronkite, the highly respected American TV journalist, was heard to say, "I thought we were winning the war."[61] The lack of resolve concerning the war even reached the inner circle of the administration. In 1967, Secretary of Defense Robert McNamara had begun advising the president that troop strength in Vietnam should reach a ceiling number, bombing should be reduced or eliminated, and the United States should seek "a new American peace initiative." Johnson would not hear of such "defeatism" and ousted McNamara (officially, McNamara resigned November 29, 1967), appointing him to a position at the World Bank, and naming Clark Clifford to the Secretary of Defense post.[62] Secretary of State Dean Rusk also held some of the same sentiments and "recognized that Tet had sapped much of the remaining grassroots support for continuing the war."[63]

Advised by Secretary Rusk, CIA Director Helms, and Under Secretary of Defense Nitze, Johnson was convinced that the *Pueblo* incident was linked to the Vietnam War effort, meant to divert attention to Korea, enabling the North Vietnamese to take advantage of the distraction to mount the Tet offensive.[64] Regardless of Johnson's thinking, the American public began retracting their support for the war, while urging that action be taken to retrieve the *Pueblo* and crew, certainly a political dichotomy. Public dissatisfaction rose to the point that the Secret Service advised the president not to travel, and Johnson became a virtual "prisoner in the White House, losing his freedom to travel in the country."[65] As 1968 passed into mid-year, Johnson's focus was less and less drawn to the plight of the *Pueblo*.

During the Johnson presidency in 1968, other events pulled at the nation's heart. On April 4, the Reverend Martin Luther King, Jr., was killed by an assassin's bullet as he stood on the balcony outside his room at the Lorraine Motel in Memphis, Tennessee. King was in Memphis to support the city's striking sanitation workers. His killer was James Earl Ray. The murder drew the attention of the nation and gave rise to violent protests in the streets of over a hundred cities, thereby forcing President Johnson

At the White House

to focus on that incident rather than the Vietnam War and his social program plans. He pleaded with the rioters to reject blind violence and follow the lead of their slain leader. Johnson and King had a complicated relationship, often placing them at odds with one another over social reform tactics, but they respected each other and worked toward mutual goals. To honor King, Johnson signed the Fair Housing Act on April 11.

Only two months later, on June 5, 1968, presidential candidate Robert Kennedy was also killed by an assassin, once more bringing the nation's attention to the horrific murder of one of its leaders while diverting President Johnson's attention. Kennedy was killed in Los Angeles by a Palestinian who had Jordanian citizenship. Sirhan Sirhan killed Kennedy in protest of Kennedy's support for the Israelis during the six-day war the previous year. These and other incidents in 1968, such as the capture of the USS *Pueblo* caused the American public to continually scrutinize the actions of their president, leaving him under the scornful spotlight of the public and the media.

Because of the intense scrutiny of the public and the unforgiving media, "It was increasingly difficult to find public forums for the president that avoided disruption from demonstrators opposing the war or demanding more money and programs for blacks and poor people."[66] Just finding a secluded location for a brief vacation for the president presented a challenge. One such place was found in April at the Hawaiian luxury estate of the late industrialist Henry Kaiser, where Johnson took the occasion to combine business with pleasure, meeting with South Korean President Park, following the January Tet offensive. The meeting did not go well as the two men argued. Park was asking for more assistance and aid from the United States, while Johnson wanted an absolute commitment from Park that he would send more South Korean troops to Vietnam. Park was convinced that earlier firefights across the DMZ were a dire warning that North Korea would not hesitate to attack South Korea in force. He was also convinced "that America simply was losing its nerve in Asia." He was totally against Johnson's new policy of diminished and/or cessation of bombing in North Vietnam. There was another lesson that Park had taken on board. He had watched as the United States had made a big show over the capture of the *Pueblo*. Battle groups had been formed in the Sea of Japan, and American air squadrons were placed on standby. Yet, the United States had taken no action in response to the hijacking of their spy ship. Was it any wonder then, that Park had great concern over whether the

Three—Reactions

United States would come to South Korea's aid if North Korea decided the time was right for an all out assault on their neighbors to the South? Park had lost patience with Johnson, and finally blurted out to the president, "At the time of the capture of the *Pueblo,* wasn't it due to your weakness that you could not give assistance to the ship?"[67] It would have been worth the price of a cup of tea to see the expression on Johnson's face at that gibe.

Just two weeks prior to this, Johnson had announced to a stunned nation that he would not run for reelection in the fall. In his address he stated that he would spend the last months in office with the overall intent to end the war in Vietnam, an intention that would not be fulfilled. Only four days after making his announcement, Martin Luther King, Jr., was murdered, soon followed by rioting, looting, and arson in several American cities. Those riots served to produce "a backlash against his support of minority programs that seemed unlikely to soften in the next two years."[68] In Washington, to quell the civil disturbances, Johnson called up 15,000 Federal troops to put down the riots.

Historian Nancy Bernkopf Tucker wrote that President Johnson was "dominated by the Cold War stereotypes of his time." So deep were Johnson's convictions that he once confided to Richard Goodwin, one of his speech writers, "...that he was the target of a gigantic communist conspiracy in which his domestic adversaries were only dupe players—not conscious participants, perhaps, but unwitting dupes.... You know, Dick, the communists are taking over our country." And "he told his staff that 'the communists already control the three major networks and the forty major outlets of communication.'"[69]

The international Cold War stereotype that the communists were attempting to carry out the "domino theory" of dominance over small countries was believed by President Johnson so fervently that he was determined to personally stop the spread of communism by its defeat in Vietnam. Perhaps wishing Vietnam to be his legacy for halting the spread of communism, instead it became his legacy for flawed leadership.

As Tucker wrote, Johnson lost "his way in the jungles of Vietnam."[70] By 1968, Johnson and his advisors saw every world event and every decision made by the White House in its relation to the war in Vietnam. "Vietnam governed choices made, expenditures apportioned, and challenges accepted...."[71] As a result, the seizure of the *Pueblo* was also looked at through the Johnson administration's Vietnam filter, thereby coloring all

At the White House

Pueblo discussions and decisions, placing them in the context of the war in Southeast Asia.

On January 23, 1968, the president held his usual Tuesday luncheon meeting with his national security team. Notes from that meeting reveal the lack of knowledge of both North Korea and the USS *Pueblo*, and consideration of military retaliation options. President Johnson voiced his opinion that one of the options included, "Hitting the North Koreans with U.S. forces," and perhaps "Capturing one of their [North Korean] ships." The president also stated that he thought the incident a plot to disrupt actions world wide, and that he "would not be surprised if something happened in Berlin to coincide with what is going on in Vietnam and Korea." At the same meeting, General Wheeler informed the group that "the man who lost a leg [during the attack on the *Pueblo*, fireman Duane Hodges,] was engaged in blowing up equipment, inferring that Hodges was injured by an explosion in the process of destroying intelligence documents and equipment."[72] In truth, Hodges was severely injured by North Korean gunfire. Both the president's and Wheeler's observations were untrue and are perhaps indicative of their naivety and paucity of knowledge of North Korea and details of the *Pueblo* capture.

Possibly on that same day, Richard Helms, Director of the CIA, penned a report following the request of the Secretary of Defense. It is unclear whether that report was part of the meeting agenda on the 23rd or the 24th. In the report, Helms was assessing the intentions of the North Koreans. He wrote that the circumstances of the *Pueblo's* capture "indicated that this was a deliberate act and not the result of a local North Korean commander exceeding his instructions." On that point, Helms was correct. The incident was surely orchestrated out of Pyongyang, likely by Kim Il-sung, himself. Helms' report went on to state, "...the North Koreans were prepared to face a period of sharply heightened tensions." Helms may have been speculating, though, when he further wrote, "...the North Koreans would probably not release the crew or the ship ... unless they judged that the United States would resort to retaliatory action, such as an air attack against [North Korea]." Helms went on to opine that he believed the Soviets would become involved and advise North Korea to conclude the unfavorable situation. And finally, Helms predicted that the North Koreans would initiate "a heavy propaganda exploitation of the affair for some days at least."[73] On that point he was correct.

On January 24, a corollary *Pueblo* meeting was held at the State

Three—Reactions

Department, with virtually the same attendees, along with George Christian, the White House Press Secretary. Taking notes at the meeting, Christian wrote that McNamara wanted the group to analyze the North Korean objective, suggesting that they may have wanted to "tie down the United States." Nitze believed that North Korea was trying to pressure the United States to negotiate an end in Vietnam. Katzenbach disagreed and suggested that the *Pueblo* was just "a monkey wrench," and that the most "plausible conclusion" was that it was "simply a North Korean action."[74] Surprisingly, though Nicholas Katzenbach was not considered a foreign policy expert, he correctly assigned responsibility: the North Koreans acted on their own. But Walt Rostow, a firm believer in Soviet conspiracy, remained unconvinced. Referring to the North Koreans he said, "They were going for a vessel in which the Russians are much interested."[75] Everyone had an opinion and most proved incorrect. In light of the fact that the CIA, NSA, and other entities had intelligence assets stationed around the world, how was it that there was such a lack of knowledgeable, informed leadership at the very pinnacle of American government?

At 1:00 p.m. that day, the president met once again with his National Security Council. This meeting produced statements that were indicative of some of the brash, unfounded statements made by senior leadership as they advised the president. Secretary McNamara, for example, stated that "the Soviets knew of it [the attack and capture of the *Pueblo*] in advance." Secretary Rusk echoed this sentiment, stating that he thought the "incident was pre-planned," and that the "Soviets may have had advance notice of what was planned." At the same meeting, the attendees also discussed the alleged confession made by CDR Bucher. Perhaps not surprisingly, finger pointing began. Secretary Rusk stated that he simply could not believe that the North Koreans could ever get a "U.S. Navy Commander to make statements like that." He implied that something was amiss in Lloyd Bucher's record or character. The president jumped in with the same sentiments, stating, "Look very closely at his record."[76] This seems to be an unfair assertion considering that the *Pueblo* had broadcast SOS messages and requested military assistance. Why question Bucher's character at that point in the investigation? Walt Rostow, ever believing the Soviets to be puppet masters, stated without evidence that the "confession by the [*Pueblo's*] captain appears to be written by the Soviets." And finally, Richard Helms, Director of the CIA, stated that, "It looks ... like collusion between the North Koreans and the Soviets ... to divert us from our efforts in Vietnam."⁷⁷ Initially, Helms' remark reflected the general belief within President Johnson's inner circle. Historian and author Mitchell Lerner described this theory as a "virtually unanimous assessment." In January 1998, Lerner interviewed Walt Rostow who stated to Lerner, "'We all agreed it was a diversionary effort. We did not wish to be diverted.'"⁷⁸

Bucher's alleged confession received a great deal of discussion among members of the Johnson administration. Johnson's advisors, for the most part, believed that Bucher had written such a document. The point on which they were understandably most unsure was whether Bucher had voluntarily written the document or whether he was coerced by the North Koreans. When the confession was broadcast, allegedly with Bucher reading it, NSA speech analysts compared the reading to Bucher's voice patterns. They concluded that it was Bucher reading the document on air. Bucher's wife, Rose Bucher, "however, upon hearing the broadcast, adamantly denied that it was her husband's voice." Rose Bucher would be proven correct after the return of the crew.⁷⁹ But the inner circle of President Johnson, and officials of the Navy, had initially believed that Bucher had broadcast the confession.

If Johnson and his advisors had more closely studied Bucher's alleged confession, they would have been able to discern that the document was rife with untruths. For example, Bucher "confesses" that the CIA had promised him "a lot of dollars" if his "task would be done successfully." North Korea also alleged that Bucher wrote that the *Pueblo* "did not hoist the U.S. flag and sailed at the highest speed...."⁸⁰ Expert analysis of such statements would surely have raised doubt as to the veracity of Bucher's forced confession.

The president's top advisors made baseless assertions, convinced that they held substance. Subsequent analysis would not bear out many of their rash statements. Did each advisor wish to impress the president by appearing to have powerful information to convey? Was it flawed leadership that led them to link known facts with speculation to project an assumed possession of powerful knowledge to please the president?

Later that evening, the president met again with Rusk, McNamara, Clifford, and Rostow. It was at this meeting that Secretary Rusk suggested that the *Pueblo* matter be taken to the U.N. Security Council. The president concurred, saying, "I think we should get [U.N.] Ambassador Goldberg down here tomorrow morning...." And while U.N. diplomatic efforts were discussed and formulated, military options were also discussed in detail.⁸¹

Three—Reactions

Even though the President's Breakfast Meeting on the 25th set out to consider using the U.N. diplomatic channels with Ambassador Goldberg, Rostow still preferred military reprisal, asserting that "international law states that the seizure of a ship on the high seas justifies counteraction and equivalent reprisal." Rostow seemed to reject the president's expressed desire for a diplomatic solution. Ambassador Goldberg, along with the president, Rusk, and McNamara were in agreement that taking the case to the U.N. would give them more time to plan their course of action. It was also hoped that this time could be used to work with the Soviets, and "give the Soviets an opportunity to try to bring their influence to bear on the North Koreans." Ambassador Goldberg was certain that taking the matter to the Security Council would "take care of our diplomatic situation." It was also at this meeting that the attendees began to grapple with the problem of winning over Congress in formulating a military retaliatory course of action, including activating a large number of military reserves. And while McNamara had the draft executive order calling up the military reserves prepared for the president to sign, Johnson was concerned about a call-up without concurrence from Congress, and stated, "We need to go to the Congress on this matter." He was also concerned that this overt action might "jeopardize our position elsewhere, particularly in Berlin."[82] The president's innuendo suggested that the Korean incidents were part of a world-wide communist plot, with the next possible step being an attempt to take over all of Berlin. Perhaps because of this fear, President Johnson stayed the course of using diplomatic channels and sent a follow-up telegram to Soviet Chairman Alexi Kosygin, asking for his help in influencing the North Koreans and reminding Kosygin of their shared objectives: "I am sure that we must agree that our common interests in preserving world peace would not be served by increased tensions in this area of the world."[83]

At the president's luncheon meeting that day, while the same discussion points arose, several new items were considered. Rostow reported that he had received information that the Soviets had loaded a cargo plane with 792 pounds of cargo, allegedly with "equipment taken from the *Pueblo.*" This further reinforced his notion of a Soviet plot. President Johnson, showing a bit of impatience, asked the group, "what I want to know is how we are going to get that ship out." Although the president preferred diplomacy, he still harbored the belief that somehow the *Pueblo* could be forcibly removed from Wonsan Harbor. CIA Director Richard

At the White House

Helms made a prophetic statement, saying that one of his [North Korean] sources had told him that the North Koreans "will exploit the incident and then turn the ship loose for humanitarian reasons." Time would prove him correct on the first assertion, but wrong on the second. In the midst of military advisors still advocating military action, the most sage advice at the meeting was probably given by Under Secretary of State Nicholas Katzenbach, who stated, "Mr. President, the only way to get that ship out with the crew is talking through diplomatic channels."[84] His words would be proven partially true when after months of rigorous negotiations with the North Koreans, the crew members were released. During that same meeting, after a verbal discussion and suggestion by Clark Clifford, the administration agreed that the *Pueblo* incident would be submitted to the U.N. Security Council.

Ambassador Goldberg addressed the U.N. Security Council on January 26, stating, "...a virtually unarmed vessel of the U.S. Navy, sailing on the high seas, has been wantonly and lawlessly seized by North Korean patrol boats and her crew forcibly detained. [This] warlike action carries a danger to peace which should be obvious to all." He went on to emphasize that the *Pueblo* was "about 25 miles off the port of Wonsan." He bolstered his statement by saying that a North Korean report from one of the DPRK patrol boats confirmed that position, as they were within a mile of the same location when *Pueblo* was attacked.[85]

President Johnson also made a recorded statement that day, his first regarding the *Pueblo*. Among several items he stated: "This week the North Koreans committed yet another wanton and aggressive act by seizing an American ship and its crew in international waters. Clearly this cannot be accepted."[86] Johnson went on to say, "We have taken and we are taking certain precautionary measures to make sure that our military forces are prepared for any contingency that might arise in this area. The United States will not back down."[87]

Another interesting meeting occurred the following day, January 26, 1968. In that meeting, President Johnson ordered General Wheeler to have General Andrew Goodpaster speak with ex–President Dwight Eisenhower to "ask Ike what is our best constitutional way to proceed."[88] The president also related that he had received a response from Soviet Foreign Minister Andrei Gromyko, in which Gromyko urged restraint and cautioned against overreacting.

General Goodpaster reported back to the president on January 29.

Three—Reactions

In his memo to Johnson, he wrote that former President Eisenhower had asked a number of questions. Perhaps not surprisingly, Eisenhower made military suggestions initially and then proposed a quarantine and a movement of military assets closer to Korea. He also suggested strongly that the administration "should do everything possible to press for action on the diplomatic front and in the U.N. Security Council, and should even ask for a special session of the General Assembly if we thought anything useful could be achieved," and concluded by expressing his "hope for the president's success in this matter."[89]

Only one day later, on January 30, approximately seventy to eighty thousand North Vietnamese troops launched one of the largest military operations of the Vietnam War, the Tet offensive. Over one hundred cities in South Vietnam were attacked, with heavy losses inflicted on U.S. troops, South Vietnamese troops, as well as the North Vietnamese and Viet Cong troops.[90] "U.S. losses were 3,895," South Vietnam lost 4,954 military personnel and an untold number of civilians caught in the chaos of battle. The number of communist soldiers killed was 32,000.[91] The U.S. military and the Johnson administration had led the American people to believe that the United States was progressing toward ultimate victory in Vietnam. As a result of the Tet offensive, the backing of the United States public waned further as scenes from multiple Vietnam battlefields were televised, and American war casualties continued to mount. As could be expected, perhaps, U.S. generals "asked for additional troops ... believing that the U.S. was now in a position to defeat the North...." President Johnson did not acquiesce. Instead, he announced that bombing in North Vietnam would be curtailed, and he set a limit on the number of U.S. troops in South Vietnam.[92] Walter Cronkite, a "moderate and balanced observer of the war's progress," returned in February from the battlefield in Hue, and stated "that it seemed 'more certain than ever that the bloody experience of Vietnam is to end in a stalemate.'"[93] The year 1968 had the highest number of American deaths in Vietnam, reaching 16,899.[94] The psychological and political fallout of the Tet offensive, coupled with the mounting U.S. military death toll, forced the Johnson administration to turn its full attention to the political nightmare caused by the quagmire in Vietnam.

Naturally, the consequences of the Tet offensive in Vietnam occupied center stage at the White House for several days. But, if Washington had been listening, they would have heard an interesting speech given in North Korea on January 31. Mr. Kim Kwang-hyop, secretary of the communist

At the White House

Korean Workers' Party stated bluntly that the issue of the *Pueblo* incursion could not be solved militarily and that U.S. officials would be better served "if they want to solve this question by methods of previous practice."[95] The last four words of that statement by Mr. Kim would prove to be foretelling and the future key to the release of the *Pueblo* crew.

Discussions of the *Pueblo* continued for a few more days with the same topics under discussion, but the Tet offensive moved the Johnson administration to place discussions of the *Pueblo* incident on the back burner, with Vietnam resuming the primary position. This is evidenced by Tom Johnson's meeting notes. Immediately following the seizure of the *Pueblo*, discussions in meetings generally began with *Pueblo* issues. After the Tet offensive, discussions always began with items regarding the Vietnam war, meaning *Pueblo* issues received less discussion time and, if discussed at all, were placed later on meeting agendas. But the president did not entirely forget about the *Pueblo*. Johnson was quoted as declaring later that, "Every day that passed during those eleven months, the plight of those men obsessed and haunted me."[96]

Ideas from various planning meetings were consolidated and presented in a document to President Johnson and, as expected, they centered on military action. The top-secret document included available options, their advantages and disadvantages, and the possible reaction of North Korea. The ideas included placing the USS *Banner* off the coast of North Korea, escorted by U.S. warships. Apparently this idea met with approval, as the USS *Banner* was ordered to proceed to Korea and join up with the aircraft carrier USS *Enterprise,* destroyers *Ozbourn* and *Higbee* and guided missile cruiser *Canberra*. In addition, at least two dozen aircraft were armed and put on alert in South Korea to protect the *Banner.*

Perhaps planners had learned some post-incident lessons from the poor planning related to the *Pueblo* missions. Even so, as the *Banner* made its way from Yokosuka to Korea, it was shadowed in the Tsushima strait by a Soviet *Riga*-class escort vessel, which approached within "450 yards and illuminated the *Banner* with flares for ten minutes."[97] The Soviet ship then followed the American spy ship for approximately two hours before breaking off to resume its own mission. The Soviets were watching the deployment of these U.S. Navy ships with interest. As an answer to the build up of American naval forces, "five additional Soviet naval ships deployed from Vladivostok to the southern Sea of Japan (initially)," and the Soviet intelligence collector *Protraktor* returned to the area. By Feb-

Three—Reactions

ruary 7, the Soviets had thirteen surface ships, a cruiser, and "a possible submarine" in the area.⁹⁸

Another idea of the Johnson advisors was to make a show of force by repositioning military assets closer to North Korea and intensifying airborne reconnaissance over the Korean peninsula. Both the military and the president favored calling up reserve military forces in anticipation of further military conflict with North Korea. (This was done by Executive Order on January 25, 1968, the first time the reserves had been called up since the Berlin crisis of 1961.)⁹⁹ Another idea was to conduct military raids across the DMZ into North Korea using both American and ROK troops. Suggestions also included immediate action to use U.S. Navy divers to recover the classified material jettisoned by the *Pueblo* crew. Other ideas involved a quarantine or blockade against North Korean naval units, electronic jamming operations against the North Koreans, and seizing a North Korean merchant or fish factory vessel.

One of the more audacious suggestions involved sending a U.S. tug boat into Wonsan Harbor, grabbing the *Pueblo* by military force, and dragging her back to sea.¹⁰⁰ Another bold option came from Walt Rostow. He was so convinced that the North Koreans had acted on suggestions from the Soviet Union that he hatched a retaliation-in-kind idea, which he repeatedly referred to as a response of "symmetry." His plan was to lure the Soviet spy ship *Gidrolog*, which was shadowing the USS *Enterprise*, into South Korean waters where the ROK military would then capture it.¹⁰¹ Rostow's suggestion understandably received no traction from the committee.

A similar plan was formulated by the Navy. Their plan involved the USS *Ozbourn*, a destroyer under the command of Captain John Denham. The destroyer had joined the USS *Enterprise* off the coast of Korea. The audacious plan involved the *Ozbourn* rushing into Wonsan harbor after the *Enterprise* aircraft and others had pounded the area around Wonsan. The *Ozbourn* was to land a crew of sailors who would attach lines to the *Pueblo*, jerk it from its berth at the pier, and hightail it out of Wonsan with the *Pueblo* in tow. The plan had been approved by Admiral Horace Epes, commander of task force 71, and who was riding the *Enterprise*. And though the *Ozbourn* crew practiced for the recovery action, the plan was never implemented.¹⁰²

It is of interest that these options considered the possible reactions of North Korea to U.S. action, but not possible repercussions from the

At the White House

Soviets or Chinese. Yet, it was believed by many within the administration that the *Pueblo* capture had hallmarks of possible instigation by the Soviets or the Chinese. It would follow, then, that on the surface, at least, this lack of consideration of Soviet or Chinese reaction is another example of defective leadership.

Even though President Johnson also thought that the Soviets or the Chinese might have influenced the North Koreans, to his credit, in the first seven hours after Johnson learned of the *Pueblo's* capture, his reaction was one of measured, deliberate consideration, carefully weighing all options. "President Johnson did not want to open a military conflict with North Korea." Opening another war front would seriously undermine efforts in Vietnam where the United States was not faring well in a conflict that was already sapping American support and resources. According to Secretary of State Rusk, in an interview for the Lyndon Baines Johnson Library Oral History Collection, Johnson had "made a prompt decision to try to get the ship and its men back by diplomatic means rather than by military means."[103] The President consistently stayed with this course of action throughout negotiations with the North Koreans for the release of the *Pueblo* and crew. Aside from being his own man, his methodology may have been influenced by his lack of complete dependence on advisors. Just as his predecessor, President Kennedy, who "learned skepticism about intelligence estimates the hard way" (Bay of Pigs), President Johnson relied greatly on his own self-counsel, stating in 1966, "I can't think of a thing I know that the press doesn't know right now. There isn't one important activity we are in that I haven't seen in the papers or on TV in some way."[104]

During the captivity of the *Pueblo* and its crew, President Johnson received a daily briefing from the CIA. In addition to daily briefings, the CIA continued to monitor all aspects of the *Pueblo* incident, including efforts at the negotiating table and world-wide sentiment regarding the issue. These findings were provided to the president in numbered "Pueblo Sitreps," (situation reports). They offer insight to the multiplicity of issues brought before the administration at the time of the *Pueblo* incident. For example, the briefing book for January 23 contained a cryptic untimely remark, considering that the CIA and the president already know that *Pueblo* had been captured. It read, "The North Koreans have long shown extreme sensitivity to U.S. and South Korean 'spy ships' operating in the area. Pyongyang's propaganda during the past few weeks has taken a par-

81

ticularly harsh line against the [United States]."[105] The briefing on the following day contained discouraging news. Referring to negotiations that had begun with the North Koreans, the president read, "The U.S. got nowhere at Panmunjom today." The briefing also stated that the North Koreans were defiant regarding the release of the *Pueblo* and the crew of the spy ship.[106] News on the 26th was no better. The CIA briefing stated, "Pyongyang is now talking about bringing the *Pueblo's* crew to trial," and that the crew must "receive due punishment."[107] This was certainly not news the administration hoped to hear, and the North Korean stance in negotiations would remain resolute for months to follow.

The CIA sitrep of January 27, 1968, reported that the Neutral Nations Supervisory Commission, which had been established by the Korean Armistice Commission at the end of the Korean War, could do nothing to assist in the release of the *Pueblo* and crew, and that Communist East European nations were taking a pro–North Korea stance in the situation. The report also stated that on the previous day another U.S. soldier had been killed along the Korean DMZ by a North Korean infiltrator, and that the U.N. Security Council had devoted only two hours of debate on the *Pueblo* situation.[108]

In CIA sitrep #14 of January 28, the president learned that Pyongyang had flatly rejected the idea of "U.N. consideration of the *Pueblo* problem." It also became apparent that the administration was attempting to solicit help from the Soviets in resolving the issue. Boris Batrayev, an operative for the Soviet Committee for State Security (KGB) in New Delhi, had conveyed to the CIA that the "USSR is interested in working behind the scenes to resolve it" [the *Pueblo* issue]. Batrayev also made it known that Chairman Kosygin was of the opinion that "the *Pueblo* incident could have been a 'genuine mistake,'—without saying on whose part...."[109]

The sitrep on the following day seemed to take exception to Johnson's preferred one-on-one negotiations with North Korea. In fact, Ethiopia had proposed inviting North Korea to the United Nations to "tell its side of the story." The idea of giving North Korea a world platform to convey their version of the *Pueblo* events was probably not well received by the Johnson administration. Further in the report, the CIA reported that the North Vietnamese had "voiced its [their] support for its North Korean 'brothers and comrades in arms....'" The CIA alleged that North Vietnam went on to claim that the "dispatch of the *Pueblo* to Asian waters" was provocation "designed to provoke a new war...."[110] This language appears to demonstrate the CIA's attempt to bolster the Johnson administration's perceived link between the *Pueblo* and the war in Vietnam.

The CIA also had its hands in another aspect of the *Pueblo* capture. Apparently the Johnson administration found it hard to imagine a Navy commanding officer giving up his ship. Whether tasked by the administration or self motivated, the CIA began examining the record of the *Pueblo's* Commanding Officer. By January 29, the agency had completed what it termed a "psychological and political analysis" of CDR Lloyd Bucher.[111] It simply seemed inconceivable to the Johnson administration, the military, and the CIA that a U.S. Navy ship had been taken without a single defensive shot fired. Did it follow that there must be something psychologically amiss with Bucher? One of their findings is almost comical. In their report of January 29, they wrote that Bucher was very involved with the fitting out of the *Pueblo*, working very long hours to get the ship ready for sea. "Indeed, he pushed so hard that he was criticized for being too demanding with the civilians outfitting the ship."[112] The ship was outfitted in Bremerton, Washington, and was found by Bucher to be rife with errors by the Navy and the shipyard workers. A glaring example was that all of the radio gear in the security spaces had been installed upside down. One can certainly see why a new skipper would be hounding the shipyard workers who were making such flagrant errors.

In addition, the CIA drew certain "inferences" from their investigation, but those inferences are to this day redacted from the report. Fully two pages of the report are blanked out. The other sections of the report revealed nothing out of the ordinary and stated that Bucher's "performance was average," wording that the Navy would consider less than stellar. In the remainder of the report the intelligence agency does its best to analyze the propaganda value to the North Koreans by their capture of the *Pueblo* and their intent in overseeing the wording of Bucher's "confession." On yet another point, they follow the Johnson administration party line as they tried to connect the dots to make a connection between Bucher's statement, the capture of the spy ship, and the war in Vietnam. It might be argued that the CIA report on Bucher was yet another stab in the dark by the Johnson administration, another effort to find a culprit for blame.

In the same CIA "psychological report," the CIA wrote a summary statement. The gist of that statement was that North Korean "propaganda statements indicate that North Korea will press for at least an implicit

Three—Reactions

U.S. admission of guilt before taking such action [,the release of the *Pueblo* crew]."[113] On that point, the CIA was spot on. It would be months before progress was made to release the crew, and only then, after the United States admitted its guilt, at least on paper.

President Johnson's calendar was full every day, and January 30th was no exception. The president held meetings from early morning to late in the evening. In the afternoon of the 30th, an interesting gathering took place. Secretary of State Rusk reported that he had been told by his sources at the United Nations that the North Koreans did not favor U.N. involvement. Rusk stated, "The North Koreans said it was not the United Nation's business."[114] That statement is significant because it confirmed that a major avenue in Johnson's wish for a diplomatic resolution had been closed by the North Koreans.

Later that day, the president met again with his Foreign Affairs Committee. And once again, Johnson asked General Wheeler, "What about the possibility of this officer having turned [voluntarily assisting the North Koreans]?" Wheeler tried to discourage that line of thinking, telling the president that the possibility was "very small." But the president could not drop it, stating, "This officer doesn't look like the normal, prudent, alert officer I would have handle Air Force One if it were on alert. We must always bear in mind the possibility that we are in the wrong."[115] It seems that Johnson had a nagging proclivity to focus the blame for the international incident on Commander Bucher. Yet his action seems greatly unfounded, especially because he had been briefed by NSA, CIA, and other advisors that the evidence did not bear out his position. There is a leadership flaw in his continuing to pursue his speculative theory in hopes of directing culpability from himself or his administration.

The president was not finished with business on the 30th. At six p.m. he met with Senate Minority Leader, Illinois Republican Everett Dirksen, and House Minority Leader, Michigan Republican Gerald Ford to discuss the *Pueblo*. Also attending were Secretary of State Rusk, Secretary of Defense McNamara, Chairman of the JCS General Wheeler, and Ambassador to South Vietnam, General Maxwell Taylor. The two congressional leaders gave little quarter to the president and his advisors with their questions. Ford started out by asking the president if he would have done things differently with "the benefit of hindsight." The president responded that he would not have waited "52 minutes to file the first message." It is unclear whether the president was referring to his own administration, military officials, or the *Pueblo*. The very next statement Johnson made was telling. He said, "I have looked into the background of this commander. It was his first command." Johnson once again revealed the leadership flaw of implying that Commander Bucher should be targeted for placement of blame for the loss of the spy ship because it had been Bucher's lack of command experience. Ford did not respond to Johnson's insinuation and turned the conversation by stating, "I would have gotten rid of all that [classified] equipment, even if it required sinking our own vessel." Johnson deflected Ford's comment by stating that he was just lucky not to "have another Bay of Pigs." Ford would not drop the line of questioning, however, asking, "First, why was there no more certain way of destroying the ship?" Johnson answered obliquely, using a football analogy of holding "the ball a second too long and [getting] tackled."[116]

Ford knew very well that culpability did not rest entirely with Bucher and counseled the president, saying, "I think you should take a good look at where we made mistakes on this." Rather than admitting any responsibility, however, Johnson again demonstrated his arrogant leadership style by countering Ford's statement, saying, "I think the mistake was made by the North Koreans. History may prove it wrong. I do not think the mistake was made by us." Ford, a former college football player, naval officer, and veteran of the Second World War understood ship-board protocol and did not acquiesce to the president, instead stating, "If I had known what was on that vessel I might have blown it out of the water myself." Ford finally had heard enough and addressed all those in the room, including the president, stating, "All of you seem to have a good reason for not doing something. We need a thorough going over of this matter to see what were the facts. It seems to me your attitude is one of excuse rather than how to prevent it from happening again. I do not like the attitude that this was a helpless ship. It appears that we should have been better prepared with a contingency plan. We ought to raise some very serious questions." For some unknown reason, Senator Dirksen then asked, "What information do we have about the Captain?" The president answered that he believed that Bucher was loyal to the United States, but he could not refrain from adding, "Bucher did have certain emotional traits which might have been exploited."

It is interesting to note that well past the January meeting with President Johnson, Ford, who would later become president, remained focused on the plight of the *Pueblo* and its crew. In a July 18, 1968, press release,

Three—Reactions

Ford showed his displeasure in President Johnson's handling of national defense, stating that the Johnson/Humphrey administration had "weakened our ability to respond to emergency situations such as the seizure of the USS *Pueblo* by concentrating attention on Vietnam."[117] Still later, after the *Pueblo* crew had been released, Ford issued a news release to constituents informing them that the House Committee on Armed Services had opened hearings on the capture of the USS *Pueblo*. He wrote that the committee would look at "the concept of single, unprotected, intelligence-gathering ships ... who generated the particular mission of the *Pueblo*, who characterized it as low risk, and who determined the ships to be used, their configuration, their armament...."[118]

President Johnson held an almost delusional belief in a world-wide communist plot and tended to see each issue as it related to the war in Vietnam. Hence, he looked at the Blue House attack and the capture of the *Pueblo* as further evidence of a communist master plan. He was certain that both events were intended to infuriate the South Koreans, inducing them to bring home their two divisions that were fighting alongside the Americans in Vietnam.[119] The president was correct that both incidents infuriated the South Koreans, but there was no proof of that being the intent of the North Koreans.[120] Meeting notes of initial discussions reveal that like the president, some of his advisors were of the opinion that either the Soviet Union or China was behind the North Korean actions. Johnson had witnessed what he felt was a part of the communist domination theory, as "50,000 People's Liberation Army (PLA) from China took up positions in North Vietnam from which they 'engaged in combat, inflicted losses, and suffered casualties.'" And then the North Koreans "reached out from behind [their] cloistered frontiers to seize the USS *Pueblo*."[121] The Johnson administration was convinced that it was the communist bloc that had acted once again, and that such action was linked to the war in Vietnam.

On February 7, 1968, Under Secretary of State George Ball's ad hoc committee had completed their work and produced the sixth draft of their "Report to the President." After weeks of work, their report in some instances appeared sophomoric, and, if it were not for the seriousness of the subject, almost comedic in its efforts to avoid any direct accusations. The committee report stated that "a balance must be struck between the need for ... the intelligence, and the risk involved in obtaining it." After writing that they believed the spy missions were essential for intelligence collection, they also wrote that "the responsible officials had at the time a valid basis for approving the mission," and that "North Korean warnings ... were in form and content simply the latest reiteration of familiar North Korean charges that hundreds of 'fishing boats and armed espionage boats' were intruding in North Korean waters." The report also warned that "[spy vessels] should not be used near North Korean territorial waters without protection." That advice seems self-evident. And finally, the committee advised that perhaps there should be "a gradual erosion of secrecy in order to produce greater mutual understanding between nations ... [thereby] dispelling suspicion, [and] creat[ing] a condition of greater mutual confidence."[122] One can only wonder what President Johnson, the NSA, and the JCS thought of that nugget.

The war in Southeast Asia overrode the president's thought processes on every issue brought before him. Not only did the president struggle to find a solution to the *Pueblo* problem, but with the exception of two or three advisors, he was surrounded by well-meaning hand-wringers, leaders who were hampered by their narrowly focused solutions, which did not always consider inherent risks. Yet in their defense, those advisors had never before encountered the seizure of an American warship by a foreign state and, therefore, could only speculate on a resolution. Yet each man was convinced that he held the best solution to President Johnson's spy ship problem.

Reaction of Congress

Congress reacted predictably upon learning of the *Pueblo*'s seizure. Members aligned themselves with either of two courses of action regarding the capture of the *Pueblo*. "The *Pueblo* seizure risked strengthening the position of [congressional] 'hawks' such as Senators Strom Thurmond (R–SC) and John Stennis (D–MS), Representative Mendel Rivers (D–SC), and Governor Ronald Reagen (R–CA), who had long demanded more forceful military actions in Vietnam."[123] Some advocated immediate military action against North Korea, while others urged restraint and diplomacy. "But, with few exceptions, even the hawks in Congress were moderate in their reaction."[124] Apart from the hawks and doves were a small number, such as Arkansas's Democratic Senator and Chairman of the Senate Foreign Relations Committee, J. William Fulbright, who seemed to be one of President Johnson's harshest critics on Vietnam, wishing to gain the spotlight by being nettlesome and accusing the president of not being forthright with the Committee.[125] All of these actions were played out on the floor of Congress, in snippets to the media, and in letters to the president.

In the Senate, Strom Thurmond of South Carolina, a strong advocate of the military and a Vietnam War hawk, rose to the occasion on January 24th when he said, "Seizure of the USS *Pueblo* on the high seas is a calculated test of the will of the American People." Apparently Senator Thurmond also believed there may have been an underlying communist plot as he stated, "In effect, the North Koreans and the Soviet Union are trying to give the United States a 'Yankee go home' suggestion." He continued, "There should be no doubt that the United States will fight if necessary to obtain the immediate release of this ship and all of its personnel." He informed his colleagues that he had sent President Johnson a telegram advising him to send North Korea an "ultimatum that the *Pueblo* will be taken by force if it is not delivered within a specified period of time." He did not elaborate on the time allowed or the method for carrying out the consequences of his ultimatum. Thurmond went on to say, "There is no question in my mind that the seizing of the *Pueblo* and its crew by the North Koreans was not an isolated incident but was closely tied in with the war in South Vietnam."[126] Countering cautionary remarks were voiced by strong Vietnam War critic and Democratic Senator Mike Mansfield of Montana. On January 29, 1968, he stated, "[we must use] caution, coolness, and restraint," and "any rash action would not only ... seal the doom of the 83 Americans of the U.S.S. *Pueblo*, it could also bring about another bloody and prolonged involvement in Korea." He went on to say, "We ought to keep our shirts on and not go off half-cocked until we know more about the details of this incident."[127]

Like the Senate, members of the House of Representatives made their feelings known in peaceful or blustery orations. Republican Representative Durward Hall of Missouri seemed to equivocate as he referred to himself as a "peacemaker in perilous times," and stated that "it is time for level heads." He then stated, "These provocations require-indeed demand-an immediate response. The president should make clear ... that the American ship should not be ransacked and should be released at once, or North Korea be prepared to suffer needed and dire consequences. We are acting too little as a proud nation to the loss of too many fine citizens."[128] Hall's thoughts were echoed by California's Republican Representative Bob Wilson, who stated, "the seizure of the U.S. patrol boat *Pueblo* ... is an obvious violation of the Korean truce and is an act of war. If this means sending in military and naval forces, including air cover, it must be done—and done at once. It calls for immediate and adequate response."[129] Democratic Representative Paul Rogers of Florida stated, "Not in 100 years has the U.S. flag been forcibly lowered from a Navy ship. The seriousness of the situation requires an immediate response by the United States."[130]

Alabama Republican Representative Jack Edwards was more direct in his remarks pointed at President Johnson and voiced his displeasure at the inaction of the administration:

> Failure of the Johnson administration to face up to foreign problems around the world encourages the Communists to become even bolder in their aggressive adventures as they sense that any reaction from us is unlikely. We should now give the Korean Communists just 3 minutes to release the USS *Pueblo* and its men. And if that fails, then we should go into North Korea and get that ship and our men—now.[131]

Voicing a less hawkish view than Edwards was Hawaii's Democratic Representative Spark Matsunaga, who opposed the Vietnam War, but as a military veteran did not wish to undercut the efforts of the soldiers fighting in Vietnam. Matsunaga stated, "let us not respond too hastily and do what we may later regret. Let us turn to that international machinery set up to settle disputes such as this—the United Nations."[132] Matsunaga's reasoning seemed logical, but the administration would soon learn that North Korea was averse to interaction with the U.N.

Members of Congress were not immune to belief in communist collusion, nor from conspiracy by the Johnson administration. On February 8, 1968, Indiana Republican Representative William Bray stated, "The Soviet Union and North Korea are certainly working together now to make the whole incident as humiliating and difficult for the United States as they possibly can." He then suggested that the administration was hiding facts about the *Pueblo* from the American people, stating, "release [of facts] might tell the American people more about our lack of military preparedness and foresight than the administration cares for them to learn."[133] The lack of proper leadership, preparedness, and planning for the *Pueblo* mission seemed apparent to Representative Bray.

So prevalent was the theory of a communist conspiracy that many congressional members concluded that rather than blaming Pyongyang, Moscow should be chastised. For example, Tennessee Republican Representative Daniel Kuykendall demanded that the administration "bring the

Soviets to immediate responsibility for the provocative excesses not only of North Korea but of all Communist nations." The conspiracy theorists in Congress wished to have the Soviet Union placed on notice that further communist aggression would not be tolerated.[134]

While the posturing and puffery continued on both sides of the aisle and in both the house and senate, on January 30 the leadership of those chambers met privately with the president. House Majority Leader Carl Albert, Democrat from Oklahoma, attended and summarized the *Pueblo* incident by stating, "This has many aspects of a kidnapping case. You want to get the victim back, but you do not want to do anything that would get the victim killed." The president answered, "We will keep our hands out and our guard up. We are going to protect ourselves. We are going to pursue the various diplomatic alternatives."[135] President Johnson was clearly putting the congressional leadership on notice of his intention to continue a diplomatic course of action.

Reaction of the Public

It was not long after the capture of the *Pueblo* that the world learned of the plight of the American spy ship and its crew. The State Department, Department of Defense, and the White House all held news conferences on January 23, 1968. After Rostow's 2:25 a.m. phone call to brief President Johnson, the Department of Defense issued the first press release some time between 8:30 and 9:00 a.m. At 11:58 a.m., White House Press Secretary George Christian held a news conference, followed at 12:26 p.m. by a "press and radio news briefing" at the State Department.[136] Secretary of State Rusk stated that every effort to get the ship and crew released would be made "through the channels that are available to us."[137] The world and the U.S. Congress now knew that North Korea had attacked and forcibly taken a military ship belonging to the United States. Keeping the U.S. public and Congress informed and placated now added to the many multi-faceted problems on the president's desk.

Print media and radio and television news swarmed around the *Pueblo* story. Monitoring written and broadcast news regarding the *Pueblo* incident, as well as the remarks of members of Congress, mattered greatly to the Johnson administration. On January 24, Bob Fleming, Deputy Presidential Press Secretary, submitted a memorandum to the president that

Reaction of the Public

summarized that day's major television network broadcasts. He wrote that NBC's John Chancellor used remarks from the State Department briefings to address the question of why no U.S. military assistance had come to the spy ship. ABC's Frank Reynolds advised the public that, "the president not only had to be concerned about losing face in Korea, but even more in avoiding a new war in Asia." Dan Rather of CBS described the mood at the White House as "grim," and reported that "diplomatic efforts continue with no military retaliation expected now." Fleming continued by citing syndicated columnist and self-proclaimed liberal, Carl Rowan, who may have been waxing hawkish when he was quoted as asking, "why the 'ponderously slow' reaction," and wondering "why the captain did not report

The Navy repositioned several warships closer to North Korea while the Johnson administration weighed retaliatory action. Headline from the *New York Daily News* of January 24, 1968 (photograph from USS *Pueblo*.org web site).

Three—Reactions

activity sooner, and why no supporting help arrived quickly."[138] Perhaps unfortunately, that same day, Secretary Rusk made an off-hand remark to the press, stating that he felt that the seizure of the *Pueblo* could be interpreted as "an act of war."

From the White House's point of view, Rusk's comment was a dangerously inflammatory misstep. An act of war, that is, one nation bombing or invading another for example, made the use of reciprocal violence justifiable under international legal doctrine. Shooting up and commandeering an American Naval vessel on the high seas in peacetime certainly seemed to qualify as an act of war. But for a high-ranking government official to openly describe the incident in that manner ratcheted up the political pressure on the president to respond in kind. Neither Rusk nor any other administration official uttered such incendiary terminology in public again.[139]

Initially the press seemed to take a wait-and-see attitude, almost assuming a pedantic tone to inform the American public. David Lawrence, for example, founder and writer for the *United States News*, informed readers of the subject of "sea coast surveillance" by describing the *Pueblo* and explaining that the United States was being watched by the Soviets from "fishing vessels ... in waters off the ports of Charleston, SC, and Boston, Mass." The media were not immune to the idea of a global communist plot. Lawrence continued, opining that the plot may have been initiated "by the Red China regime...." He went on to write that North Korea claimed that the *Pueblo* was "carrying out hostile activities." Lawrence then wrote, "This is the kind of propaganda that would naturally be expected from Communist sources," and he concluded by writing, "The whole incident illustrates how readily small conflicts can be generated that could lead to international complications."[140]

An editorial in the *New York Times* of January 24, 1968, urged caution by reminding readers of the circumstances that led to America's involvement in Vietnam. It stated, "Remembering the Gulf of Tonkin, Americans would be wise to keep cool and not leap to conclusions ... about the North Korean capture of the American naval intelligence ship."[141] The Washington, D.C., *Evening Star*, knowledgeable of normal legislative theatrics, suggested, "the *Pueblo*, has touched off a mighty roll of rhetorical thunder in Congress." Its editorial warned against unnecessary military puffery, stating, "The ultimatum and the application of military power are—quite literally—the last actions the United States should take...." and "the

Reaction of the Public

instinctive reaction of outrage must be tempered by a realization of the awesome power that this nation possesses and of the consequences of a major war to all mankind. Military force should be applied only as a last resort." The editorial continued: "So North Korea continues to tweak Uncle Sam's beard. And in recognition of the size and strength of the diminutive aggressor, we have—so far—managed quite properly to hold our temper in check."[142] So, initially, the press, mirroring the president's stance, remained receptive to learning more about the entire incident and refrained from throwing barbs of blame. However, not all print media was so patient. The *Milwaukee Sentinel*, for example, blasted the Johnson administration and the government when it wrote; "North Korea's bold seizure of the *Pueblo* is not nearly so outrageous as ... the pusillanimous American reaction to it. Our official bird is not eagle, hawk, or dove. It is chicken."[143]

President Johnson, still waiting for further information, was interviewed on January 26 by Hugh Sidey of *Time* magazine. Instead of sticking with the known facts, Johnson threw out an object of distraction he had been pondering. When asked by Sidey if the military had done all it could, Johnson stated, "Three or four things could be true. Bucher could be a traitor. I do not think that is true. He could be doped up." The president went on to say that he could find no fault with "superior officers in the field."[144] If the president did not think it was true that Bucher was a traitor, it seems odd that he would express the possibility. Whatever the reason, this statement demonstrated a not-so-subtle leadership flaw. Once again, the president had seriously besmirched the character of Bucher, laying a possibility of Bucher's culpability at the feet of the American public. The president's purpose was unknown, especially in light of the fact that there was no factual basis for that statement. By that libelous remark, it seems that Johnson was ready to point the blame finger at anyone to deflect the investigative spotlight from his administration and his closest military advisors.

An influential faction of the American public met with President Johnson on January 27, 1968. It was probable that the magnates of America's leading businesses had a vested interest in how the Korean and Vietnam issues would effect their global operations. The group was comprised of presidents or chairmen of Coca-Cola, Burlington Industries, Levi Strauss, McDonnell Douglas, ALCOA, Ford, and LTV, as well as publishers and bankers. They met with the president, who tried to assuage their con-

Three—Reactions

cerns, telling them, "I know what is on your mind is the crisis in Korea. I know you are also concerned about prices and the state of the economy and the state of our nation." Johnson then proceeded to have Clark Clifford brief the businessmen on the need for electronic surveillance and the necessity of having spy ships at sea. Oddly enough, the subject of business and the effect on the U.S. dollar were scarcely discussed.[145]

Secretary of State Rusk and Secretary of Defense McNamara informed the American public of the status of the *Pueblo* when they appeared on *Meet the Press* on February 4, 1968. Elie Abel of NBC reminded Rusk that in the previous week he had stated that the *Pueblo* and crew needed to be released and "spoke of the seizure as an act of war." Rusk responded that there had been no moderation, but "President Johnson has made it clear that we would prefer to get these men back through diplomatic process," and the "administration was [first] using diplomatic contacts through capit[o]ls; secondly, the Military Armistice Commission machinery at Panmunjom, Korea; and third, the United Nations Security Council." Abel then asked Rusk if he hoped "to continue on the diplomatic route for some time?" Rusk responded that he did "not want to put a time factor on it."[146] By that statement, Secretary Rusk conveyed President Johnson's wish for a diplomatic solution and let the American people know that such a solution could take quite some time. But the press was not finished. Max Frankel, from the *New York Times* asked McNamara if the Navy knew whether the *Pueblo* "at any time had entered North Korean waters." McNamara hedged slightly, answering:

> No, I think we can't say beyond a shadow of a doubt, at no time during its voyage it entered North Korean waters. ... at the time of seizure, we are quite positive it was in international waters ... there was a period of radio silence appropriate to its mission from the period of roughly January 10 to January 21, and it is in that period that we lack knowledge, and we will not be able to obtain knowledge of that until the crew and the commander are released.[147]

Because McNamara would neither confirm nor deny *Pueblo's* position at the time of capture, his answer created more speculation in the American public and provoked the anger "of Japan, South Korea, and some NATO countries" as it appeared that the United States was hedging on "its previous statements concerning the location of the *Pueblo*."[148] It seemed to some that McNamara had indirectly admitted that the spy ship may have been in North Korean waters. This seemingly uncertain answer by McNamara prompted NSA into action, and by reanalyzing data and

Reaction of the Public

actual voice tapes of the North Koreans, as well as SIGINT evidence of the ship's movements, it was confirmed that the *Pueblo* was, indeed, in international waters at the time of its capture. McNamara's answer had other consequences. U.N. Ambassador Goldberg was furious. McNamara's answer stripped all credibility from Goldberg's stance in the U.N. of vehemently contending that the *Pueblo* had been forcibly taken in international waters. In Korea, Admiral John Smith, who was the senior U.N. representative at the Military Armistice Commission, and who was in the midst of negotiating for the release of the *Pueblo* crew, was also irate. He knew that when he next met with General Pak, he would have to attempt to respond to Pak, who was certain to bring up McNamara's remark.[149]

Later, in the same program, moderator Lawrence Spivak asked McNamara why the *Pueblo* was not better protected. McNamara answered:

> I think that is a good question and the answer is threefold. First, to have protected it would have been a provocative act. Secondly, it would have compromised the mission. This ship went undetected by the North Koreans for ten to twelve days. During that time it carried out its mission. Not only would it have been subject to capture during that period had it been detected, but also their reaction, a reaction it was sent there to determine, would have been quite different. And finally, the protection itself always runs the risk of leading to a military escalation.[150]

There are indications that the North Koreans probably knew that the *Pueblo* was on station off their coast as soon, or very soon, after its arrival, and perhaps even when the *Pueblo* had set sail from Japan. Kim Il-sung had referred to spy ships off the North Korean coast in speeches well before the *Pueblo's* capture. It also stands to reason that the North Koreans had coastal radar that had picked up the *Pueblo*. In fact, as the ship cruised from the northern part of North Korea to the south, and days before the capture of the spy ship, Lieutenant Murphy had made a statement to one of the crew members (Photographer Lawrence Mack) saying, "Most of the crew doesn't know this, so don't say anything, but they've had fire control radar locked on us for days."[151] Murphy's statement would infer that the *Pueblo* had the technical means to determine that they were the object of North Korean radar. If so, McNamara's statement alleging that the spy ship had been undetected seems at the least, uninformed. North Korean fishing boat(s) had also undoubtedly seen the spy ship, and a DPRK sub chaser had cruised by *Pueblo* in days before the capture. As far as the remainder of McNamara's answer, it appears to be speculation, at best. The factual answer is that NSA and the military simply erred in their belief that the mission was without risk, and therefore, did not assign military assets to watch over the spy ship.

Perhaps the American public saw through the military's smoke screen answers, because their anger grew. The public's apparent embarrassment and anger subsequent to the hijacking of the *Pueblo* sparked people to take pen in hand. As a result, the volume of mail received by the White House increased accordingly. For example, by the week of February 9, 1968, the White House received over a thousand (1002) letters with reference to the *Pueblo*. Seventy-three percent of the letters that week were in favor of military action against North Korea.[152] By the week of March 22, 1968, the number of *Pueblo* letters dropped to 876, yet 81 percent of those writers advocated military action.[153]

In a Gallup poll conducted on February 6, 1968, 45 percent of the American public believed that the present situation in North Korea was likely to lead to war, and 40 percent of those responding thought that the United States needed to get the ship and crew back, by force if necessary. Even though 40 percent were hawkish, at least 46 percent approved of the manner in which President Johnson was handling the situation. Quite obviously, there was not a full consensus among Americans on the method and means of handling the *Pueblo* situation.[154]

Apparently the same beliefs of the Johnson administration, that of attributing the capture of the *Pueblo* to a diversionary tactic to draw resources away from the war in Vietnam, and that the action was a Soviet and Chinese plot, had disseminated from the White House to the American public. The same aforementioned Gallup poll asked the American public, "What to you think are the main reasons behind North Korea's action?" Twenty-nine per cent answered that it was a diversionary tactic. An equal number, twenty-nine per cent believed that Russia and/or Red China were behind it.[155]

Because of the groundswell in negative public opinion directed at the Navy and Johnson administration, the Navy and the Department of Defense found themselves in a public affairs nightmare concerning the *Pueblo* incident and were forced into a defensive position. Stoked by a grinding war in Vietnam that continued to foster a large number of antiwar demonstrations, the public assumed that the military and the administration were not divulging all of the facts surrounding the seizure of the *Pueblo*. The "*Pueblo* occurred during [a] period of dwindling confidence in the American Government" and "antimilitarism."[156] The public letters

Reaction of the Public

to the Pentagon "portrayed a marked belligerent, anti–Navy tone." Respect for the Navy had diminished to the point that the public opinion could be described as "hostile."[157] It was understandable because of the military's lack of transparency regarding efforts in Vietnam and the Navy's obfuscation regarding the role of Navy spy ships, the capture of the *Pueblo*, and the general astonishment that a U.S. Navy warship could be seized by a minor military nation. It seemed that each time the White House and Pentagon attempted to enlighten the American people about the incidents of the spy ship capture, they only made matters worse. For example, they initially said that the *Pueblo* had not asked for help, except when the ship was being boarded; a statement that is only partially true. The administration also said that the United States lacked military forces to respond to the crisis, a statement that is misleading, when in fact, the resources were available, but not prepared for quick utilization. Finally, when the public became more knowledgeable of the situation, the *New York Post's* columnist Murray Kempton wrote his opinion: "It is painful and embarrassing to me both as a person and a citizen to say so, but I cannot believe anything my government says about the *Pueblo*."[158]

This pattern of withholding facts from the press and the public may have begun some years prior when government officials and the Navy distorted "facts and deceive[d] the American public about two events that led to full U.S. involvement in the Vietnam War," that is, the allegation of events of the Gulf of Tonkin incident.[159] On August 2, 1964, North Vietnamese patrol boats attacked the Navy destroyer USS *Maddox*. Subsequently, on August 4, 1964, both the *Maddox* and the USS *Turner Joy* claimed that they were both attacked by North Vietnamese patrol craft, a claim that has since been debunked. The Navy's lack of forthrightness in those incidents resulted in a skeptical American public, rightly so, because those false allegations drew the United States into an unpopular war that would later be rued by America's political body and the American people.

Tired of the Navy's obfuscation, "Most [letters from the public] condemned the lack of support and protection for the *Pueblo*." The Navy was forced to tread carefully "to avoid further inflaming of public sentiment."[160] Apparently, their efforts to be low-key did not influence the public, because when the Navy's Court of Inquiry commenced on January 20, 1969, a full year after the seizure of the *Pueblo*, an unforgiving public and the press leaped on the opportunity to opine that the inquiry would be "a

Three—Reactions

cover-up, and whitewash, and the Navy would not tolerate ... the truth."[161] At a news conference held at Naval Air Station Miramar after the crew's return, LT Edward Murphy, who had served as the Executive Officer on the *Pueblo*, "gave his impression of life in custody." After that interview, *The New York Times* gave its impression of the suppression of Murphy's interview: "Murphy seemed 'willing to discuss the entire *Pueblo* story with newsmen but indicated he was under some sort of wraps from higher authority.'" Sensing a lack of candor on the part of the Navy, newsmen then confronted the Navy's Admiral Rosenberg, who had accompanied Murphy to the news conference, charging the Navy with keeping a "lid" on information. The news media was "stymied in their quest for individual eyewitness accounts of what actually happened."[162]

The purpose in exploring so much of the national dialogue is twofold: First, it demonstrates the depth and range of feelings of the American public, U.S. government officials, and foreign interests that resulted from the seizure of an American naval vessel. From those emotions, the resulting recommendations ranged from response by immediate and decisive military action to the more tedious, methodical diplomatic means of resolution. The president certainly could not appease all interests. Thus, President Johnson was presented with a seemingly insurmountable problem, especially in light of the unmoving and frustrating negotiations with the North Koreans and the administration's preoccupation with the Vietnam War. Second, the recorded dialogue of the media, congress, and the administration confirms a fault in leadership, which encompassed even the highest office in the United States. It is clear from the meeting notes that the president and his advisors gave no thought to the possibility that the administration, NSA, and Navy shared responsibility for seizure of the *Pueblo*. The near-desperate search for a scapegoat seemed to blind the president and his advisors to the fact that culpability started at the top with gross failure to properly plan, analyze risk, and execute the spy ship missions. The avoidance by American military and political leaders to accept responsibility for the capture of the *Pueblo* reflected poorly on them and demonstrated arrogant and flawed leadership in time of crisis.

Four

Juche—Why North Korea Seized the *Pueblo*

The Washington Viewpoint

Time would prove President Johnson and nearly all of his closest advisors incorrect in their assessments of North Korea's motive for seizing the USS *Pueblo*. But at the moment of *Pueblo's* capture, the administration's overwhelming belief was that the seizure of the spy ship was part of a larger communist plot. After all, the United States and the Soviet Union had been locked in a struggle for world dominance since the end of the Second World War. By 1968, the opposing giants had faced each other for two decades in a continuing war of words and arms escalation. During that time, four U.S. presidents (Truman, Eisenhower, Kennedy, and Johnson) watched over American interests to protect freedom and democracy, while Moscow-driven Communism expanded into Eastern Europe and Asia. President Johnson and his inner circle had witnessed the aftermath of the Second World War and the increasing polarization between the United States and the Soviet bloc.

During the Cold War, Americans were fed a steady diet of the evils of communism and were exposed to red scare tactics from the likes of Wisconsin Senator Joseph R. McCarthy. Between the print media, nightly televised Vietnam war updates, and congressional hearings, the average citizen might well have believed that the Soviets or the Chinese were behind the *Pueblo* incident. While a portion of the anti-communist liturgy from the media and Washington may have espoused the truth, some was certainly speculative. President Johnson believed that anti-communist fears were plainly based on evidence. The Vietnam War became Johnson's measure of the facts. To him, there was no better example of communist

Four—*Juche*—Why Korea Seized the *Pueblo*

tentacles reaching around the globe than the encroachment of communism into Vietnam. Historian Mitchell Lerner explained this, writing:

> The decision by North Korean president Kim Il-sung to capture the *Pueblo* made sense only when considered within a global Cold War framework. Lyndon Johnson viewed the seizure as part of a world-wide challenge to the United States, a coordinated communist plan to divert U.S. military resources from Vietnam and to pressure the South Koreans into recalling their two divisions from that area.[1]

As early as January 24, 1968, however, some officials such as Under Secretary of State Nicholas Katzenbach held a different opinion. He stated in a State Department meeting that the spy ship's seizure was "simply a North Korean action."[2] While the reasons for Kim Il-sung's action are complex, one explanation resides in Kim's allegiance to the ideology of *Juche*.

The North Korean Perspective

To grasp Kim Il-sung's reasoning and adoption of *Juche*, we must first understand that throughout its history, Korea had been subjugated by the Mongols, the Chinese, Japan, and Russia.[3] In addition to living under foreign authority, the country was party to detrimental trade agreements with both Eastern and Western nations, thereby crippling Korea's economy. Hence, the Korean people have maintained a great distrust of foreigners because multiple foreign nations attempted to dominate the Korean peninsula over centuries. Some scholars, therefore, "argue that *Juche* is a reflection of a centuries-old tradition of independence from foreign powers."[4] It was this drive for self-independence that drove Kim to push North Korea into its isolationist stance, i.e. the hermit nation after he assumed power. In spite of the various attempts to subjugate Korea, the nation maintained a "streak of autonomy [in the midst of foreign domination] and a deep desire for independence...."[5]

One trading partner, Japan, forced its influence to the point that it annexed Korea in 1910, a situation that was politically acceptable to the United States.[6] Under Japanese rule, every aspect of Korea was controlled. A later example of the Japanese oppression was the forced shipping of millions of Korean men and women to Japan to be used as slave labor for the Japanese war effort during the Second World War. Yet, in the midst of Japanese rule, mass protests took place in Korea and splinter resistance groups formed, some of which embraced Communism. The Japanese could not eliminate all guerrilla resistance fighters in Korea, and from these fragmented groups of soldiers, a leader emerged, Kim Il-sung, an adherent of Communism, who would later rule North Korea for nearly a half century. The Japanese considered Kim Il-sung to be the most dangerous of the guerrillas because of his military prowess, and they made numerous attempts to locate and eliminate him. In 1939, Kim's guerrilla tactics were achieving results against the Japanese military. His bands of soldiers were destroying entire "convoys and companies," while they received aid from the general Korean population. But the Japanese were too powerful for Kim's guerrillas. When the guerrillas were in danger of elimination, Kim Il-sung fled north and was afforded sanctuary in Russia. While in Russia, with the sponsorship of Joseph Stalin, Kim and two divisions of guerrilla fighters were trained in Siberia to retake Korea.[7] The history of the subjugation of Korea by foreign states and the draconian Japanese measures to enslave all of Korea, became the stimuli for Kim Il-sung's adoption of the Juche ideology.

By the end of the Second World War, the Soviets had crossed into the northern part of Korea, and the U.S. Army had moved onto the peninsula from the south. With Hirohito's surrender, the Americans and the Soviets each moved to fill the void of the departing Japanese. Once again, Korea was occupied by foreigners. Under the subsequent Armistice Agreement, the Soviets would retain the northern part of Korea while the Americans held the south,

Kim Il-sung, the autocratic ruler of North Korea, following the close of the Korean War. He ruled, using the *Juche* ideology as his guide for decades, allowing no dissenters to thwart his draconian leadership (https://origins.osu.edu/article/image/kim-il-sung-premier-dprk-1948–1972-president-1972–1994-primarily-responsible).

Four—*Juche*—Why Korea Seized the *Pueblo*

with each side restricted to their side of a hastily designated line. Hastily formulated because the Americans were afraid that the Soviets would rush to occupy the entire peninsula before the Americans could settle into the country. Consulting no Koreans, it was Colonel Dean Rusk (future Secretary of State) and Colonel Charles Bonesteel (future general in charge of all U.N. forces in South Korea) who had been assigned to find a suitable dividing line. Their rather unsophisticated approach used a *National Geographic* map. Knowing that Seoul was to remain the capital in the South and remain within the American sector, Rusk and Bonesteel looked for a possible dividing line above Seoul. They could find no natural geographic line, so instead, they chose the 38th parallel. Their commanders along with the Soviets accepted the 38th parallel, and that dividing line remains today.[8] Within a few weeks, the United States had moved nearly 25,000 military troops into South Korea.[9] Shortly thereafter, two leaders were installed by the opposing sides. The Americans designated Syngman Rhee to head South Korea. The returning guerrilla fighters considered Kim Il-sung to be their "general commander, great leader, sagacious teacher, and intimate friend ... and their trust, self-sacrifice, and devotion are such that they [would] gladly die for him." Thus, the guerrillas "pushed Kim Il-sung forward" as their choice for leader of North Korea, and the Soviets concurred.[10] By 1948, with his cadre of guerrilla fighters at its core, Kim formed the Korean People's Army (KPA) and subsequently was "referred to as '*suryong*,' a term meaning supreme or maximum leader."[11] North Korea would, from then on, be called the Democratic People's Republic of Korea (DPRK) and South Korea would be referred to as the Republic of Korea (ROK).

Whether due to centuries of internal conflict or domination by outsiders, Korea's history reveals that a great many forces have influenced the country. "That Korea had been frequently under foreign rule is acutely felt by all Korean People."[12] Driven by more than a decade of personal resistance to Japanese colonialists, and later fighting as a Communist in the Korean War, Kim Il-sung would have been well aware of that history. Besides adhering to communist ideology, Kim was a Korean nationalist, and he surrounded himself with many of his old guerrilla fighters and other nationalists. To Kim, one Korea meant "the nation as an indivisible and deified sacred entity. The notion that individuals are not worthy of living if they are deprived of their nation has been promoted [by Kim] so persuasively that complete loyalty to the nation is considered natural."[13]

Juche

The ultimate nationalistic goal for Kim and his Central Committee was the reunification of the Korean peninsula into one nation, a goal that was blocked by South Korea and the United States. The result was Kim's intense hatred for those two nations.[14] "Kim's hatred of the United States was apparently matched only by his frustration over the unattainability of his ambition to rule all of Korea, and he endeavored, with marked success, to instill the same hatred in the minds of all the North Korean people as well."[15] More than anything else, the North Korean leader sought self-determination and governance over a unified Korea, without being influenced by the Soviets and Chinese.[16]

Juche

The exact origin of *Juche* is subject to debate. Various scholars attribute the philosophy to Karl Marx, Friedrich Engels, Vladimir Lenin, Joseph Stalin, or Mao Tse-tung. More likely, it was an evolutionary "Asian view of Marxism-Leninism with significant overtones for the future development of Communist doctrine in Asia."[17] In North Korea there is no doubt about *Juche's* origin; it is attributed to Kim Il-sung and is said to be Kim's "original, brilliant, and revolutionary contribution to national and international thought. Kim first promulgated *Juche* in a speech to party propaganda and agitation workers in 1955."[18] He contended that while Marxism-Leninism was valid revolutionary thought, it needed his interpretation "to define a new set of practical ideological guidelines appropriate to the revolutionary environment in North Korea."[19] In other words, Kim molded Marxism-Leninism to fit the communist politics of North Korea. Thus, North Koreans see *Juche* as "uniquely Korean." In addition, *Juche* "is claimed to be an 'eternal truth' … meant for all the oppressed peoples in the world."[20] And while self-sustainability is the base of *Juche*, coincidentally this ideology placed Kim Il-sung, "the guerrilla fighters of the liberation struggle," the Korean Workers Party (KWP), and the North Korean military at the apex in North Korean society.[21] Kim "saw himself as an absolutely essential figure in the struggle of the working masses against the oppressive middle class."[22] He became "the one-man distillation of the North Korean regime itself, to whom all of his people must pay unlimited and unending homage.[23] As a result, Kim became the North Korean "absolute communist dictator" for life.

Four—*Juche*—Why Korea Seized the *Pueblo*

For Kim, the ideology of *Juche* became a blueprint for achieving the unification of Korea.[24] Kim was "determined to forge a Korea that could resist foreign domination-while at the same time opportunistically allying with communist forces."[25] The foundation of *Juche* is national self-determination instead of foreign intervention, exactly what Kim advocated for Korea.[26] It is an ideology that demands that North Korea "take charge, subvert external interests, and strengthen its grip on its own population."[27] North Korea's policies and behavior are governed by the "state ideology of *Juche*. An understanding of the origins, components, and philosophical underpinnings of the *Juche* ideology is essential to an understanding of the North Korean state and its people."[28] Understanding *Juche* reveals the philosophy of Kim Il-sung, and the reason for the North Korean seizure of the USS *Pueblo*.

Elements of Juche

According to Kim Il-sung, *Juche* must have two key factors to achieve *chaju* (political independence). Kim believed that *chaju* meant complete equality and mutual respect among nations. In addition, he believed that "every state has the right of self-determination in order to secure the happiness and prosperity of its people as it best sees fit."[29] But Kim also held that in order to reach *chaju*, the nation must first have an independent, self-sufficient economy, termed "*charip*, or self-sustainability [of the economy]." Kim believed "that economic dependence on foreign aid would render the state a political satellite of other countries" and that "it would be impossible to successfully build a socialist republic without the materiel and technical foundations that would come from an independent national economy." Kim believed that his industrial base would come from the formation of a machinery-building industry, which would in turn, "equip light industry, agriculture, transport, and all other branches of the economy."[30] Of course, as we see today, this economic plan of *Juche* has never been attained, as North Korea is heavily dependent on Russia and China for handouts, and the population suffers greatly from lack of food.

Finally, Kim Il-sung believed that *chaju* and *charip* both required protection for self-sustainability. For this, he stated that the nation must have a formidable military to defend itself from domestic conflict and outside aggression, a condition called *chawi*.[31] To ensure that *chawi* is achieved,

Elements of Juche

the military is positioned just below the country's leader and "above the working class and the peasantry." In addition, the "DPRK Constitution calls for 'arming all the populace [and] turning the entire country into a fortress.'"[32] In *Juche* ideology, "*chawi* is critical" and will remain a tenet "as long as imperialist countries continue to exist...."[33] Understandably, having been a guerrilla fighter for many years while opposing the invading Japanese, Kim was determined that North Korea would never be a colony again. To this end, Kim mobilized the entire country, with a military completely infused with the *Juche* ideology. "Those who were not directly taking up arms were to contribute to the construction and maintenance of the domestic defense industry and remain ideologically prepared, so that the home front would be united in a sense of socio-political superiority."[34] In order to focus his country's belligerence, Kim needed a perceived threat. And because he believed that imperialist countries should not be allowed to exist anywhere in the world, rightly or wrongly, he chose the United States to be the designated imperialist enemy of North Korea soon after the Korean War armistice was signed in 1953. The United States remains the focus of North Korea's perceived external threat even today.

Kim Il-sung faced several challenges to implementing the Juche ideology: First, *Juche* requires the elimination of political rivals in order to achieve complete subservience, cooperation, and participation of the North Korean people. Kim allowed no other ideology to be discussed or formed in North Korea. Workers became part of the state, instruments to achieve national independence and self-reliance. All workers toiled for the state, all in harmony for the greater good of North Korea. Under Kim, the state now owned most of the land and all production. In true communist fashion, all commercial and agrarian production was forcibly taken from the largely rural population, centralized, and managed by the government. To instill a sense of worth in workers, Kim formed the Korean Workers Party (KWP), which he said, "empowered the North Korean worker by including all workers in one organization for the good of the state." Membership in the KWP was meant to demonstrate a condition of equality among the populace.[35]

Under Kim's rule, dissenters either quietly disappeared or were publicly executed. Killing off dissenters, of course, was one of the techniques Kim used to maintain power. The late political scientist and professor, R.J. Rummel wrote in *Statistics of Democide: Genocide and Mass Murder Since 1900*, that Kim Il-sung's regime was estimated to have executed, or killed in work camps, from 710,000 to slightly over 3,500,000 dissenters.[36] In addition to the work camps, Kim was responsible for forcing 400,000 South Koreans to serve in the North Korean Army, capturing these conscripts when the North was moving into the South during the Korean War. It is estimated that over half of these men were killed while being forced to serve North Korea.[37] Elimination of dissenters would ensure that the North Korean populace remained loyal "supporters" of the dictatorial regime.

Second, *Juche* requires the populace to be isolated from outside influences. In North Korea, interaction with foreign communities was, and continues to be, forbidden, and the government controls all media and the access to foreign cultures. Professor Han S. Park pointedly wrote, "North Korea's achievement of ideological consensus on *Juche* would never have been possible without the deliberate and methodical manipulation of the mass media by shielding off the entire society from the external world."[38] Kim could never achieve self-reliance for North Korea because failed crops, "massive scale" starvation deaths, and an inability to obtain credit on the world market for trade and commerce forced North Korea to solicit hand-outs from China and the Soviet Union.[39] Even today, the North Korean Army receives unpaid leave periods of up to a month or more to forage on their own through recently harvested fields to gather unharvested kernels of grain to augment their meager food rations.[40]

Yet, "the North Korean elite has elevated *Juche* to a sacred doctrine, an end in itself. The *Juche* ideology was to be Kim's guide [for raising his nation to world equality. But in order to keep himself in power], *Juche* ultimately became a straitjacket [for Kim], spawning such deleterious effects as a propensity toward chauvinism, bragging, [mass murder], and even deception," some of which were clearly evident as the United States struggled to work with the North Koreans for the release of the *Pueblo* and crew.[41]

The Propaganda of North Korea

Kim Il-sung's propaganda machine served several purposes. Because of failures in self-sufficiency, a keystone of *Juche*, Kim resorted to propaganda aimed first at the North Korean people to elicit their loyalty; second, to keep himself in power; and third, to ensure that the world would recognize the alleged formidability of North Korea, in essence, to project the idea that North Korea was equal to all other world powers. Propaganda initiated following the seizure of the *Pueblo* served all three of these purposes.

A ludicrous example of Kim's propaganda techniques was his claim that only North Korean citizens enjoy "free will." Kim claimed that it was "free will" that "motivated people's actions independent of [any capitalist] economic imperative." Author Paul French wrote his opinion on Kim's thinking:

> The notion of free will in Party-dominated North Korea is almost as absurd as the notion of self-reliance. However, it is politically useful in establishing that philosophically North Koreans, through *Juche*, are capable of independence [when] contrasted [with] the servility of the South Koreans dominated by American imperialism. Within this theoretical paradigm the DPRK appears the free country and the ROK the enslaved chattel [of the United States].[42]

Another of Kim's dictums held that the disproportionate military expenditures for a strong military were necessary to achieve sufficient *chawi*, the ability to protect the country and elevate the North Korean military to an even basis with all nation states, even if it was at the expense of a starving population. As further justification, Kim Il-sung continued to insist that *chawi* was necessary because of a constant threat from imperialist nations, specifically the United States. His proof was the continued occupation of South Korea by U.S. forces.[43]

Kim's propaganda also included a boast that North Korea was militarily the equal of any other nation, reinforcing this contention with blustery threats against coastal water incursion by capitalist countries, specifically the United States. In 1968, perhaps in an effort to reinforce his image as a strong leader, Kim's blustery threats continued, but were summarily dismissed by U.S. officials involved in the cursory risk analysis for the USS *Pueblo* mission.[44] A major purpose of those threats was to propagandize and reinforce Kim's role as the North Korean people's protector. By broadcasting the warnings on Radio Pyongyang to the North Korean population, Kim assured the citizenry that he was protecting the country, while proving to the people that North Korea was the equal of any world power.[45] In other words, Kim constantly marketed himself first to the North Korean people, and then to the rest of the world in order to glorify *Juche* ideology and reinforce his power. In doing so, he established

Four—*Juche*—Why Korea Seized the *Pueblo*

what Korean historian Wayne S. Kiyosaki terms "The Cult of Kim Il-sung." As an example, Kiyosaki described Kim's speeches as vehicles intended to glorify himself to the populace and keep him in power:

> As the spokesman for a country that generates higher expectations than guarantees of self-realization, Kim Il-sung apparently believes that it is necessary for the masses to believe that his leadership will hold at bay or even subdue the forces that threaten to thwart the national goals of Korea.[46]

Kiyosaki insisted that a great deal of theatrics were included in Kim's manipulation of the masses:

> [Kim's] theatrics of leadership are part of the national act that must be played out to pry the country loose from old moorings and outmoded beliefs. It is [Kim's] conviction that fears must be dispelled by the undaunted, timidity by heroics, conservatism by progressivism, and egotism by patriotism. Only total mobilization under a strong leader will bring about the cohesiveness that North Korea needs to unify the country and assert itself internationally.[47]

However, even Kim Il-sung's blustery speeches could only carry popular support so far. Kim needed to demonstrate the infallibility and continuance of *Juche* as the nation's ideology and to prove to the North Korean people, and to the world, that because of *Juche*, he and North Korea were formidable. Actions were necessary because Kim needed to assure the North Korean people that *Juche* ideology was necessary for North Korea's survival against imperialist aggression, that the huge North Korean military expenditures were necessary, and that he was the leader to ensure the welfare and safety of the people and nation.

It was under his *Juche* ideology and through *Juche* propaganda that Kim's "North Korean regime hardened more than ever before its 'anti-imperial' ... attitude toward the United States and South Korea; from mid–1965 North Korea accelerated its campaigns for 'unification by means of revolution,' that is, revolutionary guerrilla warfare against the South [and the United States]."[48] Kim carried out several bold actions in 1968 meant to reinforce *Juche*, to educate the world, and to assure the continuance of his autocratic leadership. The seizure of the USS *Pueblo* on January 23, 1968, was one of those actions. Two others were the attempted assassination of the South Korean president in an attack on the Blue House on January 17, 1968, and on April 15, 1969, Kim initiated the shoot down of a U.S. EC-121 spy plane killing 31 U.S. airmen, "the deadliest such incident during the entire Cold War."[49] Kim obviously capitalized on the seizure of the USS *Pueblo*. While the *Pueblo* contained an immense amount of clas-

The Effect on the Treatment of the Pueblo Prisoners

sified material and communication coding machines, the DPRK military "largely ignored this trove of information and instead sought to use the incident only for domestic propaganda."[50] The propaganda value of the capture of a U.S. warship was immense to Kim, as the government-controlled media lauded the bravery of Kim and the North Korean military as they faced down and then defeated the U.S. imperialists who had been allegedly invading North Korean waters.[51] "What mattered [most] was the fact that Kim perceived the seizure as a tremendous boost to his prestige."[52] During the eleven months that the *Pueblo* crew was held captive, Kim issued "ninety-one *Pueblo*-related propaganda statements of over three hundred words [each]."[53] It was apparent that Kim's propaganda machine was operating at a high level in 1968.

The Effect of Juche *and Kim's Propaganda on the Treatment of the* Pueblo *Prisoners*

Actions directed toward the crew of the *Pueblo* by the North Koreans may be more easily understood knowing the principles that comprise *Juche* ideology. The fact that the North Koreans sent armed naval vessels to intercept the *Pueblo* would indicate that the American spy ship had been under surveillance by the DPRK military as the ship idled off the North Korean coast. It is likely that the North Koreans knew the mission of the *Pueblo* and also knew the armament capability (or lack thereof) of the small ship, factors that would have been weighed in their decision to intercept the minimally-armed U.S. ship. In Kim's *Juche* ideology, North Korea is vaunted as the equal in military might to any other country, and the United States is held to be the imperialist villain that had caused innumerable deaths and injuries to the Korean people and must, therefore, be destroyed. Against the threat of exile or death, it follows that members of the North Korean military held these principles as truth. With four North Korean ships surrounding the *Pueblo* and two aircraft overhead, it was clear to the North Korean captors that North Korea was, indeed, more powerful than the imperialist American spy ship. After receiving orders from their military chain of command, the DPRK Navy ships fired on, boarded, and hijacked the *Pueblo*. In accordance with the *Juche* ideology, the North Korean captors had shown that through *chawl*, the implementation of a strong national military, at least in this instance, they were superior in military strength to the United States, and were, therefore, able to subdue the United States on the high seas.

In the sequence of events in the *Pueblo's* capture, the first communication from the North Korean sub chaser crew demonstrated their intention to engage and attack the American ship. With the sub chaser's crew lining the deck in full battle dress, each man holding a rifle, the sub chaser signaled in flag code, "Heave to, or I will fire."[54] On the surface, such a signal might be attributed to overzealous audacity. That audacity was fueled by North Korea's firm belief in the power of the *Juche* ideology, so fervently embraced by their leader, Kim Il-sung. By virtue of signaling their intent to fire on the American ship, the North Koreans demonstrated that they were the superior force, with a duty to subdue the American trespassers.

After a punishing, completely one-sided gun fusillade by the North Koreans that repeatedly strafed the *Pueblo,* Commander Bucher had little option other than to stop the *Pueblo,* thereby allowing the North Koreans to board the U.S. spy ship. Reports from Commander Bucher and others relate the arrogance of the North Koreans after boarding the spy ship. Bucher and the crew were held at gunpoint, struck by fists and gun butts, prodded with bayonet points, kicked, and karate chopped to ensure compliance and submissiveness. After boarding the *Pueblo,* North Korean Colonel Scar (a nickname assigned by the Americans) stated to Bucher, "Why are you spying on Korea? You are a CIA agent bringing spies to provoke another war."[55] Of course, this was not entirely true, but to the North Korean military, which was required to adhere to the tenets of *Juche,* this was the only logical conclusion. It is also interesting to note that at no time during the North Korean capture of the *Pueblo* did the North Koreans demonstrate any trepidation or fear while confronting and subduing the Americans. Their belief in *Juche* and leader Kim Il-sung drove them to believe that they had a duty to be victorious over the imperialist enemy. So deeply ingrained was this belief, that the captors showed little inclination for caution or compassion.

The North Korean military was not the only group of people demonstrating strict adherence to *Juche.* As the *Pueblo* crew was taken off their ship near Wonsan, they were met by a vocal mob of North Korean civilians. The mob was held back by soldiers, but persons in the crowd could be seen spitting toward the crew and yelling insults. They "acted as if they would have delighted in tearing us to pieces if it had not been for the

The Effect on the Treatment of the *Pueblo Prisoners*

restraint imposed by their military, who did not hesitate to knock down ... [their fellow North Korean citizens if they became] overzealous." Bucher was probably correct when he wrote that the "vociferous reception" was "a put-up job," a propaganda stunt by the North Korean government.[56] A short time later, as the Americans were being transferred from buses to a rail station in Wonsan, they were met by a second mob of North Korean citizens. Bucher recalls seeing an angry mob shaking their fists and spitting at the Americans. "Guards had to knock some of them to the ground to clear a path for us to move off the bus."[57] Both incidents served to demonstrate the strong hold that Kim and the *Juche* ideology had on the psyche of the North Korean people. As previously stated, the *Juche* ideology demands at all times that the North Korean leadership "strengthen its grip on its own population."

While the crew was on the train platform, Kim's propaganda machine, a keystone for Kim to maintain his autocracy, wasted no time, demanding that the *Pueblo* crew remove their blindfolds and raise their hands while cameras flashed, recording the moment for North Korean posterity. But Kim had broader propaganda plans than just an ever-present influence in North Korea. His propaganda unit soon distributed a picture of the captured crew that was published beyond North Korea and subsequently appeared on the cover of the February 5, 1968, *Newsweek* magazine in the United States. With that picture, Kim ensured that the world would know the prowess of the North Korean military and see the imperialist United States being humbled on the world stage, thereby proving the complete superiority and self-reliance of North Korea, primary tenets of *Juche*. It certainly helped to bolster Kim's perceived superiority that he and his top commanders believed that the Johnson administration was unable to adequately support South Korea because it was so mired down in Vietnam. This was reinforced by a CIA estimate stating as such.[58] Kim would continue to exhibit the captured Americans, as his prison staff held several staged press conferences where the crew was prominently displayed while North Korean propagandists spoke from scripts to international press correspondents, and the crew answered pre-scripted questions that glorified the "greatness of North Korea."[59] Pictures of these press conferences were broadly disseminated, thereby ensuring that the world knew of North Korea's self-perceived power and domination over the imperialist aggressors.

During the first two days of his imprisonment, Commander Bucher

Four—*Juche*—Why Korea Seized the *Pueblo*

February 5, 1968, *Newsweek* photo showing the *Pueblo* crew on a railroad station platform as they were transported to prison. The photo was released by the North Korean propaganda officials and made its way around the world (photograph from USS *Pueblo*.org web site).

wrote that he endured nearly sixteen hours of constant beatings.[60] In their eleven-month period of imprisonment, the entire *Pueblo* crew was beaten, mistreated, starved, and tortured by their captors on a daily basis. These actions served to intimidate, but more importantly, to subjugate every member of the crew, from the Commanding Officer to the lowest ranking

The Effect on the Treatment of the *Pueblo Prisoners*

enlisted man. Referring again to the *Juche* ideology, North Korea was to take charge and subvert external interests. Kim Il-sung explained this to mean dominating and/or eliminating his avowed adversary, the United States. On January 23, 1968, eighty-three U.S. military men on a virtually defenseless Navy ship were found on Kim's doorstep, and he did not hesitate to carry out their capture. Thus, he was demonstrating his *Juche*-inspired dominance over his archenemy, the United States.

On the second full day of their imprisonment, Bucher and his junior officers were told that they were going to be "shot at sundown."[61] The threat of imminent death by shooting was a recurring theme shouted at the prisoners by prison officials. Several times, prisoners were made to kneel and a pistol was placed against their heads. A senior prison officer then told the holder of the gun to shoot the American. Each time, the trigger was pulled, resulting in a loud click. The DPRK soldier holding the gun would then appear to reload the gun, and the action was repeated. The *Pueblo* crewmen never knew whether or not there would be a real bullet in the firing chamber of the pistol.[62] Commander Bucher recalls such an incident while being interrogated and after he had refused to sign a confession. A North Korean colonel (whom the crew nicknamed "Super-C") told another officer to, "Kill the SOB [Bucher]." After the gun clicked against Bucher's head, the DPRK interpreter said, "Well, it was a misfire. You will have another two minutes. You were lucky the last time."[63] Bucher then heard the slide on the pistol draw back to place another bullet in the gun's chamber, and he closed his eyes and waited. In seconds, he realized that he had not heard the misfire bullet eject from the pistol and hit the floor. He then became somewhat certain that this was just a game. When asked again to sign the confession and again refusing, Super-C said, "You are not worth a bullet." The guards then beat him into unconsciousness. Later, Bucher came to in his room. In a great deal of pain, he asked to go to the bathroom, where he urinated blood. Subsequently, Bucher was told that if he did not sign the confession, the North Koreans would begin shooting *Pueblo's* crew members one by one, starting with the youngest man. With that, the North Koreans sent for Fireman Apprentice, Howard Bland, allegedly to shoot him. At that point, Bucher agreed to sign the bogus confession.[64] As noted earlier, that confession drew a great deal of discussion within the Johnson administration. Bucher's confession, written under a great deal of duress, contained the following:

Four—*Juche*—Why Korea Seized the *Pueblo*

> I am Commander Lloyd Mark Bucher, Captain of the USS *Pueblo* ... who was captured while carrying out espionage activities after intruding deep into the territorial waters of the Democratic People's Republic of Korea ... the U.S. Central Intelligence Agency promised me that if this task would be done successfully, a lot of dollars would be offered to all crew members of my ship. Particularly, I myself would be honored.... I have no excuse whatsoever for my criminal acts.... The crime committed by me and my men is entirely indelible....[65]

Just the last word, "indelible," should have told American analysts that perhaps this was not a bona fide, self-generated confession. In addition, the same analysts should have known that the *Pueblo* missions were not tasked by, nor had any relation to, the U.S. Central Intelligence Agency. The ship was tasked by the Navy and the NSA. Though the confession contained errors, which could be detected by U.S. government officials, Super-C was elated at the confession and would force Bucher to write a second confession as the weeks passed by.

Bucher spent untold hours facing Super-C and listening to the tirades of the rabid North Korean. Super-C started his sessions with Bucher by asking the same question, "How is your life these days?" Bucher was not sure whether Super-C's blind faith in Kim Il-sung's ideology made him less credible, but Bucher knew that the interrogator was not unintelligent. During the course of their time together it became apparent that Super-C had "read Shakespeare, knew Greek and Roman mythology, and spoke of attending a Moscow military academy." He also had a fondness for "western style leather shoes" and was familiar with U.S. history and current events. Super-C also had stamina. He could go on a tyrannical lambasting speech that blasted either the American government or Bucher himself, and continue speaking for three to four hours, all the while keeping Bucher standing at attention in front of him. Bucher stated that he would lie awake at night after such a session trying to analyze all of the strange ideas that Super-C had spewed.[66]

In addition to Bucher, the other officers on the *Pueblo* were beaten and tortured by the North Koreans to obtain written confessions. Lieutenant Edward Murphy, the ship's executive officer and navigator suffered the same mistreatment as his commanding officer. The North Koreans wanted him to admit that the *Pueblo* had entered North Korean waters. Murphy knew the position of the ship at the time of capture was in international waters. Therefore, he refused to sign a confession. He was stripped to his shorts and made to kneel on the floor while a stick was placed behind his knees to cut off blood circulation. He was kicked,

The Effect on the Treatment of the *Pueblo Prisoners*

punched, smashed in the face and kicked in the back until "he doubled over in pain." Because Murphy did not initially sign a confession, he was dragged to Super-C's office, where a pistol lay on the colonel's desk and this dialogue took place:

> "Are you ready to die?" asked Super-C.
> "Yes, sir, I am," answered Murphy.
> "You know I have the authority to kill you."
> "Yes, sir, I'm sure you do."
> "I'll give you twenty minutes to write your will."
> "I've already written a will."

As Murphy stated later, "I wasn't bluffing. At that point I had lost my fear of death. And I could look him straight in the eye and tell him to shoot me...." Later that same day, Murphy was again tortured so brutally that he estimates that he "lost consciousness at least six times, [and] remembers waking up and feeling the warmth of blood on his shorts and the cold of the room at the same time."[67] Murphy later signed a pre-written confession.

Lieutenant Steve Harris, the officer in charge of the Communication Technician (CT) detachment, was also beaten and told that he was responsible for the lives of his CT's. Believing that the North Koreans would harm those enlisted men assigned to him, he agreed to sign a confession. Examples of some of the inane questions asked by the captors of Harris and the false answers given by Harris are:

> "Where is Washington, D.C.?
> "One hundred miles north of Rhode Island," answered Harris.
> "Where is the Air Force Academy?"
> "In Texas."
> "On Johnson's ranch?"
> "Of course," answered Harris.

Harris was tortured with the same sticks behind the knees technique, but was also made to sit on a steaming radiator. He also signed a bogus confession, as did LTJG Skip Schumacher.

Like the officers, many of the enlisted crew members were also mistreated. They too were subjected to the squatting stick behind the knees torture, forced to sit on steaming radiators, beaten with table legs, beaten with two by fours, kicked in the face and groin, clubbed, whipped with belt buckles across their eyes, and made to crawl on the floor until their knees were bloody. They also signed meaningless confessions to satisfy

Four—*Juche*—Why Korea Seized the *Pueblo*

their captors. It should also be pointed out that during their early days in prison, several of the crew members suffered from the wounds they had received during the attack on the *Pueblo*. Some of the wounds had become infected and were "open and draining," creating a horrible stench in their respective sleeping rooms.[68] Whenever a guard entered their room, the crew was to jump up to attention, but never look at the face of the guard. They were to keep their heads down. Their living conditions were deplorable.

When members of the crew were allowed to go to the latrine, they were not allowed to talk to one another. If they spoke to each other in their rooms, the guards would want to know what they had been talking about. Communication among the crew was sometimes limited, but somewhat by chance, they worked out a system whereby they could communicate with crew members in other rooms. Communications Technician Second Class Charles Ayling used a comb to tap out a message in Morse code on a radiator pipe. He was answered, and so began an internal communication system tapping on the radiator pipes.[69]

During their first week of captivity, members of the crew were interrogated individually. When he returned to his cell after one such interrogation, one of the crew members asked LT Stephen Harris what was to happen to them. He responded that he did not know what the North Koreans wanted with them, "except maybe to make propaganda mileage."[70] There is irony in Harris's remark, in that he had probably never heard of Kim's glorious ideology of *Juche*, yet he had managed to state the very core of Kim's objective in capturing a U.S. Navy ship and crew. For Kim Il-sung, the resultant propaganda from the ship's capture would prove to the world and to his own people that North Korea was self-reliant, and the equal of any world power. It would prove by concrete evidence that Kim's *Juche* ideology was successfully bringing North Korea to a condition of self reliance. In addition, it would show the North Korean population that *chawi*, the building of a military force, was necessary to enable North Korea's military to defeat any real or perceived aggressor nation, even if it was at the expense of the non-military and non-governmental classes of the population. Kim's propaganda extolled that the attainment of *chawi* could only come about through his enlightened guidance and the hard work and sacrifice of the North Korean people. What he failed to mention was that the sacrifice included thousands of North Korean people starving to death.

The Effect on the Treatment of the *Pueblo* Prisoners

After several interrogation sessions, Commander Bucher came to the conclusion that the continual line of questioning by the North Koreans seemed to have little to do with the technical aspects of the *Pueblo*. He stated that his interrogators acted out their tantrums and never asked him for technical information. "Instead, they seemed completely hung up on a propaganda line for purely political purposes…."[71] Bucher further stated that the verbiage used by the prison officials seemed staged, with the speaker seeming to follow a script. Interestingly, the script did not contain questions regarding the intelligence capabilities of the ship and crew. The North Koreans tortured and beat the crew only to obtain confessions of spying. Either they had no idea regarding the "vast knowledge and experience" of the crew, or they simply did not have an interest in the intelligence capabilities of the ship and crew. It is also possible that the North Koreans were lacking in intelligence analysis capabilities, and therefore, simply handed the *Pueblo's* intelligence assets to the Soviets. Strangely, the guards who continually beat the Americans seemed to be "deeply interested in what American women wore to the beach," rather than military or intelligence data and capabilities.[72]

There was another factor that convinced Bucher that he, his crew, and ship were being used primarily for propaganda purposes in North Korea. At no time during the months of captivity and prolonged interrogations did officials from the Soviet Union or Communist China make an appearance. Bucher felt that if that had happened, the Soviets or Chinese Communists would have taken over the interrogations in order to learn more of the technical capabilities of the American spy ships. "It seemed an entirely North Korean show run in the narrow spirit of nationalistic bombast."[73] Through propaganda, Kim Il-sung was able to disseminate his story of the Americans intrusion in North Korean waters, American espionage against the people of North Korea, provocation of the peaceful nation of North Korea, collaboration in landing of South Korean infiltrators into North Korea, and blatantly violating the Korean armistice. After all, did he not have the actual spy ship to prove his propaganda points? Kim's accusations, of course, are inane. After all, the North Koreans repeatedly violated the Armistice Agreement by their furtive guerilla attacks across the DMZ.

LTJG Schumacher came to the same conclusion as his commanding officer. During his interrogations, he was not asked for details of the ship's mission. Schumacher concluded "that the Koreans were playing us for propaganda, not hard military information." He then asked himself, were we "pawns in a diplomatic struggle, rather than war criminals to be given a kangaroo-court trial before the world and then shot?"[74] Further evidence of the crew's value to Kim's propaganda machine came on February 13. On that day, all six of the officers and oceanographer Dunnie Tuck were taken to a large room where they would be the focus of a staged press conference. The questions and answers were carefully rehearsed, and none of the officers could stray from the accepted answers. On a table in the room were bowls of fruit, candy, cookies, and cigarettes, articles to which the prisoners had no access in their confinement. Naturally, the reporters present were all North Koreans. Super-C thought the press conference was a huge success. After all, he had staged it all himself. This was the first of several staged press conferences held, and at future such meetings, other Soviet-bloc reporters were allowed to attend. Super-C, because he believed the press conferences were great propaganda devices, then conceived the idea that perhaps the crew should sign a letter which admitted their intrusion into North Korean waters and send the letter to President Lyndon Johnson. Subsequently, the North Koreans drafted the letter to Johnson, writing as if the *Pueblo* crew was admitting their intrusion into North Korean waters, asking forgiveness from the DPRK, and additionally asking for the help of President Johnson. They then showed the letter to the *Pueblo* officers. After pointing out several mistakes in the letter, the officers were told to rewrite the letter, which they worked on for two weeks. After revisions had been made to the document, the North Koreans accepted it, and it is reported that President Johnson received the open letter in early March. Those close to the president said he was very unhappy with the letter.[75]

 In later debriefs and in their written accounts, both Bucher and Stephen Harris make reference to a term repeated ad nauseam by their captors. During interrogation, after interrogation, and in remarks made to the prisoners in their confinement rooms, the North Koreans told the American prisoners that they must be "sincere." The English language has one definition for the word, but the North Koreans had a different interpretation. To the North Korean captors, when they told the *Pueblo* crew to be sincere, they meant that if the Americans would apologize, admit to their spying, and tell their interrogators truthfully what was asked of them, things would go much easier for them. But this was not as simple as it sounds. The Americans had to listen carefully to the North Korean ques-

The Effect on the Treatment of the Pueblo *Prisoners*

Photograph of one of the press conferences held by the North Koreans with Commander Bucher standing at the center of the picture. North Korean Colonel "Super C" thought that these canned news conferences were a great idea (U.S. Navy photograph).

tions posed in a broken English dialect and attempt to reach a conclusion as to what the questioner was asking or trying to learn. Going along (being sincere) to get along was not easy for the Americans. In the American definition, sincerity means lack of deceit and telling the truth. Yet, when the Americans were interrogated, it seemed that the North Koreans were fishing for specific answers, not necessarily the truth. At times, it became a game for the Americans to develop an answer to a question based upon what the Americans thought the interrogator wished to hear. Such an answer, many times, was an outright falsehood, but one that the interrogator believed to be true based upon the interrogator's preconceived knowledge. LT Harris wrote, "Truth to Communists [their North Korean captors] is what best serves the party line. Facts are of no importance to them unless they happen to suit ideological purposes."[76] In other words, the answers given to their captors by the Americans were of little significance unless they met the framework of the North Koreans' pre-conceived ideas and opinions. To the North Koreans, this strange repartee, false as it ofttimes was, constituted sincerity on the part of the Americans. To

Four—*Juche*—Why Korea Seized the *Pueblo*

their credit, the crew members made an untold number of attempts to "bend" the truth, knowing that the North Koreans did not fully understand the English language or grasp nuances used by the Americans. In some instances, the North Koreans found out that the Americans had duped them in their testimony, and the result was even more severe beatings. Such was the case when the North Koreans learned that an extended middle finger aimed at their captors was not an Hawaiian "good luck" sign, a falsehood the crew had told their captors.

The physical beatings and mistreatment by the North Koreans was always accompanied by blustery shouts, name calling, harangues on the

The North Koreans are having a hard time proving to the world that the captive crewmen of the U.S.S. Pueblo are a contrite and cooperative lot. Last week Pyongyang's flacks tried again—and lost to the U.S. Navy. In this class-reunion picture, three of the crewmen have managed to use the medium for a message, furtively getting off the U.S. hand signal of obscene derisiveness and contempt.

The *Pueblo* crew learned that the North Koreans did not know what an extended middle finger signified, and the crew began using the gesture in their dealings with the North Koreans. After the North Koreans learned the meaning of the gesture, punishment inflicted on the crew ramped up. In the picture the front row from the left is Howard Bland, Donald Peppard, James Layton, and Monroe Goldman. Back row: Ronald Berens, Harry Iredale, William Scarborough, and Charles Law (photograph from USS Pueblo.org web site).

The Effect on the Treatment of the Pueblo *Prisoners*

virtues of communism, the shortcomings of democracy, and verbal threats. Some senior North Korean military members were so adroit at their haranguing speeches that they could keep up the tirade for hours, thereby terrifying the Americans, who never knew whether such performances were a prelude to execution, or simply more bluster. LTJG Skip Schumacher described the savagery and the "unbelievable dialogue" during interrogations. He stated, "Hatred and fear had been thick in that room, actually making it painful to breathe."[77] He went on to say that the "beatings and tortures were coldly programmed and calculated to break us into total submission. They [DPRK] did nothing from passion or impulse. Guards would come to my room, for example, with instructions to administer ten kicks on the ankles and shins."[78]

A diatribe by North Korean prison officials might be aimed at a specific subject, or could cover a number of subjects. A favorite topic of the DPRK Colonel in his tirades was the fact that there was truly only one Korea and that the United States was "solely responsible for the Korean people being divided into two separate countries." The interrogator would tell Bucher and the other *Pueblo* officers that they must not refer to his country "as North Korea, that South Korea was only a figment of [America's] warped Imperialist imagination and that we must recognize none but the one and only indivisible Democratic People's Republic of Korea."[79] And from there, the colonel would branch into the "bestial treatment of North Korean patriots who fell into the hands of American troops occupying South Korea." Commander Bucher relates that he never believed for a moment that "American troops had been guilty of the atrocities [that the colonel] and his interpreter were turning themselves inside-out to describe."[80]

On March 4, the American prisoners were told to wrap up all of their belongings. The following day, the Americans were once again loaded onto buses and driven to another location on the outskirts of Pyongyang. This would be their second prison location. It was bigger and newer than the Barn, and the crew dubbed it the Farm. Upon arrival, and through an interpreter, Super-C told the crew that they would remain in this prison until the United States apologized. He also told the crew that they were not to blame for their imprisonment. Instead, he said that it was the fault of "the expansionists ... and imperialists" [within the U.S. government].

Almost immediately after arriving at the Farm, the crew was given a

Four—*Juche*—Why Korea Seized the *Pueblo*

list of orders, which the North Koreans called the "Rules of Life," and the crew was told that they must obey each order in the list. They were:

- Obey all orders
- Show respect to all people in charge
- Do not sing in the room
- Do not lie on the floors
- Do not lie on bed with clothes on
- Do not resist interrogation
- Do not encourage others to resist interrogation
- No communication between rooms
- Do not write anything except what is authorized
- Keep clean
- Take good care of public property
- Observe public morality[81]

At the Farm, Bucher continued to be isolated from his men, yet one enlisted man, Fireman John Mitchell, had been assigned to clean Bucher's room, and he became the liaison between Bucher and the crew.[82] There were other differences between the two prisons. At the Farm, the crew could look out their windows and see other military facilities nearby, and according to Commander Bucher, the roads they observed nearly always had military vehicles passing.[83] The crew was fed in a mess hall, where by being careful, the crew was able to communicate among themselves by whispering and passing notes. The crew became more adroit at telling lies to their captors. For example, the ship's corpsman, Baldridge, told his captors that he was "acquainted with Drs. Casey and Kildare," popular TV show characters in the United States. Another crew member told his captors that the "National Guard kept all their weapons at home ... even the tanks," because they didn't want to have the tanks' hubcaps stolen.[84] But the crew members suffered for their insolence and disrespect. In April, the North Korean prison officials cracked down on the crew. Beatings intensified with several of the crew members beaten into unconsciousness.

By June, nearly the entire crew was suffering from dysentery. "Sailors collapsed in the corridors, doubled over in pain, unable to control their bowels. With only one toilet, always occupied, the men had no choice but to relieve themselves on the floor." They were losing astonishing amounts of weight. For example, Charlie Law went from 215 pounds to 125. The

The Effect on the Treatment of the *Pueblo* Prisoners

food became worse, with many of the men contracting scurvy from their poor rations. Running sore scabies formed on many men, and some men began having trouble walking. Many of the men had become convinced that they would die if conditions did not improve soon. Commander Bucher was no exception to the failing health of the crew and was sick for at least a part of June, slipping in and out of depression, and having lost nearly 80 pounds. "One day he collapsed in the latrine; a sailor dragged him back to his cell, unconscious."[85]

Super-C took perverse pleasure in passing American or international news to the crew, news that was usually slanted to cast aspersion on the United States. On April 20, he called the crew together to inform them that the Reverend Martin Luther King, Jr., "had been shot down" on orders from President Johnson. He went on to say that there were riots in every American city, that the United States was losing the war in Vietnam, and that the capitalist American dollar was doomed.[86] But Super-C gave out one more piece of information. He said that the United States and North Korea were holding talks at Panmunjom.[87] Whether or not he realized the consequences of his remark, it was the first time that the *Pueblo* crew had learned that talks for negotiating their freedom were taking place. It gave the crew a morale boost to know that they had not been forgotten.

Super-C's impromptu meetings were not always the same. In Washington, Senator Stephen Young had delivered a speech in which he had stated that the *Pueblo* incident was a result of "CIA agents in charge of the vessel" sailing it into North Korean waters.[88] The statement was false, of course, but the damage to the *Pueblo* crew ensued. Because of that public congressional speech, Super-C was convinced that Young's speech confirmed that there was a tie between the *Pueblo* and the CIA, and therefore, he believed that the *Pueblo* crew had lied to him when they had denied such a relationship during interrogations. Therefore, the entire crew would have to be punished. The beatings continued.

In the North Korean closed society of 1968, the citizens were given no access to the current world news. What passed for news in North Korea was the carefully crafted propaganda issued by the Communist party's propaganda agency. All such "news" items were written to bolster the Kim Il-sung *Juche* ideology and venerate the nation's image of their leader. The crew of the *Pueblo* received the same biased falsehoods as those given to the North Korean populace. The only difference was that the Americans were given only the bleakest of news that painted the United States in the

Four—*Juche*—Why Korea Seized the *Pueblo*

worst possible light. Examples as described by Commander Bucher included "The March of the Poor on Washington, the assassination of Martin Luther King, Jr., and the riots that followed, the assassination of Robert Kennedy, giving us the impression that the nation was on the brink of anarchy and revolution." Prison officials lied, telling their captors that in the Vietnam War, the United States was "losing 14,000 airplanes and helicopters a week, 5,000 tanks, and also had lost the battleship *New Jersey*." None of these claims were true, of course, but the prison officials would believe anything that came out of Kim's propaganda machine. Bucher wrote that the various claims fed to the prison officials, who in turn, spewed them to the Americans, became so preposterous that the crew began suspecting that it was "*all* a pack of lies."[89] But what would be the purpose of the North Koreans fabricating so many propaganda lies and selectively feeding them to the American captors? The answer points directly at the *Juche* ideology. In order for Kim's grand ideology to be successful, the North Korean population has to be completely controlled in every aspect of their lives. The citizens are given no access to any news or stimuli that would be in conflict with *Juche*, and therefore, for all practical purposes there is no independent thinking among the populace. Any thoughts contrary to Kim's ideology carried heavy consequences, including death. Is it any wonder, then, that in order to keep control of the crew of the *Pueblo*, crew members were treated much the same as North Korean citizens. Learn the party line, learn the *Juche* ideology, revere Kim as the glorious leader, recognize the sacrifices necessary for the country to become self reliant and militarily powerful, then take your place as a happy North Korean citizen. Kim's administration and prison officials may have been naive enough to believe that the same techniques used on North Korean citizenry could be blindly applied to the *Pueblo* crew.

Apparently North Korean prison officials felt that American people, specifically the *Pueblo* crew, could be persuaded that the communist way of life was better than democracy if it were not for Lyndon Johnson and the American capitalist moguls. So, like any good hucksters, the prison officials looked for opportunities to sell communism and the *Juche* way. For example, the "black and Filipino crewmen were lectured [to by prison officials] on American segregation and white supremacy policies," in order to sway them to communism.[90] According to Commander Bucher, this attempt was to no avail as the *Pueblo* crewmen remained loyal to the United States.

The Effect on the Treatment of the Pueblo *Prisoners*

Religion and a belief in God became ever more important to the crew. Even many of the men who had not been strong believers began praying while in prison. The men surreptitiously wrote Bible verses that they remembered and shared these scraps of paper with one another. They called it *The Pueblo Bible*.[91] The prison officials could "not understand the faith of the *Pueblo's* crew. The North Koreans held no reverence for God." One of the guards made the statement, "We are no longer slaves to superstition. We are atheists."[92] The *Juche* ideology placed Kim Il-sung in the place of a divine being. He was the Korean god. *Juche* replaced the former North Korean beliefs in Buddhism and Confucianism with Communism. LT Harris wrote, "[the North Korean] antithesis to Christianity was communist ideology; to the Gospel, the party line; to elders and deacons of a church, the Central Communist Committee of the Party; the Virgin Mary, equated to Kim Il-sung's mother, Kang Ban Sock; [and] to Christ, Premier Kim Il-sung."[93] It was no wonder that the prison officials could not understand the theological faith of the spy ship crew. The *Juche* ideology was their religion, and their deity was Kim Il-sung.

Perhaps it was for this reason that the prison officials took opportunities to ridicule the *Pueblo* crew's belief in a supreme being. The prison officials' attempts at debunking Christianity were comical in their simplicity. Prison guards argued that, "the Russians had explored space and couldn't find God." Another of the guards' favorites was, "We dug holes all over this country and never found hell," and, in reference to Soviet space exploration, the guards said, "The Soviets have shot your God out of the sky."[94] In spite of the numerous North Korean propaganda films and the arrogant belittling of Christian ideology by their captors, LT Harris observed that while he was unable to "assess the depth of every man's commitment," it was his opinion that "instead of becoming less religious because of communist indoctrination, the *Pueblo* crew became more religious." He went on to say that crew members from a variety of religious backgrounds "became acutely aware that a vital relationship with God was more important than anything else when the sea got rough."[95]

It is relatively easy for an American to understand the chasm between life in North Korea and the United States. Aside from the complete dichotomy of life styles in the two nations, one only needs to look at the difference in information of world events shared with the respective populations. In the United States, our news services provide up to the minute reports from around the world. And while the news may be biased at

Four—*Juche*—Why Korea Seized the *Pueblo*

times, it is laid out before the American people to analyze and form their own opinion. No such thing could occur in Kim Il-sung's regime. His people were fed only the most basic of news, and only fabricated news that glorified his dictatorial leadership. Of course, the other freedoms that Americans take for granted were lacking in North Korea at the time of the capture of the *Pueblo*. Therefore, I would argue that North Korean prison officials could never understand the psyche of their American prisoners and treated the *Pueblo* crew in the same manner that they would treat a North Korean *Juche* dissident. But what were the facets of the Americans' psyche that enabled the Americans to hold hope of their rescue and return to the United States? What were the coping mechanisms utilized by individual crew members to endure their torture and captivity?

Navy Captain Raymond C. Spaulding, Medical Corps, a researcher for the Center for Prisoner of War Studies, Naval Health Research Center in San Diego, wrote a report in January 1975 in which he described some of the attributes of the *Pueblo* crew, their experiences, and their coping skills in surviving their nearly year-long captivity. Aside from Commander Bucher, the crew was housed in cells with four to eight crew members per cell. The officers were housed in individual cells to prevent them from communicating with one another. Spaulding noted that in each of the enlisted men's cells there was a leader with whom the men could confide and gain encouragement. This group support was essential to the men coping with their daily horrors. The support provided by the leaders in each group helped to instill hope and faith in the other men, much like a "group therapy session."[96]

In Spaulding's post-prison interviews with crew members, it became apparent that the chief coping skills used by the men were their "faith in their commanding officer, [faith] in their religion, and [faith] in their country." Contrary to the blind adherence to *Juche* and their glorious leader Kim Il-sung, which governed the lives of North Korean prison officials, the Americans had a far more worldly view, a far greater perspective of the world events and politics. Perhaps because of this perspective, the men had inborn ego defensive mechanisms that were foreign to their prison tormentors. Spaulding lists these as "faith (as described above), reality testing (analyzing the outrageous claims and statements made by prison officials), denial (the ability to compartmentalize those statements made by prison officials that they held as false), rationalization (the ability to analyze facets of their imprisonment and treatment), and humor (acting

The Effect on the Treatment of the **Pueblo** *Prisoners*

out, assigning derogatory names to their captors, playing pranks on prison officials, devising methods of communication, breaking prison rules, issuing false statements, etc.)." Spaulding went on to write that:

> [The men] sized up the situation, made decisions as to how they would individually handle the stress, and then stopped being preoccupied with the subsequent event. In effect, they consciously allowed themselves to use more primitive defenses. These men were secure in their identity as Americans, were confident they would not be abandoned, and maintained important object relations through fantasy and anticipation of rescue. A quality of confident self-identity characterized the group.[97]

The *Pueblo* crew passed their time in various ways. There were long discussions in their rooms, drawing from various subjects. They spoke of girls, their romances, food, and sports. Others talked about escape, a subject that was given great attention, although most of the crew knew it was a plan that could never be carried out because the tight security and language barrier were simply too formidable. However, knowing the odds, Bucher still asked his officers to form an escape committee, whose head would be Skip Schumacher. Other discussions involved sports, or food and the favorite food dishes they missed or would relish when they returned home. Some of the men created mental projects in their heads. For example, Gene Lacy, the ship's chief engineer, tore down his 1937 Ford in his head, and then began to reassemble it, telling one of the crew members that he would have it "finished" in two or three days. Skip Schumacher designed and built a house in his head. While some of these activities might appear trivial, they all served a greater purpose, to help the crew assuage their deplorable treatment at the hands of their captors.

By the time the *Pueblo* crew was moved to the Farm, there had been ten meetings between the American and North Korean negotiators. There had been no movement other than General Pak finally giving the American negotiator the names of the dead and wounded members of the crew. General Pak was in no hurry to settle any issues between his government and that of the United States and would do so only when instructed by higher authority.

During the relentless interrogations, there was another subject that was favored by prison interrogators, a topic that created great debate within the military and the government of the United States. During the early interrogations, many members of the crew attempted to give the interrogators only their names, ranks, and service numbers, a practice

Four—*Juche*—Why Korea Seized the *Pueblo*

that the military ingrains in all of its members. The crew was under the assumption that they were to be treated as prisoners of war under the Geneva Convention rules. But their North Korean captors made it known to the men that they were not to be considered prisoners of war. Their interrogators shouted at them, "No! You are not a prisoner of war. You are a political prisoner."[98] With that parameter, North Korea obviously felt free to beat and torture the *Pueblo* crew. The definition of a political prisoner is generally that of a person who is a political dissenter within his/her own country. The American prisoners did not fall under this parameter, but the *Juche* ideology depended on propaganda to bolster the country's dictatorial politics as prescribed by Kim Il-sung. Thus, perhaps it might more accurately be said that the Americans were prisoners of the North Korean propaganda machine.

The ferocious and vicious nature of the North Korean interrogations continued throughout the duration of the crew's imprisonment. During such a long period of captivity, the crew was able to begin to understand a bit of the North Korean interrogators' psyches. For example, Commander Bucher relates that during one such furious session, performed by a senior DPRK colonel, he found himself analyzing the performance of the colonel. Bucher felt that the furious performance was carefully scripted. "For all his yelled insults and profanities, their wording had been carefully memorized," and the colonel was not "really losing control of himself."[99] At the end of his performance, the colonel asked that Bucher sign a confession attesting that he was an American spy. The hate-filled, terrifying lecture had one purpose, to intimidate Bucher to the point of signing a trumped-up confession. The harassment by the DPRK military officials conformed with the *Juche* tenet of self-reliance and being in charge of any situation and placing the American prisoners in a demeaning, subservient role. Ultimately, Bucher and other members of the *Pueblo* crew signed confessions of guilt, but laced the confessions with enough nonsensical remarks to show the American people that they were being coerced to sign such documents.

The North Korean colonel who had forced Bucher to write and sign the bogus confession was elated with the results of his efforts. Within a day following the confessions, he came up with another propaganda-related project for the *Pueblo* officers. After calling together Bucher and the other *Pueblo* officers, he instructed them that they must write another letter of confession and appeal to President Lyndon B. Johnson of the

The Effect on the Treatment of the **Pueblo** *Prisoners*

United States. "The KORCOMs [Korean Communists] wanted [such a letter] to convey to President Johnson our guilt in violating their territorial waters for the purpose of committing espionage. [In this letter] we were to ask the President to admit his responsibility, as head of the United States government, for a 'provocation against the peace-loving Korean people.'"[100] As a student of Kim Il-sung and *Juche*, the colonel was taking charge of the situation, placing North Korea on an even plane with the United States and naively believing that a humbled President of the United States would follow his wishes. Commander Bucher remarked that he found it incredible that the North Koreans "seriously expected positive results" from such a letter to Johnson.[101] But if we look at the North Korean colonel's demand, it is obvious that if a letter to Johnson were answered by the U.S. administration in an apologetic manner, it would be an enormous propaganda coup, demonstrating to the world that North Korea had humbled the United States and its leader, a bedrock goal of Kim Il-sung's *Juche* ideology.

Whether it was by voluntary assimilation, or adoption of the *Juche* ideology in fear of consequences at the hands of Kim's military or secret police for dissention (untold numbers of North Korean non-believers were killed by Kim's regime), North Koreans had no choice but to live Kim's party line. Some were enamored enough with Kim's ideology that many became *Juche* apostles. Whether they sincerely believed in the North Korean ideology or relished a debate with their American captives, some of the prison officials argued that their way of life was superior to that of Americans. According to Commander Bucher, prison officials would often begin these discussions by stating that it was not the American people that North Korea hated. Instead, it was the "Johnson clique" (the Johnson administration) that was "controlled" by the CIA. During one of his tirades, Super-C stated:

> We do not hate the American people who are in the clutches of the Johnson murder clique ... and the Rockefeller gluttons and hobnailed boots of bloody-handed Wall Street warmongers.... We know that American workers are whipped slaves of Morgan Steel. We know that Americans will be our friends when they overthrow the CIA. But first, the Johnson dogs must be dealt with. You must show your gratitude and sincerity to the Korean people by honest confessions of your crimes.... Then you may go home to your loved ones.[102]

In contrast, however, the *Pueblo* crew was shown numerous propaganda films. In one of these films, a Korean boy is asked "What do you

Four—*Juche*—Why Korea Seized the *Pueblo*

want to do when you grow up?" He answered, "To honor our glorious Comrade Kim Il-sung by killing 100 Americans."[103] The American crew was forced to attend four-hour indoctrination classes twice per week and were shown political films every Friday night.[104] As if the films and lectures might not be enough *Juche* propaganda, the North Korean prison officials constructed a picture gallery with images designed to show the atrocities committed by the Americans during the Korean War and after. Another display depicted the "Glorious Anti-Japanese Guerrilla Movement Led by Our Leader Comrade Kim Il-sung." The display was accompanied by a guest book that the Americans were encouraged to sign and enter comments. Perhaps the prison officials sought to determine whether or not they were successful in converting members of the crew to communism. Of course it was a complete failure as the Americans wrote glowing comments, attempting to show their "sincerity."[105] Fabricated, favorable comments from the Americans were the demonstration of "sincerity" that the North Koreans craved.

LTJG Schumacher related an incident that might be construed to be the high point in the propaganda indoctrination of the *Pueblo* crew. He wrote that the crew was taken from the prison and bused to the "Sinchon Museum of American Atrocities," where the crew was supposed to see the "documentary proof of American butchery during the Korean War." But of course, there was no real proof, "merely allegations made through captions on what could be stock photographs from the war." Schumacher also related that when they asked their North Korean guide pertinent questions, they were answered with outrageous responses that in reality were absurd, impossible, or farcical. For example, when the crew was shown a captured Catholic rosary, they were told that the number of beads "revealed to American Intelligence the number of soldiers in the Korean Army."[106]

While *Juche* drove all actions of the prison officials during the captivity of the *Pueblo* crew, the overt brutal treatment of the crew by the *Juche* adherents did not break the Americans' innate ego defense mechanisms. LT Stephen Harris summarized the North Koreans' blind fidelity to *Juche,* writing, "I began feeling pity for the KORCOMS [North Koreans]. They're slaves of a Satanic ideology and a brutal system."[107] While many men of the *Pueblo* crew later carried physical and mental scars of their ordeal at the hands of the North Koreans, amazingly, for the most part, the men were able to withstand their imprisonment and resume their lives following their return to the United States in December 1968.

The Washington Viewpoint

The North Korean captors were relentless in their naive attempts to "indoctrinate" their American captives. Propaganda was their tool for teaching the *Pueblo* crew. For example, one day the crew was told to board buses. They were then driven into Pyongyang to see a stage play. Even the title of the play oozed propaganda. Like the theme of other movies the men had previously been forced to watch, the play was titled *How Glorious is our Fatherland.* The theme of the propaganda was usually the same. A poor menial worker, male or female, finds success and satisfaction from working like a slave to build Kim Il-sung's glorious dream of a utopian communist country.

Five

Negotiations for Freedom

Kim saw *Juche* as the vehicle to move Korea to *chaju*, self-independence, with a heavy overlay of nationalism. He held that in *chaju*, all nation states must be viewed as equals, a fact that comes into play when outsiders try negotiating with the North Koreans. This was in evidence as the United States, thinking itself dominant, toiled to negotiate freedom for the *Pueblo* and crew. Chuck Downs, former deputy director for Regional Affairs and Congressional Relations in the Pentagon's East Asia policy office wrote, "Dealing with North Korea is a tough proposition." The North Koreans are "especially adept at brinkmanship. They make a show that convinces us they mean business. Then they extract their price and celebrate. They take from the negotiating table what they are unable to win in any direct conflict [and] survive not just to fight another day, but to create a new crisis when they are better equipped and stronger. At many occasions [of negotiating] North Korea demanded everything but actually took whatever it could get."[1] Such was the case in the negotiations for the release of the *Pueblo* and crew.

Rear Admiral John Smith was the initial U.S. negotiator in talks with North Korea for the release of the spy ship and crew. Smith was a Naval Academy graduate who considered himself to be the wrong man in the wrong place at the wrong time. He had never felt comfortable in the DMZ truce village. He was well aware of the continued belligerency of the North Koreans and considered them to be "savages...dangerous and unpredictable." He harbored premonitions of the North Koreans hiding a machine gun that could possibly fire on him some day, or the possibility of his being kidnapped."[2] Early in negotiations, and attempting to show dominance, Smith vehemently denounced the Blue House raid and demanded the release of the ship and crew with compensation to the U.S. government. When he looked up from his prepared script, he saw that he

Five—Negotiations for Freedom

was literally being laughed at by his North Korean counterpart, Major General Pak Chung Kuk, who, by his actions, considered North Korea to be the equal of the "imperial aggressors" and took charge of the meeting(s).[3] "Pak was a thin, dark-haired man with Occidental features and a mole beneath his right eye." Apparently Pak's appearance lent itself to some of Smith's aides who referred to Pak as "frog face."[4]

In answer to Smith's opening remarks demanding the release of the *Pueblo* and crew, Pak went into his own diatribe, stating;

> Our saying goes, "A mad dog barks at the moon." I cannot but pity you who are compelled to behave like a hooligan, disregarding even your age and honor to accomplish the crazy intentions of the war maniac Johnson for the sake of bread and dollars to keep your life. In order to sustain your life, you probably served Kennedy, who is already sent to hell. If you want to escape from the same fate of Kennedy, who is now a putrid corpse, and of Johnson, who is a living corpse, don't indulge yourself desperately in invectives....[5]

General Pak Chung-kuk is facing U.S. General Gilbert Woodward, lower left (dark hair and glasses; other officials unidentified). Woodward would remain until the final negotiations were completed and would sign the final agreement releasing the *Pueblo* crew (U.S. Navy photograph).

Five—Negotiations for Freedom

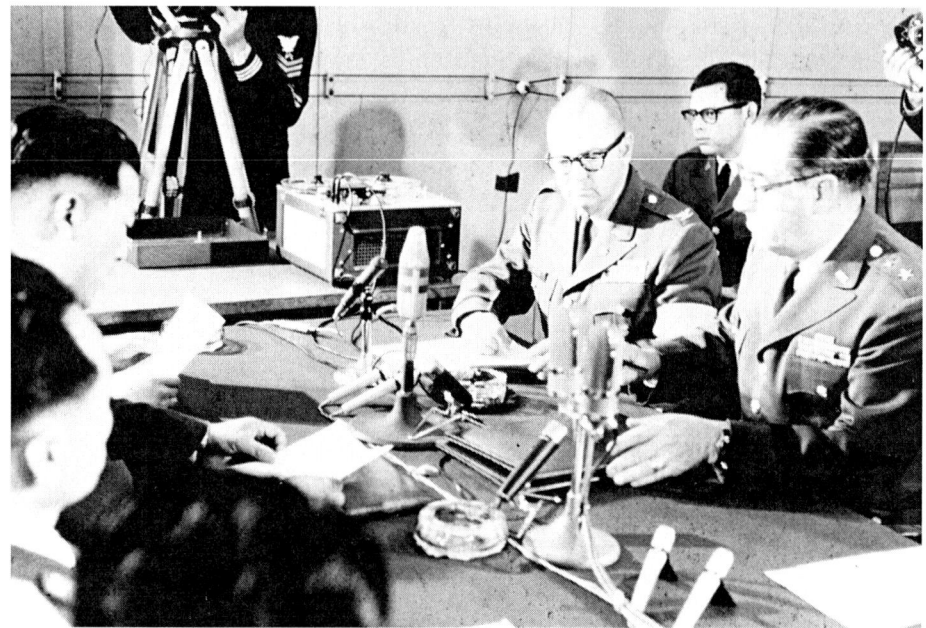

A different angle of General Pak Chung-kuk facing U.S. General Gilbert Woodward.

Pak also said to Admiral Smith,

> Notwithstanding that you have committed overt aggressive acts, you have indulged in an attempt to cover up the truth ... by distorting the facts as if your armed ship had been in international waters. Your preposterous charge graphically reveals the barbarous and shameless nature of the U.S. imperialist aggressors....

Not to let it lie, Smith replied:

> [Your] wild statement and the distorted version of your piracy off Wonsan were an attempt to divert attention from your regime's attempt to assassinate the President of the Republic of Korea and your actual capture of a U.S. vessel in international waters.[6]

Throughout the negotiations, General Pak employed strong words, but they gave an indication of the preferred mode of aggressive negotiation tactics used by the North Koreans throughout the drawn-out talks to release the *Pueblo* and its crew. Pak was at the table to carry out the wishes of Kim Il-sung and would not give quarter to the Americans without instructions from Kim. His primary job was to keep the Americans at the

Five—Negotiations for Freedom

table, but at bay, not conceding anything to Admiral Smith, and later, General Woodward.

The initial few meetings between Smith and Pak amounted to nothing more than the two men denouncing each other and their respective governments. They were getting nowhere. President Johnson, on learning of the lack of progress, was disappointed. He was hoping that the talks would obviate the need for military action. Secretary of State Rusk and Ambassador Porter began to have misgivings as to Smith being the U.S. negotiator, but no change was made until Smith's tour in Korea came to an end. Johnson's disappointment was apparent when he was asked at a press conference if "he was confident of being able to bring home both sailors and ship (*Pueblo*) and he answered, 'No, I am not.'"[7]

More than likely, Pak's instructions came directly from Kim, whose hatred for the United States was voiced by him while negotiations were underway.[8] Kim wrote the following in the *Nodong Sinmun*, the Workers' Party newspaper of November 21, 1968:

> If more countries, even if small, pool their strength and fight resolutely against imperialism, the people can knock down U.S. imperialism with decisively overwhelming power at each and every front. The peoples of all countries making revolution should tear the limbs off of the U.S. beast and behead it all over the world. When the peoples of many countries attack them from all sides and join in mutilating them in that way, they will soon become impotent and bite the dust in the wind.[9]

Under the leadership of Kim Il-sung, the North Korean strategy at the negotiating table "require[d] iron-fisted control by one side of the negotiating table and clever manipulation of the other."[10] "Secretary of State Dean Rusk referred to the ten months of negotiations with North Korea after the seizure of the USS *Pueblo* as the most frustrating episode in his career."[11]

"The holding of hostages as a means of coercing an enemy or an ally into complying with your will is at least as old as the recorded history of human conflict."[12] Kim Il-sung would surely have known the value of his *Pueblo* hostages and use the American propensity for recovering captured Americans to his advantage. By negotiating with the United States for the release of the *Pueblo* crew, Kim Il-sung could show the world audience that his country was on equal footing with the more powerful imperialist aggressor, the United States. It was not in Kim Il-sung's interest to complete the negotiations quickly. He would ensure that the talks spanned many months.

Five—Negotiations for Freedom

At the negotiating table, the North Koreans demonstrated their mastery of *Juche* ideology. To show their ability to take charge of a situation, the North Koreans, in the final days of negotiations, demanded that the U.S. negotiators sign a letter of apology and admit to criminal acts. A precedent for this manner of resolution had been set when a U.S. helicopter pilot had been forced down in North Korea on May 17, 1963. In that incident, Kim Il-sung, in a letter to General Hamilton H. Howze, the United Nations Command (UNC) commander in chief at the time, outlined the demands to be met prior to the release of the American pilots. The UNC would be required to admit to "criminal acts," guarantee that such acts would not occur in the future, and strictly abide by the Armistice Agreement. The U.S. negotiator in this instance was a fiery Major General named Richard Ciccolella. The negotiations dragged on with no movement by the North Koreans. They insisted that the United States sign a confession attesting to the fact that the helicopter crew had been spying, which was not true. The pilot had simply gotten lost and veered into North Korea by mistake. General Ciccolella was finally able to receive permission to give a signed confession to the North Koreans for the release of the Helicopter crew. But he insisted on having the last words as he handed the signed confession to the North Koreans. He said, "Here you sons of bitches is your goddamn sheet of paper. It isn't worth the paper it is written on." Ciccolella continued, "The only reason I am giving it to you so that we can get the body of this man back." Continuing to harangue the North Koreans, he added, "You people should be ashamed of your conduct. You are not worthy of wearing the uniform of a soldier. I spit on you."[13] The North Koreans were not fazed by the General's lambast. They looked at the paper, saw that it was what they wanted, and subsequently released the body and the crew. After U.S. officials signed a letter admitting their intrusion into North Korea, the army crew was released on May 16, 1964, nearly a year after their helicopter had crossed into North Korea.[14]

The 1963 helicopter incident and the absurd negotiations that took place to release the U.S. crew are mentioned because of the audacity of Major General Ciccolella, and because the negotiations regarding the release of the *Pueblo* crew were nearly identical in their frustrating, absurd negotiations with the North Koreans. Major General Pak Chung Kuk remained the North Korean negotiator for the duration of the negotiations. The Americans facing him across the table knew that even as chief spokesman for the North Koreans, Pak did not have the authority to make

Five—Negotiations for Freedom

decisions. This was apparent when the Americans posed questions and/or solutions, but would have to wait until the next day to get answers. Obviously Pak was being debriefed and fed the discussion points for each day.

In May 1968, Admiral Smith, who had reached the end of his term in Korea, was replaced by Major General Gilbert Woodward. Shortly after becoming the American negotiator, Woodward asked General Pak to put his demands down in writing and give it to him. Surprisingly, on May 8, Pak gave a written document containing the demands to Woodward, who sent it to Washington. The document went all the way to the White House, where President Johnson reviewed it. After arguing the pros and cons with his aides, Johnson simply said, "I don't want that."[15] The grinding negotiations would continue.

Even while the talks dragged on, the North Koreans continued their skirmishes along the DMZ with guerilla firefights occurring regularly. On November 3, fifty guerillas, a force larger than that which had attacked the Blue House in January, made their way inland from the sea to the South Korean village of Ulchin. The infiltrators took control of the village and held propaganda rallies and killed a villager who tried to escape. The villagers were able to sound the alarm, and 5,000 South Korean troops swarmed the area, killing thirty of the infiltrators, and scattering the others.[16]

During the *Pueblo* negotiations, Pak had insisted that the U.S. negotiator sign a document containing what the UNC and American officials referred to as the "three A's," admission of guilt, apology to North Korea, and assurance that it would never happen again.[17] Perhaps because it would imply an admission of wrongdoing, the United States did not wish to sign such a document. As a result, the negotiations dragged on for months. Ever mindful of the value of propaganda, Kim Il-sung had no intention of moving more quickly in negotiations with the Armistice Commission and the American negotiators. He used the vehicle of the Armistice Commission for his own purposes. The negotiations became a sounding board for his *Juche* ideology. By holding a more powerful country at bay at the bargaining table, he was demonstrating to the world that his country was the equal of perceived nations of power. It was the North Koreans who "summoned the United States to meetings," thereby forcing the United States to accept Kim's schedule of negotiation meetings. In accordance with *Juche* philosophy, forcing the United States to acquiesce during negotiations brought prestige to Kim Il-sung in the eyes of the

Five—Negotiations for Freedom

North Koreans and the world, while demonstrating to North Koreans the global prominence of their country and the esteemed guidance of their leader. Did the North Koreans simply wish to humiliate the United States? Perhaps, but more important to the North Koreans was the fact that the antagonistic "relationship gave them international status in their own eyes, and that the depiction to their own people of the United States as North Korea's chief adversary reinforced their propaganda of the imminent threat to the security of the state."[18] If American negotiators learned nothing else in their talks with North Korea, they came to the realization that they "[could] do little to prevent North Korea's continued utilization of [Armistice Commission discussions] for political purposes," that is, the demonstration to the world of Kim's *Juche* ideology.[19]

In late October, General Woodward had reached the end of his six month tour as head negotiator for the Americans. Instead of leaving Korea, Woodward decided to stay on as negotiator. He stated, "After coming this far, I was sort of enmeshed in the thing. I figured it was a shame to have to bring in somebody else." He told his superiors, "I'll see it through, no matter how long it takes."[20] One can only imagine how long it would have taken to bring Woodward's successor up to speed and learn the nuances of the North Korean negotiating style of General Pak. Woodward stayed through to the completion of the negotiations. In the words of James F. Leonard, who had been named the State Department's "country director" for Korea, "Woodward was a godsend—a tough, patient man who appreciated the situation's subtleties."[21]

Finally, in an odd set of circumstances, U.S. negotiators recalled the signing of a similar meaningless piece of paper in 1964, took a lesson from history, and reached an agreement when Woodward signed a written document, and Pak permitted Woodward to read a complete refutation of the signed agreement into the record of the negotiations. In other words, the United States had agreed to North Korea's demands of the three A's, and North Korea had allowed the U.S. negotiator to verbally reject the three A's agreement. It was James Leonard of the state department, with a subtle tip from his wife, Eleanor, who came up with the idea to follow the lead of the hostage agreement reached with Korea in years past. Eleanor suggested that if they told the North Koreans up front that they were going to sign the document but would consider it a false document, perhaps the North Koreans would still agree to it.

On October 17, Woodward finally met Pak again after a gap of forty-seven days, during which time President Johnson was criticized for not being engaged in the *Pueblo* negotiations. This was not true, as it was General Pak who had been staying away from any new negotiation meetings.[22] The absence of the negotiators at the table had even given birth to private U.S. citizens volunteering to go to the DMZ to take the place of General Woodward. Many of these uninformed folks were convinced that they could do a better job than Woodward. One such dreamer had the gumption to travel to Moscow and several Asian countries in an attempt to speak with the North Korean ambassadors to request permission to come to the bargaining table. His plans, of course, came to naught.

At the meeting of the 17th, Woodward presented the new proposal to Pak, after which, they recessed for nearly an hour. During that time, Pak undoubtedly contacted Pyongyang and returned to the table. Pak then stated, "I note that you will sign my document. We have reached agreement."[23] On December 23, at nine o'clock in the morning, General Woodward took his place at the negotiating table. Pak sat across from him, while Woodward read a statement, a statement that had initially been suggested by Eleanor Leonard to her husband, James. Woodward read:

> The position of the United States Government with regard to the *Pueblo* ... has been that the ship was not engaged in illegal activity, that there is no convincing evidence that the ship at any time intruded into the territorial waters claimed by North Korea, and that we could not apologize for actions which we did not believe took place. The document which I am going to sign was prepared by the North Koreans and is at variance with the above position. My signature will not and cannot alter the facts. I will sign the document to free the crew and only to free the crew.

After further negative remarks by Pak, the North Korean general acquiesced and wrote the time and date on the document and tossed it back to Woodward. The *Pueblo* crew would be going home. They would line up and cross the Bridge of No Return in single file at thirty second intervals later that day, exactly eleven months after their capture.

The fact that the North Koreans demanded a written document proving that the United States had agreed to the "three A's," and then agreed to allow General Woodward to verbalize a refutation of the agreement seems ludicrous. Secretary of State Dean Rusk called the agreement "bizarre." He went on to say, "It is as though a kidnapper kidnaps your child and asks for fifty thousand dollars. You give him a check for fifty thousand dollars and you tell him at the time that you've stopped payment

Five—Negotiations for Freedom

on the check, and then he delivers your child to you."[24] General Woodward also commented on the strange circumstances of the acceptance by the North Koreans of the agreement. When he was asked to sign and then refute the agreement he stated his thoughts:

> I said right then and there they'll buy it.... It satisfied their one condition, a signature on a piece of paper. The North Korean people would never hear about the repudiation. Their propaganda boys would take care of that. And as for the rest of the world, well they just didn't care.[25]

Nations outside of North Korea knew of the dichotomous nature of the agreement, but with Kim Il-sung controlling all media within North Korea, the North Korean citizens would never know about it.[26] Woodward signed the agreement on December 23, 1968, and within hours, the *Pueblo*

General Woodward signs the final document agreeing to the North Korean "Three A's" demand after verbally refuting the validity of the document. The *Pueblo* crew was released within hours following the signing (U.S. Navy photograph).

Top: December 23, 1968, *Boston Herald Traveler* headline announcing the release of the *Pueblo* crew. *Bottom:* The Bridge of No Return. The *Pueblo* crew crossed this bridge in the area of the border near the Joint Security Area on December 23, 1968, to return to South Korea and to the care of the U.S. military and the U.N. Armistice staff. Commander Bucher crossed the bridge first, followed by the crew and the remains of Fireman Duane Hodges (photographs from USS *Pueblo*.org web site).

Five—Negotiations for Freedom

crew and the remains of Fireman Duane Hodges, who had died from gunfire injuries during the attack on the *Pueblo*, were taken to the DMZ at Kaesong and released to walk across the Hangul Bridge, more commonly called "The Bridge of No Return."[27] While members of the press on both sides of the bridge observed, Bucher was made to walk across the bridge first. He was followed by North Koreans carrying the plain wooden coffin containing the remains of Hodges. One by one, the crew then followed Bucher to freedom and were quickly moved away in U.S. buses to undergo physical examinations and debriefing at an Army hospital in Seoul.[28] It was here that Bucher received a telegram from "President Johnson, who declared the crew's release, 'a source of the deepest satisfaction to me and to all of your fellow countrymen.'"[29]

After eleven months of the *Pueblo* crew's captivity in two different prisons in Pyongyang, and after Lyndon Johnson announced that he would not seek reelection, Kim was faced with "accepting [Johnson's] offer" to release the *Pueblo* crew or face continued confrontation with "an unpredictable U.S. administration at some future point in time."[30] For Kim and North Korea, the propaganda value of the *Pueblo* and its crew had served its purpose, and the issue of the ship and crew could be resolved under conditions agreeable to North Korea.

Kim Il-sung's propaganda machine made full use of the release of the *Pueblo*

Commander Lloyd Bucher crosses the Bridge of No Return to the waiting U.S. military and the U.N. Armistice staff (U.S. Navy photograph).

Top: A U.N. Armistice commission bus carries the *Pueblo* crew away from the Bridge of No Return. Crew members can be seen waving in the bus windows. *Bottom:* General Charles Bonesteel on the left in the hat and jacket, greets and shakes hands with CDR Bucher as he arrives at the Armistice Commission headquarters (U.S. Navy photographs).

Five—Negotiations for Freedom

crew. "The North Koreans believed they had won a clear victory." The North Korean Foreign Ministry spokesman summed up the North Korean sentiment by stating: "This means the ignominious defeat of the U.S. imperialist aggressors and constitutes another great victory for the Korean people. Today in Panmunjom ... once again the U.S. imperialists knelt to the Korean people and apologized for the incident of the armed spy ship *Pueblo*."[31]

State propaganda ensured that the North Korean people knew their leader was working to achieve *chawi*, a basic tenet of *Juche*. Kim's propaganda affirmed that he was fully capable of backing up his claim to place North Korea on an equal military footing with the United States. By using the seizure of the U.S. spy ship, Kim Il-sung had achieved *chawi*. In addition, Kim had his "war trophy," a lasting legacy of his facing and defeating the imperialists in the form of the United States spy ship permanently on

Three of the *Pueblo* officers eating at the Armistice Commission headquarters after their release from the North Koreans. Left to right, Chief Warrant Officer Gene Lacy, LT Stephen Harris, and LTJG Carl "Skip" Schumacher (U.S. Navy photograph).

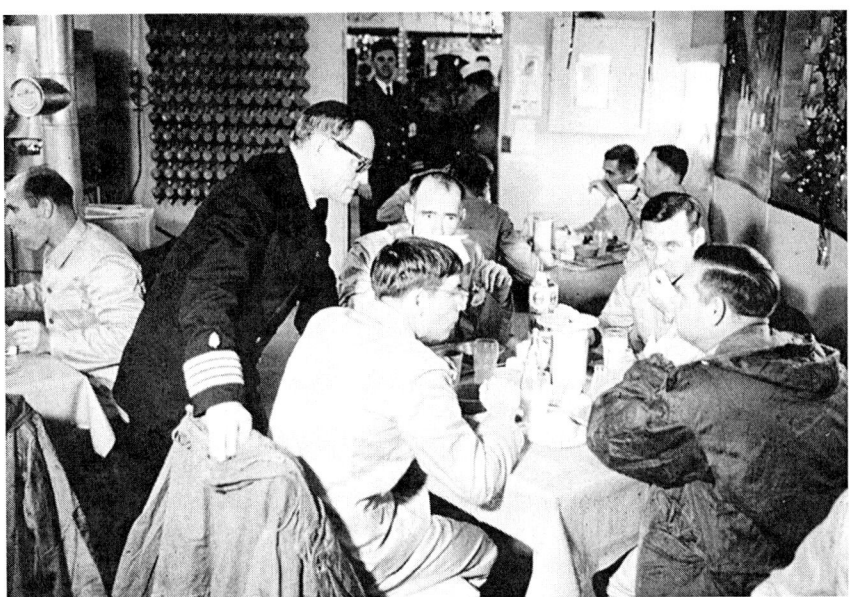

Top: A U.S. Navy medical officer speaks to crew members while they are eating at the Armistice Commission headquarters. The two men facing the camera are believed to be Engineman Rushel Blansett on the left and Marine Sergeant Robert Chicca on the right. *Bottom:* Commander Bucher is taken from the Joint Security Area mess hall for debriefing and medical examination (U.S. Navy photographs).

Five—Negotiations for Freedom

The crew attends a memorial service for Duane Hodges at the 121st Evac. Hospital (photograph from USS *Pueblo*.org web site).

display as a part of a military museum in Pyongyang, the capital of North Korea. On January 20, 2003, the thirty-fifth anniversary of the ship's capture, the DPRK's Central News Agency issued a news release commemorating the capture of the *Pueblo:* "The spy ship *Pueblo*, a trophy captured by Korean seamen from the U.S. imperialists, is on display on the river [T]aedong in [P]yongyang [and] since the spy ship was brought to the river, it has been visited [seen but not boarded] by 360,000 Korean people including servicemen and schoolchildren, and more than 7,000 foreigners." That news statement is followed by an almost comical next paragraph. It states, "Pak In-ho, an officer and hero of the republic who was the head of the seven-member death-defying corps that captured the ship, briefs visitors on what the ship did, the combat for capturing it, and the brazenfaced and crafty nature of the U.S. imperialists."[32] A sardonically humorous passage, considering that the *Pueblo* never fired a shot in "the combat." In late 2013, the ship was cosmetically refurbished and opened to the North Korean public. The *Pueblo* serves as a permanent marketing tool aimed at the North Korean people, reinforcing Kim Il-sung's belief that through

Five—Negotiations for Freedom

Juche, he and the nation had achieved *chawi*, defending against their imperialist enemy, the United States. The capture of the *Pueblo* "provided Kim with coveted domestic propaganda. In short, Kim wanted only the symbolic value of the American humiliation for display to the people of his own country."[33] The "North Korean press today continues to trumpet both [the *Pueblo* incident and the EC-121 shoot-down] as badges of national honor."[34]

In reality, Kim's grand design of uniting Korea by military force had failed miserably. After his plan to disrupt South Korea, to be followed by the unification of the two Koreas, was unsuccessful, his capture of the *Pueblo* ensured his stature with his citizenry. But he also recognized his failures and wasted no time in deflecting the blame. Immediately after releasing the *Pueblo* crew, Kim's purge began anew. He focused blame on his military elite, firing his defense minister, at least a dozen generals and admirals, and had them executed or thrown into prison. Two of those

The captured USS *Pueblo* has been converted to a North Korean war museum, depicting the glory of humbling the United States. Thousands of North Koreans visit the ship annually (https://commons.wikimedia.org/wiki/File:USS_Pueblo_(AGER-02)_02.jpg Attribution-By Nicor[CC BY-SA 3.0 https://creativecommons.org/licenses/by-sa/3.0)], from Wikipedia Commons).

Five—Negotiations for Freedom

generals were his own brothers. His subsequent statement regarding his actions attributed full blame to others by saying that his generals had "deliberately sabotaged his campaign plan, wrecking it beyond reclamation, and overturned the military line of the party, and that the generals did not fully utilize the military assets at their disposal."[35]

Kim's assignment of blame to his generals for their failure to subdue South Korea and win the hearts of his Southern neighbors may or may not have had substance, but his military actions, including the capture of the USS *Pueblo*, had long-lasting repercussions, all of which were actually counter to Kim's goals. "In the final analysis, North Korea's militant policy toward the South [and the United States in 1966–69] became counterproductive by hardening the South Koreans' fear and distrust of the Pyongyang regime and providing a rationale for the continued presence of U.S. troops until the ROK would develop a sufficient deterrent force against the North."[36] Even as early as May 1968, the CIA learned that there was a "growing nervousness on the part of North Korea" as a result of the $100 million in military aid given to South Korea to quell President Park's wish to invade North Korea, and because there had been a "lack of real progress in the Panmunjom talks concerning the *Pueblo*." The North Korean government also learned that the South Koreans were "receiving a squadron of F-4 Phantoms and three Navy destroyers."[37] Kim's hope for easily negotiated concessions from the U.S. negotiators for the release of the *Pueblo* and its crew did not go according to his plan.

The reaction in Washington to the capture of the *Pueblo* generally attributed the incident to a world communist plot orchestrated by the Soviet Union or China. Historian Mitchell Lerner wrote: "Almost unanimously, the Johnson administration embraced the idea that North Korean actions were rooted in a larger Communist conspiracy."[38] However, Soviet intelligence officers denied their participation. "'This was simply not something we would do,' explained former KGB Major General Oleg Kalugin."[39] Perhaps understandably, Washington continued to believe that North Korea had acted, while the major communist powers had pulled the puppet strings, regardless of the fact that the Soviets denied involvement. The Soviet Union had its own fleet of spy ships lurking off the U.S. coast and shadowing the U.S. Navy fleet. "It is highly unlikely that the Soviets would risk a quid pro quo capture of one of their spy ships by the United States and risk strengthening the position of American hawks who had long demanded more forceful actions against communist influence, especially

Five—Negotiations for Freedom

in Vietnam."[40] In addition, the U.S. and Soviet governments had been making progress in negotiations of non-proliferation of arms talks in 1967–68, the results of which were beneficial to the economies and safety of both nations. Soviet complicity in the spy ship seizure would have jeopardized further negotiations.[41] Yet, President Johnson and many of his closest advisors were convinced of a communist conspiracy, even venturing to speculate that Berlin would be the next communist objective.

We now know from Soviet and CIA sources that Kim was not taking direction from either the Soviet Union or the Chinese. He knew exactly what he was doing and, in all likelihood, gave the orders to fire on the *Pueblo* while the North Korean warships idled near the spy ship, awaiting his direction. "To Kim, such acts as piracy on the high seas and in the air over Korea seemed justifiable to dramatize the depths of Pyongyang's resentments to a world that seemed oblivious to his beliefs," even if it meant drawing criticism from both Moscow and Peking.[42]

It would be speculation to guess the nature of Kim's risk analysis before seizing the *Pueblo*. As an autocrat, Kim answered to no one, heeding only his own counsel. The CIA, in a report dated November 26, 1968, but written just before the *Pueblo* crew was released, concluded:

> In deciding to risk possible U.S. military retaliation by seizing the *Pueblo* on 23 January 1968, Kim and his aides probably calculated that Washington would not use nuclear weapons to attack the North. They were willing to risk provoking a conventional air attack (as the most probable form of retaliation, if it came) because they were confident they had a good chance of resisting and surviving it. Another important consideration probably was the North Koreans' calculation that Washington was deterred from launching an air attack because of the regime's defense treaties with Moscow and Peking. [A subjective factor in Kim's reasoning was that] Kim probably believed that by seizing the *Pueblo* he would be upstaging Moscow and Peking and scoring a point regarding the importance of small countries in the world communist movement. Kim ... "extracted ... personal political benefits from seizure of the ship. From his viewpoint, he has defied the major enemy and he has upstaged his big communist allies in the process."[43]

Kim had acted on his own in his quest to capture the *Pueblo*. He was guided by his *Juche* ideology and a fortuitous opportunity. Four years after the *Pueblo* incident Kim wrote an article for the *Pyongyang Times* that explained how *Juche* guided his actions. "The government of [North Korea] formulates its foreign policy on the basis of the [*Juche*] idea and is guided by this idea in carrying out its external activities. In a word, our republic maintains its independence in its foreign activities."[44] With *Juche*

Five—Negotiations for Freedom

as his guide, Kim may have gambled that the United States had its plate full with Vietnam and would, therefore, not risk starting another war in Korea. He won the gamble, thereby humiliating the United States and raising his esteem, all in accordance with *Juche* ideology. The idea that North Korea acted alone is supported by former U.S. Ambassador to Taiwan, Ralph N. Clough, who wrote:

> North Korea has never wavered in its determination to bring about the withdrawal of U.S. forces [from South Korea], but its tactics have varied over the years, from acts of force, like the seizure of the *Pueblo*, to proposals for direct negotiations. Hostility toward the United States has been a permanent feature of the political landscape in North Korea, serving to rally the populace under the leadership of Kim Il-sung to meet the U.S. threat, often portrayed in North Korean propaganda as a scheme to back South Korea in a military invasion of the North.[45]

Historian B.C. Koh concurred: "It is improbable that the decision [to seize the *Pueblo*] was either instigated by or cleared in advance with the Soviet Union [or] Peking.... In all likelihood, North Korea acted alone, unaided and without consulting any of its allies, for the main purpose of harassing and humiliating its archenemy, the United States."[46] Without the help of any other communist nation, Kim had focused world attention on his small country and caused a great deal of consternation within the administration of President Lyndon Johnson and great concern among the American public.

Enabled by flawed leadership within the U.S. Navy and the Johnson administration, the seizure of the U.S. spy ship *Pueblo* was a unilateral decision on the part of Kim Il-sung. Capturing the spy ship allowed him to perpetuate the *Juche* ideology and maintain his power by demonstrating to the North Korean people that he had achieved *chawi* for the nation. Lack of due diligence on the part of the Navy and Washington officials allowed a dramatic act by Kim Il-sung to be played out on the world stage, allegedly to give his government legitimacy and achieve perceived equality with the world's greatest and most powerful political communities.

Six

The Navy Court of Inquiry

The debate upon whether the *Pueblo* crew members were prisoners of war, or political propaganda prisoners, caused a great deal of consternation in the U.S. military and the Johnson administration. In what manner would the commanding officer and the crew of the *Pueblo* be treated by the U.S. government and the Navy, in particular, upon their release and return to the United States? Would they be classified as returning prisoners of war, returnees from imprisonment following a ship hijacking at sea, or victims of a scenario whereby a Naval officer gave up his ship without firing a shot in defense?

The dilemma of Americans being captured by a country with which we were not at war presented a conundrum for the U.S. Navy after the crew was released. The Navy was convinced that Bucher should receive discipline and be brought before a court-martial for signing a (bogus) confession, thereby giving the North Koreans more than his name, rank, and serial number and for giving up his ship to the North Koreans without a fight. The Navy hierarchy was intent on disciplining Bucher and other crew members for what they considered to be a violation of the military's Code of Conduct for the U.S. Fighting Man. "The Code of Conduct for Members of the United States Armed Forces" was put into effect in 1955, following the Korean War. It consists of the following five orders:

> I. I am an American, fighting in the forces which guard my country and our way of life. I am prepared to give my life in their defense.
> II. I will never surrender of my own free will. If in command, I will never surrender the members of my command while they still have means to resist.
> III. If I am captured I will continue to resist by all means available.

Six—The Navy Court of Inquiry

      I will make every effort to escape and aid others to escape. I will accept neither parole nor special favors from the enemy.
- IV. If I become a prisoner of war, I will keep faith with my fellow prisoners. I will give no information or take part in any action which might be harmful to my comrades. If I am senior, I will take command. If not, I will obey the lawful orders of those appointed over me and will back them up in every way.
- V. When questioned, should I become a prisoner of war, I am required to give name, rank, service number and date of birth. I will evade answering further questions to the utmost of my ability. I will make no oral or written statements disloyal to my country and its allies or harmful to their cause. [Note—the second and third sentences of this clause were added during Jimmy Carter's administration in 1977, after the *Pueblo* incident. Therefore, if the *Pueblo* crew had been considered prisoners of war when they returned to the United States, they might have been held accountable for failure to follow the first sentence.]
- VI. I will never forget that I am an American, fighting for freedom, responsible for my actions, and dedicated to the principles which made my country free. I will trust in my God and in the United States of America.[1]

The Code of Conduct is ingrained in all U.S. military personnel as they process through basic training. After a great deal of discussion within the Johnson administration and the Navy, it was decided that members of the *Pueblo* would not be charged with violation of the military code of conduct, that is, giving their North Korean interrogators more than just name, rank, and serial number. After all, the United States was not at war with North Korea when the ship was captured. The Navy pursued a different avenue in recommending discipline of Bucher, Harris, and one of the ship's enlisted men. Essentially, they were charged, instead, with failure to safeguard the mountains of classified documents and equipment carried on the ship. "The fact that his [Bucher's] humanity [in safeguarding the lives of his crew members] might have saved the world a war did not enter into the Navy's judgement," nor did the Navy consider the fact that the *Pueblo* was overloaded with unnecessary classified material with no efficient means to destroy it or scuttle the ship in an emergency situation.[2]

Six—The Navy Court of Inquiry

Determined to ferret out the responsible individual or individuals who allowed the *Pueblo* debacle to occur, the Navy formed a fact-finding body to conduct a Court of Inquiry. The Court of Inquiry panel members were made up of five senior Navy officers. The president (head) of the panel was Vice Admiral Harold G. Bowen. The other members were Rear Admiral Richard R. Pratt, Rear Admiral Allen A. Bergner, Rear Admiral Edward E. Grimm, and Rear Admiral Marshall W. White. Their combined biographies listed 77 medals and decorations, 184 years of service, and "presumably, unswerving belief in a hard and uncompromising system."[3]

Could the *Pueblo* crew receive an untainted examination at the hands of such an austere group? For the most part, the answer to that question cannot be answered unequivocally, because unbeknownst to Bucher and his attorney, Miles Harvey, the Navy had placed restrictions on Admiral Bowen's access to a long list of witnesses. Bowen could not call Admiral Hyland to testify regarding his actions surrounding the *Pueblo* incident, and he was also prohibited from calling anyone in higher authority to the men on the panel. In other words, no one from the JCS, CNO's office, or the White House. All of those entities had individuals with knowledge of the case, but who could not be called to testify.[4] Thus, Bowen was somewhat hamstrung from the

Prior to the start of the Navy Court of Inquiry, Commander Bucher's picture appeared on the cover of the February 3, 1969, *Newsweek* magazine. The question on the cover would become the subject of debate for decades (photograph from USS *Pueblo*.org web site).

Six—The Navy Court of Inquiry

beginning. Also, aside from one or two exceptions, it would seem that the court of inquiry panel members were lop-sidedly hard liners. As an example of their fervor, an interesting incident occurred during the proceedings. LTJG Tim Harris informed CDR Bucher that he had been approached by a Navy captain (who was involved with the panel) and was "told in so many words that he had better come up with something that would help the Court to hang his captain, or else."[5] An incident like this would appear to foretell the thinking of the panel. But, Bucher's attorney, Miles Harvey,

Above: The *Pueblo* Board of Inquiry, left to right, Rear Admiral Richard R. Pratt, Rear Admiral Marshall W. White, Vice Admiral Harold G. Bowen (standing), Rear Admiral Edward E. Grimm, and Rear Admiral Allen A. Bergner (U.S. Navy photograph). *Opposite top:* CDR Bucher was represented by family attorney E. Miles Harvey, left, and Navy JAG Officer Captain James E. Keys. Bucher sits between them (U.S. Navy photograph). *Opposite bottom:* During the Court of Inquiry, members of the board and attorneys visited the USS *Palm Beach*. Left to right are Rear Admiral Allen Bergner, Captain James Keys, and Miles Harvey (photograph from USS *Pueblo*.org web site).

Six—The Navy Court of Inquiry

informed Admiral Bowen of the incident, and to his credit, Bowen called the over-eager captain before him and relieved him of his duties.

Exactly one year after being taken by force by the North Koreans, on January 23, 1969, during the Navy's court of inquiry, and prior to his testimony, CDR Bucher was given a mandatory warning that he was suspected of violation of Navy regulations. The warning was standard procedure in a court of inquiry, but the result deeply aroused public sentiment. Letters to the Pentagon "turned into a torrent."[6] Anti–Navy sentiment rose higher yet when it was rumored that selected members of the *Pueblo* crew, including Commander Bucher, would be punished. The media portrayed Bucher as "wan and thin," speaking in "a choked voice," and "powerless before the admirals who sit behind an elevated table and watch him." The result was an outpouring of sympathy from the public and "contempt for those who would persecute him further." For example, an editorial in *The New York Times* of January 25, 1969, titled "The *Pueblo* Inquiry," stated, "Certainly now there is neither need nor excuse for subjecting Commander Bucher to the emotional trial he is being forced to endure."[7] Adding more fire to the national public furor, the Navy denied copies of the transcript of the court of inquiry proceedings to *The New York Times, Washington Post, Los Angeles Times,* and *Reader's Digest.* Public sentiment then placed the Navy, not CDR Bucher, on trial, and "public indignation [had] shifted from the North Koreans to the Government at home."[8]

Captain William Newsome, chief counsel to the investigating admirals (U.S. Navy photograph).

At the court of inquiry, Bucher was the first to take the stand and was grilled by

Six—The Navy Court of Inquiry

the five presiding admirals. Bucher carefully went through all the details of the *Pueblo's* outfitting, its perpetual mechanical and communication problems, and the details of the North Koreans firing upon his ship, the wounding of his men, the futility of attempting to man the ship's two .50 caliber machine guns, and finally, the boarding of the spy ship by the North

In this photograph, LT Stephen Harris, left, and CDR Lloyd Bucher, right, leave the inquiry hearing (photograph from USS *Pueblo*.org web site).

Six—The Navy Court of Inquiry

Koreans. He was asked some key questions, one of which was whether or not he had at any time entered North Korean waters. Bucher answered, "At no time." The questions continued, most of which asked indirectly why Bucher had not taken more drastic action to fight the North Korean aggressors, to destroy the classified material on the ship, and scuttle his own ship rather than turn it over to the North Koreans. Bucher had answers to all of these questions, answers that for the most part explained his actions as those taken to save the lives of the ship's crew, rather than having the North Koreans destroy the ship through additional gunfire, probably killing the majority of the crew in the process. After a short recess, the panel members returned to the room and advised Bucher that based upon his answers to that point, he was now suspected of a violation of Navy regulations, article 0730, which stated that a Navy commanding officer shall not allow representatives of a foreign government to board his ship, search it, and will not allow those foreign representatives to take members of the ship from the ship, as long as he has the power to resist.

Commander Bucher was represented in the court of inquiry by his civilian attorney, Miles Harvey, a friend of the Buchers. Immediately after Bucher was informed of article 0730, Harvey asked Bucher, "Commander Bucher, at the time the North Koreans set foot on your ship, did you any longer have the power to resist?" Bucher answered, "No, I did not."[9] The probable outcome of the hearing would prove to hinge on that question and Bucher's answer as defense against a charge of violation of article 0730.

Many times, however, such thorny questions are not easily answered. Retired Vice Admiral James Stockdale wrote, using an example: "To say, 'I spilled my guts because I was being tortured,' is never an adequate explanation. To what degree were you incapacitated? How much information did you give. These questions must be answered." Stockdale went on, "Aristotle would say the same to the man who says, 'I stole the money because my kids were starving.'" Stockdale's point is that "more information is required before the act is justified."[10] And that is the path that the Navy inquiry panel followed. Bucher was not about to get off easy by simply saying that he took the action he did to save his crew. The panel would require further information. Stockdale went on to write, "Moral responsibility cannot be escaped," and, "...you cannot use your profession as a shield from responsibility for your actions. A person is the sum of his deeds, and the responsibility for them rests squarely on his shoulders."[11]

Six—The Navy Court of Inquiry

At no time while Bucher was being grilled by the North Koreans or by the Navy's court of inquiry, did he fail to accept his moral responsibility, knowing full well that it might not be acceptable to the Navy.

There was another interesting series of questions and answers when Rear Admiral George L. Cassell was called before the court of inquiry. When Cassell took the stand, Bucher did not look at him. It should be remembered that it was Cassell who had previously told Bucher in Honolulu when he visited the CINCPACFLT headquarters that there were contingency plans in effect that allowed for military resources to come to the aid of the spy ship. Since he had made that statement to Bucher, Cassell had been promoted to rear admiral. Admiral Bowen addressed Cassell and stated, "I must conclude that the whole operation of the *Pueblo* was planned without any external means for her protection, that international law was her only protection. When this basic assumption was violated, did you expect that ship (*Pueblo*) to protect itself?"

"Yes, we did," answered Cassell.

Bowen then asked, "Did you think that *Pueblo* could defend herself adequately with two .50 caliber machine guns?"

Cassell answered, "Yes I did."[12]

This testimony is interesting. Cassell was a distinguished Naval Officer, having received many awards for gallant service, including a Distinguished Flying Cross for service during World War Two, and a Navy Distinguished Service Medal for meritorious and distinguished service. In other words, he was a highly regarded officer. Why, then, would he have made one statement to Bucher while he was assistant chief of staff for CINCPACFLT, but change his story while testifying at the Court of Inquiry? One can only conclude that is must have been done for a self-serving reason, and to continue the Navy's pointing to Bucher as the Navy's scapegoat.

One by one, the other *Pueblo* officers and members of the spy ship's crew testified at the hearing. Without exception, the men backed up the actions of their captain. They testified that if they had been in the same circumstances as Bucher, they would have taken the same course of action. For example, when the panel queried Lieutenant Edward Murphy, Bucher's executive officer on the *Pueblo*, they asked, "In your opinion, at the time the North Koreans boarded the *Pueblo*, did Commander Bucher any longer have the power to resist?"

Murphy answered, "I can say the decision that I was aware of ... would

Six—The Navy Court of Inquiry

have been essentially identical.... I can see no difference in the end result, sir."[13] In other words, Murphy stated that he would have made the same decisions as his commanding officer, Bucher.

Bucher and Harvey were winning their struggle against the court of inquiry panel. The press was allowed to be in the court room, and they became so disgusted with the pompous panel members that the press even refused to stand when the court convened each day. The press corps also "sensed an undercurrent of social caste running through the inquiry. Bucher had come from a very humble upbringing, having grown up as an orphan in Father Flanagan's Boy's Town in Nebraska. He had served in the Navy as an enlisted man before being commissioned through ROTC at the University of Nebraska. The Navy term for an officer with prior enlisted service is "mustang." In stark contrast, all of the panel members were Naval Academy graduates, a difference not taken lightly by academy men. With the press knowing of this social chasm, and through the efforts of Harvey, Bucher was becoming an antiestablishment hero to Americans following the hearing's progress.[14]

Congress, of course, was aware of the proceedings. Representative Edwin D. Eshleman (R-PA) expressed his anti–Navy sentiment by urging "newly appointed Secretary of the Navy, John Chafee, to halt [the court of inquiry]." Congressman L. Mendel Rivers (D-SC) began procedures to establish a subcommittee to "conduct a full and thorough inquiry into all matters arising from the capture and internment of the USS *Pueblo* and its crew by the North Korean Government."

The court of inquiry, which had begun in January, was completed on March 13, 1969. Prior to the announcement of the Navy's findings, this post-inquiry editorial appeared in the *Wall Street Journal* of March 17, 1969:

> If the court of inquiry's findings are as fair as its hearings have been, they will show that whatever questions there may be about the commander's conduct, the big mistakes were made at far higher levels. For the Navy, the lesson of the *Pueblo* is an old one: If you send men on a difficult mission ill-equipped, ill-prepared, and ill-trained, you cannot expect exemplary performance.[15]

The Navy took a hard line in its recommendations for discipline of the *Pueblo* crew. "The Navy couldn't condone its commanders giving up without a fight. If surrendering to preserve sailors' lives became the norm, the Navy couldn't do its job; it would fall to pieces."[16] It was this reasoning that caused the Navy to insist on punitive measures for Bucher and others.

Six—The Navy Court of Inquiry

The panel came to a quick decision that CDR Bucher had the ability to resist the North Koreans, but had failed. As a result, he had lost his ship, or, in the antiseptic words of Admiral Bowen, "...he let government property get away." CDR Bucher, and LT Stephen Harris, who was in charge of the ship's intelligence personnel, were recommended for disciplinary letters of reprimand. In addition, it was recommended that *Pueblo's* XO, Edward Murphy, receive a letter of admonition.[17] But then, the task of meting out discipline became a bit more complicated for the inquiry panel of admirals. Because they were taking the hard line, they were forced to examine one of their own. Admiral Grimm had been a friend of Admiral Johnson for many years. But, for disciplinary consistency, he would now have to review avenues of discipline for his friend. As a result, Admiral Johnson was also recommended for a letter of reprimand along with Captain Everett Gladding who headed up the Naval Security Group Pacific.

Contrarily, "Americans embraced Bucher for the reason that he hadn't thrown away lives for the sake of some quixotic notion of military honor or tradition."[18] It seems plausible that public reaction and sentiment played a significant role in forming Secretary of the Navy John Chafee's post-hearing decision to drop all charges against the *Pueblo's* crew and those in the Navy chain of command above the spy ship. Writing his decision, Chaffee stated:

> [In relation to the accusation of] failure to anticipate the emergency that subsequently developed [, this] accusation could be leveled in various degrees at responsible superior authorities in the chain of command and control ... the common confidence in the historic inviolability of a sovereign ship on the high seas in peacetime was shown to be misplaced. The consequences must in fairness be borne by all, rather than one or two individuals whom circumstances had placed closer to the crucial event. In light of the consideration set out above, I have determined that the charges against all of the officers concerned will be dismissed.... The Navy's leaders are determined that the lessons learned from this tragedy shall be translated into effective action.[19]

Perhaps Navy Captain William Newsome, who assisted the inquiry panel, and who then put together the entire inquiry report for the board, summed up the national opinion when he discussed the outcome after he retired. As reported in a *New York Times* interview, Newsome said, "[the outcome of the Navy's court of inquiry ended] kind of neat, really, since they allowed the Secretary to become the nice guy and the military vindicated itself because it made the appropriate recommendation." Newsome went on to say, "You don't prosecute heroes. The public painted Bucher

Six—The Navy Court of Inquiry

Secretary of the Navy John Chafee, who made the decision to drop all charges against those whom the Board of Inquiry assigned blame for the capture of the *Pueblo* (photograph from U.S. Senate archive).

as a hero and you don't prosecute heroes."[20] Yet, while the Navy's punishment was nullified, Commander Lloyd Bucher would relive the events of January 23, 1968, in his mind every day, always wondering if he could have done anything differently to save his ship and his honor within the Navy. And in the words of author Jack Cheevers, "...that was a harsher and more crippling sentence than anything the Navy could dish out."[21]

Epilogue

While public interest in the plight of the *Pueblo* ebbed with the change of U.S. presidents in January 1969, the United States had not abandoned its monitoring of North Korea, nor had North Korea ceased its muscle flexing. In April 1969, President Richard M. Nixon and the American public learned that a U.S. EC-121 spy plane had been shot down over North Korea by North Korean MIGs, resulting in the deaths of thirty-one American airmen. Once again, an unarmed military unit that reported to CNFJ was sent into a hostile zone with faulty communication gear and without cover by escort forces.[1] Apparently, lessons from the *Pueblo* incident had been forgotten or ignored.

President Nixon's reaction to the shoot-down proved interesting. With his staff members, he discussed the idea of hijacking a large, newly refurbished North Korean fishing ship as it was transiting from a shipyard in The Netherlands to North Korea. Nixon sought revenge for the *Pueblo* and the spy plane shoot-down. In other words, the president wanted to capture a North Korean vessel in the same manner that the North Koreans had taken the *Pueblo*. After an examination of the international and legal aspects and a great deal of discussion with National Security Advisor Henry Kissinger, Secretary of State William Rogers, and Attorney General John Mitchell, the plan was abandoned.[2]

Several lessons are apparent from the seizure of the *Pueblo*. At the outset of the spy ship program, no mission-specific ship had been designed and built for intelligence-gathering. Starting with the USS *Liberty* and extending to the preparation of *Banner* and *Pueblo*, mothballed, past-prime hulls were reconfigured for use as spy ships. None of the intelligence ships were specifically designed from keel up to be used for the missions on which they were sent. This resulted in "work around" solutions, making do with available resources. For example, in the case of the *Banner* and

Epilogue

Pueblo, mission-essential electronic eavesdropping equipment was placed on top decks where space was available, causing the ships to become less stable and top heavy.

Using retired, balky coastal freighters as the platforms for *Banner* and *Pueblo* meant that they were prone to equipment break-downs. *Pueblo* experienced several episodes of steering equipment failures. Another concern that Navy leadership discounted was that the top speed of the old freighters was a paltry 13 knots at best, not nearly fast enough to quickly depart a hostile situation. It could be argued that if *Pueblo* had been capable of higher speed, it may have safely avoided seizure.

Pueblo and *Banner* were designated as auxiliary ships, not ships for the front line. Having served on auxiliary ships, I know that they are not well armed, as their mission does not normally take them into harm's way. But unlike the usual auxiliary ships, the spy ships were routinely sent into dangerous waters without proper defense. Two .50 caliber machine guns are meager arms against torpedo boats, sub chasers, and MIGs. Armament and protection for the sailors who might need to use that armament (proper gun tubs, for instance) was given scant attention. CDR Bucher was even told to stow his .50 caliber guns below deck and out of sight.

Another lesson not addressed was the failure to ensure essential communication capabilities aboard the *Pueblo,* leaving the ship in several instances unable to properly communicate with its operational chain of command, including the moments prior to imminent danger. This communication problem was apparently a lesson not learned by the Navy, as earlier the *Liberty* had been sent into a dangerous area with poor communication capability that may have been the leading factor in the attack on that ship. In the case of the *Pueblo,* this communication flaw was especially apparent off the coast of Korea. The identical problem had been previously experienced and reported by the *Banner.* Hence, the Navy had knowledge of this sporadic communication problem in the Sea of Japan, and yet it was not corrected.

Command and control of the *Pueblo* was lacking, as it was in the *Liberty* attack. Command of the ship and its mission rested at the highest levels in Washington, the NSA, and the JCS. Local administrative control of the ship was in Japan and rested with an admiral who had limited previous exposure to Naval intelligence operations. Between Japan and Washington were multi-levels of operational and administrative leadership. The vast operational and communication distance between Washington, the

Epilogue

Navy chain of command, and the *Pueblo* left far too many gaps in communication and control of the ship, the same shortcoming experienced six months earlier by the *Liberty* and reported in the *Liberty* Court of Inquiry. The deficiencies in command and control experienced in the *Liberty* incident had not been corrected when *Pueblo* sailed.

A second command and control issue was the fact that Office of Naval Intelligence (ONI) officials barred CDR Bucher from having complete control over the intelligence personnel and spaces on board the *Pueblo*, even going so far as initially denying him access to the ship's intelligence spaces. This restriction was contrary to normal Navy shipboard protocol and created a divisive atmosphere between the regular ship's crew and the intelligence personnel, and distracted from the smooth operation of the ship.

There was a distinct lack of leadership attention to details regarding the construction, operation, and mission of the *Pueblo*. At many steps in the ship's conversion from mothballed coastal freighter to spy ship, construction plans on paper did not translate easily to the actual ship's mission. Bucher's account of numerous meetings with shipyard officials clearly points out the difficulty in ensuring that the ship would be habitable and operationally sound. In his book, Bucher relates several of his recommendations that fell on deaf ears, especially with Navy and shipyard officials, who were more concerned with repair and/or reconfiguration projects involving ships destined to return to the Naval front line in Vietnam.[3] According to Bucher, it was apparent that NSA and the Navy did not devote proper attention to detail regarding the spy ship program.

Another example of lack of leadership attention to details was apparent in the misallocation of classified publications sent to the *Pueblo* prior to sailing. The disbursement of this classified material is the responsibility of the Office of Naval Intelligence Publications (ONIP) and the Naval Security Group Pacific. Through obvious mismanagement, the *Pueblo* received an allotment of classified material for the *Pueblo*, classified publications for the intelligence operators on the ship, and all classified publications that would have been required for a coastal freighter, which were superfluous. As many as ten copies of some publications were received, and on the morning of departure for its mission, the ship received yet another classified publication shipment. Even though CDR Bucher had voiced concern regarding the sheer volume of intelligence materials before leaving port, through inattention to detail by Navy leadership, at the time of its capture by the North Koreans, the *Pueblo* was carrying an inordinate

Epilogue

amount of classified material, a large portion of which fell into the hands of the North Koreans and, according to CIA sources, was turned over to the Soviets.

A corollary to this leadership failure regarding intelligence publications was the fact that the *Pueblo* was provided with woefully inadequate intelligence material destruction capability. The ship had a small capacity burn apparatus and a limited number of weighted bags, not nearly sufficient for emergency destruction of all of the classified material on board. In addition, the ability to scuttle the ship quickly in a crisis situation was also impossible. Poor attention to detail by Navy personnel provided North Korea, and ultimately the Soviets, with one of the largest windfalls of U.S. intelligence material ever collected.

Another lesson that should have been learned was that it was foolhardy to send a nearly defenseless ship into a known hostile area without providing for protection of the ship and crew. The Navy was well aware that the North Koreans were not receptive to the U.S. Navy parking a spy ship off their coast. Yet, Navy leadership made no provision for emergency response to reach the *Pueblo* in a critical situation. All U.S. military assets were either too far away, or tactically misconfigured to come to prompt assistance of the hapless spy ship.

Another lesson that was completely ignored by *Pueblo's* chain of leadership command, including the Johnson administration, was the repetitive overt and clear warnings from North Korea. Blatant military attacks against DMZ peace keepers and a daring attack on the South Korean president's residence demonstrated the brazen volatility of the North Koreans. The government of Kim Il-sung had issued multiple warnings directed toward the United States, placing the United States on notice that spy ships off the Korean coast would not be tolerated. One such clear warning from North Korea came only three days prior to the capture of the *Pueblo,* but apparently NSA, the CIA, and the Navy did not give credence or due concern to the DPRK warning and therefore gave no serious thought for protection of the spy ship. Proper analysis should have been given to the North Korean warnings.

Above all, it was flawed leadership that failed to conduct a proper risk analysis of the ship's mission. All other facets of poor leadership are secondary to the Navy's lack of proper risk analysis. Disregarding previous lessons learned, conducting no serious detailed examination of all factors germane to the spy ship mission, and failing to properly weigh the risk to

Epilogue

the *Pueblo*, the Navy, NSA, and President Johnson's administration officials relied upon the belief that no harm had occurred in previous *Banner* missions, and therefore, no harm could come to a U.S. Navy ship that maintained a thirteen mile distance from other nations' shores. As a result, the Navy assigned a routinely-endorsed rating of minimal risk to the *Pueblo* mission, a rating that proved to be foolish, indeed.

Kim's legacy, the ideology of *Juche*, which continues in practice today, has remained central to North Korea for decades. The same ideological propaganda disseminated to the North Korean people was continued by his successor and son, Kim Jong-il, and now Jong-il's son, the present ruler of North Korea, Kim Jong-un. While 30 percent of the North Korean government budget and 15–20 percent of their GNP is spent on the military, and starvation is decimating the population, the Kims have bolstered their regimes by reminding the North Korean public that all efforts of the KWP and all government action is for the good of the whole, North Korea.[4]

Today, propaganda continues to flourish in North Korea. An interesting example occurred on August 8, 2015, when North Korea announced that it had created its own time zone, called "Pyongyang Time." The new Pyongyang time was explained to the populace as throwing off a vestige of prior Japanese "colonial domination," because North Korea's previous time zone had been set during the Japanese occupation. In addition, the act of creating its own time zone served to demonstrate North Korean independence to the world community.[5]

Hatred for America continues to be a prominent theme in North Korean propaganda. Just as in 1968, North Korea is threatening military action against both South Korea and the United States. But this time, Kim Jong-un, the grandson of Kim Il-sung, is threatening to carry out an attack on Washington, D.C., using nuclear weapons. His propaganda machine has produced a video depicting intercontinental missiles "slamming into Washington, near what appears to be the Lincoln Memorial."[6] In addition, recently a number of ICBM missiles thought to be capable of carrying nuclear weapons have been test fired from North Korea in the direction of allies of the United States, including Japan and South Korea. These missile launchings are clear violations of United Nations sanctions against North Korea. Undeterred by U.N. admonitions, North Korea continues launching its test rockets.

As for the crew of the *Pueblo*, they arrived in the United States to a heroes' welcome in San Diego, where nearly a thousand well-wishers gath-

Epilogue

ered for an arrival ceremony at Miramar Naval Air Station to greet the arriving men. Among the crowd was Senator Margaret Chase Smith and Governor Ronald Reagan, who made a few remarks of welcome. The crew then received initial medical treatment and debriefing at Miramar. The families of the crew members were flown to San Diego to be reunited with the crew, and the San Diego Chamber of Commerce "provided at the chamber's expense, lodging for the families at the El Cortez Hotel."[7] The body of Duane Hodges was escorted to his hometown, Creswell, Oregon, (population nearly 1,000), where he was buried with full military honors on December 28, 1968.[8]

On the day of the *Pueblo* crew's arrival in San Diego, an editorial in the *San Diego Union* read:

Today, San Diego is again happy with tears as 82 men whose names will be permanently inscribed in history ... come home to San Diego. We are proud to represent the entire nation as the host for these gallant men. There could be no better Christmas present. It is fitting and proper that San Diego should be selected as host for the returning heroes, and a place for them to rest and relax....[9]

The term "hero" seemed to be loosely thrown about in the media and elsewhere. Indeed, in the arena of public opinion, much of the nation's public believed the *Pueblo's* crew to be heroes. Yes, perhaps they could be called heroes in that they had survived a brutal eleven months at the

The headline of the *San Diego Union* of Dec. 24, 1968 (photograph from USS *Pueblo*.org web site).

168

Top: The *Pueblo* crew was flown to San Diego's Miramar Naval Air Station upon their return to the United States. They were welcomed as heroes by the large crowd that gathered to meet them. *Bottom:* Governor and future President Ronald Reagan was among the dignitaries greeting the returning *Pueblo* crew at Miramar Naval Air Station (photographs from USS *Pueblo*.org web site).

Epilogue

hands of their North Korean captors. But, understandably, there were a great many who believed that giving up their ship without a fight, signing a number of confessions, and supplying the Soviets with a treasure trove of classified information negated any hero's classification. Of course, that dichotomy, with its parallel debate, continues today.

After an initial examination at Miramar, the men were bused to the Navy's Balboa Hospital in San Diego. In January, at Balboa, a ceremony to award Bucher and nine of his crew members with purple hearts was arranged. But it is alleged that the Navy could not even accomplish that with dignity. The music being played consisted of two Army tunes, "This is the Army, Mr. Jones," and "The Caissons Go Rolling Along." And instead of keeping with the solemnity of the occasion, as Bucher was receiving his award, a news correspondent began loudly broadcasting a news feed. To top it off, a member of the Balboa staff then concluded the ceremony by announcing that a Balboa-employed sailor had won a $50 dollar gift certificate as "Sailor of the Month." It would seem that the Navy had little regard for the *Pueblo* crew that had been incarcerated in North Korea for eleven months.

The jubilance of the San Diego public upon the arrival of the *Pueblo* crew was soon replaced by the intense scrutiny of a Naval Court of Inquiry in an attempt to assign blame for the Navy's own failure in leadership. Following the inquiry proceedings, the majority of the men left the Navy after completing their enlistments.

CDR Bucher received the purple heart medal at a ceremony held at Balboa Hospital in San Diego in 1969 shortly after release (photograph from USS *Pueblo*.org web site).

Epilogue

Commander Bucher remained in the Navy and requested and received orders to the Naval Post–Graduate School in Monterrey, California. Following completion of an advanced degree, he held two more shore-based Naval assignments before retiring from the Navy in 1973.[10]

There is a tendency for anyone familiar with the *Pueblo* incident to look past the more complicated issues swirling around the case of the captured spy ship and disrespectfully reduce the entire matter to one question: was Commander Lloyd Bucher right or wrong in his decision at the moment in time? Perhaps unsurprisingly to one who has been a Navy officer, those officers in the Navy above the rank of commander tend to believe that Bucher should have done more to resist the North Koreans. But more junior officers at the lieutenant commander level and below tend to hold a more "widespread sympathy and even admiration for Bucher."[11] Over the years the debate on the issue will fade into history. But perhaps a statement in the *Christian Science Monitor* of December 26, 1968, remains true today; "Welcome as is the news of the release of the crew of the USS *Pueblo*, that whole affair remains highly messy and unsatisfactory."[12] One

Fort Rosecrans National Cemetery, the final resting place of CDR Lloyd Bucher. Bucher died January 28, 2004 (photograph from USS *Pueblo*.org web site).

Epilogue

can hope that lessons learned regarding the flawed leadership within the Navy, NSA, and the White House would serve to improve leadership and decision-making in the future. If not, equally disastrous incidents will undoubtedly occur. Meanwhile, the *Pueblo* remains on the Navy's list of active ships, even though the spy ship is a North Korean dockside museum, a testament to the glorious North Korean Navy under Kim Il-sung that embarrassed the United States. And "although regulations say that every commissioned (Navy) ship must have a commanding officer, *Pueblo* has none. Her situation, the Navy explains, is 'not normal.'"[13]

Ironically, as this passage is written, the United States has once again been involved in another vessel seizure on the high seas, as two U.S. Navy gunboats were captured and detained by a foreign military force without a shot being fired.[14] This is yet another embarrassing incident caused, at least partially, by arrogance and lack of leadership within the U.S. Navy and the leadership in Washington. The Navy "has fired the commander" of this group of sailors for "failing to provide effective leadership, leading to complacency [and] a lack of oversight," the same leadership flaws so evident at the time of the *Pueblo*.[15]

Chapter Notes

Preface

1. Cohen, Warren I. and Nancy Bernkopf Tucker, eds. *Lyndon Johnson Confronts the World: American Foreign Policy 1963–1968*. Cambridge: Press Syndicate of the University of Cambridge, 1994. 133. Print.
2. Armbruster, William A., LCDR USN. "The *Pueblo* Crisis and Public Opinion." *Naval War College Review.* Naval War College, Newport, R.I. Vol XXIII, No. 7, March 1971. 84, 86, and 106. Web. July 23, 2015. https://www.usnwc.edu/Publications/Naval-War-College-Review/Press-Review-Past-Issues.aspx.
3. "Juche Ideology." Quoted from the web page of the Democratic People's Republic of Korea (DPRK). Web. Oct. 25, 2016. www.korea-dpr.com/juche_ideology.html.

Introduction

1. Grimes, William. "Antonio Prohias, 77, Drew 'Spy vs. Spy' Cartoon." *New York Times*, 3 March 1998. Web. 2 Feb. 2016. http://www.nytimes.com/1998/03/02/arts/antonio-prohias-77-drew-spy-vs-spy-cartoon.html.
2. Jacobson, Harold William and William Zimmerman, eds. *The Shaping of Foreign Policy*. New York: Atherton Press, 1969. 38. Print.
3. Meyer, J.A. "COMINT—Hard Facts in the Cold War." For NSA. Date unknown. pg. 5. Web. 22 Feb. 2016. https://nsa.gov/public_info/_files/friedmanDocuments/ReportsandResearchNotes/FOLDER_184/41751359079054.pdf. At the time of his writing, the author was on the NSA staff.
4. McGarvey, Patrick J. *C.I.A.: The Myth & the Madness.* New York: Saturday Review Press, 1972. 37. Print.
5. Powers, Thomas. *Intelligence Wars: American Secret History from Hitler to Al-Qaeda.* New York: New York Review Books, 2002. 230. Print. Since this book was written in 2002, it is quite possible that NSA may no longer be the largest data center in the world.
6. McGarvey. 74–75.
7. Powers. 230.
8. Bamford, James. *Body of Secrets: Anatomy of the Ultra-Secret National Security Agency.* New York: Anchor Books, 2002. 187. Print. According to Bamford, Air Force C-130s and Navy EC-121s were the primary airborne sigint platforms. Bamford's book is cited many times here within, as it is one of the best sources for information regarding the inner workings of NSA and the spy ship missions of the *Liberty, Banner,* and *Pueblo*. His various sources reveal the attitude and skulduggery of NSA and the Navy in regards to the expendability of the ship's crews versus the invaluable data gathered for intelligence purposes.
9. Cheevers, Jack. *Act of War: Lyndon Johnson, North Korea, and the Capture of the Spy Ship Pueblo.* New York: NAL Caliber (division of Penguin Group), 2013. 2. Print.
10. Powers. 237.
11. Meyer. 18.
12. *Ibid.*
13. Newton, Robert E. "The Capture of

Notes—Chapter One

the USS *Pueblo* and Its Effect on SIGINT Operations." Center for Cryptologic History, National Security Agency. Fort Meade, MD: 1992. Web. 15 Oct. 2015. http://nsarchive.gwu.edu/NSAEBB/NSAEBB278/U.S._Cryptologic_History—The_Capture_of_the_USS_Pueblo.pdf. It is unclear whether Newton was an analyst for the NSA or an historian in the NSA Center for Cryptologic History.

Chapter One

1. Meyer. 12–13. Author defines COMINT as intercepting signals and messages, which are then "sent to a central organization for analysis."
2. Bamford. 242.
3. *Ibid.* 93–94.
4. *Ibid.* 187.
5. Blau, Peter M. and Marshall W. Meyer. *Bureaucracy in Modern Society.* New York: McGraw-Hill, 1987. 59. Print.
6. Naval History and Heritage Command. *Liberty III (AGTR-5) 1964–1970.* https://www.history.navy.mil/research/histories/ship-histories/danfs/l/liberty-agtr-5-iii.html.
7. Cristol, A. Jay. *The Liberty Incident: The 1967 Israeli Attack on the U.S. Navy Spy Ship.* Washington: Brassey's, 2002. 24. Print.
8. *Ibid.* 12, 15.
9. Gerhard, William D. and Henry W. Millington. "Attack on a Sigint Collector, the U.S.S. *Liberty.*" National Security Agency Central Security Service. United States Cryptologic History, Special Series Crisis Collection, Volume 1, 1981. 19. Web. www.nsarchive.gwu.edu 1 Jul. 2015. Search USS *Liberty.* Doc. is NSAEBB24/nsa10.pdf. The document reveals that the intelligence component members on board the *Liberty* knew that they were sailing into dangerous waters, and had asked for a possible retraction of the mission.
10. Bamford. 198–199.
11. History.com. www.history.com/this-day-in-history/israel-attacks-uss-liberty, accessed 12/3/17.
12. Bamford. 217.
13. Smith, Richard K. "The Violation of the *Liberty.*" *United States Naval Institute Proceedings*, 104/6/904, June 1978: 62–70. Web. 2 Feb. 2016. www.heretical.com/miscella/liberty.html.
14. Cristol. 84.
15. Cristol. 66, 155.
16. Clifford, Clark M. "The Israeli Attack on the USS *Liberty.*" Memorandum to W.W. Rostow. 18 July 1967. LBJ Library, National Security File Memos to the President, WWR Vol. 35, Box 19. Print.
17. Cristol. 164.
18. Cohen and Tucker. 304–305.
19. Dallek, Robert. *Flawed Giant: Lyndon Johnson and His Times, 1961–1973.* New York: Oxford University Press, 1998. 431. Print.
20. Bamford. 204.
21. *Ibid.* 223.
22. *Ibid.* 228.
23. Examples of dissenting opinions have been written by many persons. Political Analyst Maidhc Cathail wrote an article entitled "Behind the USS *Liberty* Cover-Up" for the Jan/Feb 2015 issue of *The Washington Report on Middle East Affairs* pgs. 26–27 in which he makes a case for a cover-up. His article can be seen at https://consortiumnews.com/2014/11/12/behind-the-uss-liberty-cover-up. Another example is a British Broadcasting Corporation documentary which aired in 2002, titled "Dead in the Water," also alleging a conspiracy.
24. Cristol. 104.
25. Boston, Ward. "Time for the Truth About the *Liberty.*" *Union Tribune* (San Diego) 8 June 2007. Web. 2 Feb. 2016. http://www.sandiegouniontribune.com/uniontrib/20060608/news_lz1e8boston.html.
26. Bamford. 293.
27. *Ibid.*
28. Cristol. 103.
29. The Navy message traffic containing the results of the *Liberty* board of inquiry, as well as the series of follow-up endorsements (6) are contained in copies of original naval messages initially classified as "Top Secret." They have since been declassified and were accessed on line. Web.

Notes—Chapter One

15 Jul 2015. www.thelibertyincident.com/docs/courtofinquiry.pdf.

30. McCain, John S., Admiral U.S. Navy. First Endorsement on msg of RADM Isaac C. Kidd of 18 June 1967, "Court of Inquiry to enquire into the circumstances surrounding the armed attack on USS *Liberty* (AGTR-5) on 8 June 1967." Naval Message Serial 00020/00, 18 June 1967. Commander in Chief, U.S. Naval Forces Europe to Judge Advocate General. Web. 3 Aug. 2015. www.thelibertyincident.com/docs/courtofinquiry.pdf

31. Gerhard and Millington. 60.

32. Under Secretary of Defense Operational Control South (USDOCOSOUTH). Message date time group R 021734Z Jul 67. Web. 3 Aug. 2015. www.thelibertyincident.com/docs/courtofinquiry.pdf. Message states that position reports (posit) sent on June 3rd and 4th were lost by the Security Group in Morocco.

33. McCain, John S., Admiral U.S. Navy. "Court of Inquiry to inquire into the circumstances surrounding the armed attack on *USS Liberty* (AGTR 5 on 8 June 1967 (U). Naval Message Ser. 00073/J141, 6 September 1967, Commander in Chief U.S. Atlantic Fleet to Chief of Naval Operations. Web. 3 Aug. 2015. www.thelibertyincident.com/docs/courtofinquiry.pdf.

34. Cristol. 157.

35. *Ibid.*

36. *Congressional Record—House.* July 12, 1968. 21055. "Navy Communications Foulup Caused U.S.S. *Liberty's* Presence Off Sinai Coast." Web. 3 Mar. 2016. www.thelibetrtyincident.com/docs/CongressionalRecord.pdf.

37. Bamford. 240.

38. *Ibid.* 243. and Newton. 12.

39. Cheevers. 3.

40. Author Unknown. "AGER 2 Pueblo (ex-FP 344, ex-FS 344, ex-AKL 44)." Web. 12 Jul. 2015. www.globalsecurity.org/intell/systems/ager-2.htm.

41. Lerner, Mitchell B. *The Pueblo Incident: A Spy Ship and the Failure of American Foreign Policy.* Lawrence: University of Kansas Press, 2002. 11. Print.

42. Bamford. 241.

43. Newton. 11.

44. Gallery, Daniel V. Rear Admiral Ret. *The Pueblo Incident.* New York: Doubleday, 1970. 2. Print.

45. Cheevers. 3. For the most part, the same planning and building process was used for both the *Banner* and the *Pueblo* which resulted in similar problems being experienced in both ships.

46. Bucher, Lloyd M., Commander. *Bucher: My Story.* New York: Doubleday, 1970. 6. Print.

47. See abbreviation section for definition of MIG.

48. Bamford. 242.

49. Bucher. 4. Also note that Bucher was promoted to CDR after reporting to the *Pueblo.*

50. Bamford. 242.

51. Schumacher, Carl F. and George C. Wilson. *Bridge of No Return: The Ordeal of the U.S.S. Pueblo.* New York: Harcourt Brace Jovanovich, 1971. 79. Print.

52. Armbrister, Trevor. *A Matter of Accountability: The True Story of the Pueblo Affair.* Guilford, CT: Lyons Press, 2004. 13. Print.

53. Bucher. 61–65.

54. Newton. 27.

55. Bucher. 105.

56. Newton. 29.

57. *Ibid.* 43.

58. Bucher. 107–108. Emphasis added by author, as this final statement and others that echo this generalized risk assessment will be examined later in greater detail. It should be noted that according to Bucher, Cassell later attempted to recant his statement at the subsequent Court of Inquiry following the release of Bucher and the *Pueblo* crew.

59. Armbrister. 160.

60. Bucher. 406–410. Copies of *Pueblo's* operating orders and its sailing orders are in appendices II and III respectively.

61. Bamford. 251.

62. USS *Pueblo* sailing orders issued 5 January 1965. Web. 1 June 2015. www.usspueblo.org/Pueblo_Incident/Sailing_Orders.html The orders can also be found at Appendix III in Bucher's book.

63. Bucher. 410.

64. Bucher. 134.

Notes—Chapter Two

65. Bucher. 134–137.
66. Bucher. 406.
67. Aldrich, George H. "Questions of International Law Raised by the Seizure of the U.S.S. Pueblo." *Proceedings of the American Society of International Law at its Annual Meeting (1921–1969)*. Vol. 63 (1969): 2–6. Web. UTA library data base. 14 Sep. 2015. www.jstor.org/stable/256577717 Aldrich served as the Principal Deputy Legal Advisor in the Department of State in 1969.
68. *Ibid.*

Chapter Two

1. Hutchison, Phillip J., "Leadership as an Ideograph: A Rhetorical Analysis of Military Leadership Training Material." *Journal of Leadership Studies*, vol. 7, no. 3. 2013. University of Phoenix. Print.
2. Stockdale, James B., Vice Adm., "The Principles of Leadership." *American Educator*, date unknown. Web. Oct. 19, 2016. libguides.usna.edu/ld.php?content_id=17258864 Hereinafter, all quotes from Stockdale are from this article.
3. Armbrister. 267.
4. Hearings. 638.
5. Newton. 35–36.
6. Owen, David. *The Politics of Defence*. New York: Taplinger Publishing Co. 1972. 13–14. Print.
7. Hearings. 734.
8. Strauch, Ralph E. "The Operational Assessment of Risk: A Case Study of the *Pueblo* Mission." Prepared for United States Air Force Project Rand. March 1971. Rand Corporation, Santa Monica, CA. Web. 1 Dec. 2015. www.rand.org/pubs/reports/R691.html. Strauch, at the time of this article was a senior mathematician with the Rand Corporation, a think tank for NSA and the Department of Defense. Strauch holds a Ph.D. in statistics from U.C. Berkeley. Though his study was written in 1971, two years after *Pueblo's* capture, his findings bolster and support my opinion that the *Pueblo* capture was caused in great part by the flawed leadership that gave no consideration to the immense risk involved in the spy ship orders, thereby assigning a minimal risk rating to the North Korean spy mission.
9. Lerner. 52–53.
10. Hearings. 737.
11. *Ibid.* 777.
12. *Ibid.* 778.
13. *Ibid.* 797–798.
14. Hearings. 648–649.
15. Lerner. 56.
16. During the hearings, Admiral Moorer's testimony preceded that of Admiral Johnson.
17. Bolger, Daniel P. "Scenes from an Unfinished War: Low-Intensity Conflict in Korea, 1966–1969." *Leavenworth Papers Number 19*. Combat Studies Institute, U.S. Army Command and General Staff College. Leavenworth, KS, 1991. Print. 66.
18. Cheevers. 71.
19. Strauch. v.
20. Bolger. 33–36. The CIA had access to Kim's speeches and occasionally submitted excerpts from his speeches to the president in his daily briefings. CIA daily briefings can be seen at the CIA web site.
21. Bolger. 112.
22. Sarantakes, Nicholas Evan. "The Quiet War: Combat Operations Along the Korean Demilitarized Zone, 1966–1969." *The Journal of Military History*, 64, April 2000. 439–458. Web. 20 Mar. 2016. 439. www.usnwc.edu/Academics/Faculty/Nicholas-Sarantakes/Publications/QWar.aspx.
23. Sarantakes, 442–443.
24. *Ibid.*
25. *Ibid.* 443.
26. *Ibid.* 445.
27. United States Dept. of State. *Foreign Relations of the United States, 1964–1968*. Vol. XXIX, Part 1, Korea, Document 133. Web. 28 September 2015. https://history.state.gov/historicaldocuments/frus1964–68v29p1/d133.
28. *Ibid.*
29. Goldberg, Arthur J. *Report of the United Nations Command to the United Nations on the Increase in Violations by North Korea of the Military Armistice Agreement in Korea*. 2 Nov. 1967. Web. 6 Aug. 2015. repository.un.org/bitstream/

Notes—Chapter Two

handle/11176/76988/S_8217-EN.pdf?sequence=1&isAllowed=y.

30. Bolger. 61.
31. Kriebel, Wesley P. "Korea: the Military Armistice Commission 1965–1970." *Military Affairs*, Vol. 36, no. 3 (Oct. 1972). 96–99. Web. UTA Library. 21 Sept. 2015. http://www.jstor.org/stable/1985311.
32. Jenerette, Vandon E. "The Forgotten DMZ," *Military Review* 58, May 1988. Cited by Sarantakes on page 440.
33. Sarantakes. 440.
34. Bolger. 89.
35. Foster, John S., Jr. Memorandum from the Director of Defense Research and Engineering (Foster) to Secretary of Defense McNamara. Washington, December 7, 1967. Web. 28 September 2015. https://history.state.gov/historicaldocuments/frus1964–68v29p1/d138.
36. In 1967, American troop strength in Vietnam had reached 485,600 personnel. That number would only be surpassed in 1968 when 536,100 U.S. troops were in-theater. Source—American War Library, whose source is the Department of Defense Manpower Center. Web. July 28, 2016. www.americanwarlibrary.com/vietnam/vwatl.htm.
37. Strauch. 12.
38. Newton. 37.
39. Mobley. 5.
40. Lerner. 58.
41. United States Cong. House. Committee on Armed Services, Report of the Special Subcommittee on the USS Pueblo. *Inquiry Into the U.S.S. Pueblo and EC-121 Plane Incidents*. 91st Congress, First Session. Washington: GPO, 1969. 1657. Print. Hereinafter combined with with Hearings.
42. Newton. 73–74.
43. Cheevers. 344.
44. Bamford. 270.
45. Lerner. 61; Armbrister. 27.
46. *Ibid.*
47. "Two sent back to North as moles." *Korea Joongang Daily*. Jan. 22, 1968. Web. mengnewsjoins.com/view.aspx?gCat=030&aid=2947986 This is an interesting article that was written in the *Korea Joongang Daily*, a daily South Korean newspaper that reported that there were 33 attackers, and that two of the attackers were quietly sent back to North Korea to act as spies for South Korea.
48. Bolger. 62.
49. Sarantake. 447.
50. Bolger. 87.
51. Bolger. 65.
52. Bolger. 62–65.
53. Bolger. xi.
54. "3 G.I.'s Are Hurt By Seoul Raiders." (January 24, 1968). *New York Times (1923–Current File)* Web. 2 May 2016. https://login.ezproxy.uta.edu/login?url=http://search.proquest.com.ezproxy.uta.edu/docview/118208097?accountid=7117.
55. Sarantakes. 441.
56. Sarantakes. 451.
57. Sarantakes. 450.
58. Feherenbach, T. R. *The Fight For Korea: From the War of 1950 to the Pueblo Incident*. New York: Grosset & Dunlap, 1969. 157. Print.
59. Lerner. 60; Sarantakes. 450.
60. Lyndon Baines Johnson Library Oral History Collection, Dean Rusk, Secretary of State—Interview III, 1/2/70 internet copy. Tape 1–19, Indonesian Policy. Web. www.lbjlib.utexas.edu/johnson/archives.hom/oralhistory.hom/ruskOB.pdf accessed May 2015.
61. Bolger. 75.
62. "General Westmoreland's Farewell Address to ROK 9th Division." 21 May 1968, Korean Speech, Box 17, Papers of William C. Westmoreland, LBJL. As cited by Sarantakes, page 446.
63. Sarantakes. 442.
64. Tom Johnson's notes. LBJL. February 15, 1968. Box 2.
65. Bolger. 68.
66. Lerner. 60–61.
67. Hearings. 703.
68. Schumacher/Wilson. 79.
69. *Ibid.*
70. Strauch. 22–25.
71. Author unknown. "AGER 2 Pueblo (ex-FP 344, ex-FS 344, ex-AKL 44." Global Security Organization. Web. 12 July 2015. www.globalsecurity.org/intell/systems/ager-2.htm.
72. Strauch. 25.
73. McGarvey. 27–28.

Notes—Chapter Three

74. Owen.15.
75. *Cong. Rec.* "The Unprovoked Attack on USS *Pueblo.*" 24 January 1968: 816. Print.
76. Wheeler, Earle, General. "USS *Pueblo* Incident." Memorandum dated 29 March 1968. Web. 7 Jul. 2015. www.nsarchive.gwu.edu/NSAEBB/NSAEBB453/docs/doc15.pdf Web cite document contains both Nitzes memo with questions and Wheeler's memo in answer.
77. *Ibid.*

Chapter Three

1. Schumacher/Wilson. 71–75.
2. Newton. 51–52.
3. Bucher described the DPRK subchaser as a Russian-built SO-1 class ship. They are characteristically 171 feet long and heavily armed with an 85 mm (3 inch) cannon, two smaller 37 mm cannons, six heavy machine guns, other smaller machine guns, as well as mortars and rocket launchers. Web. July 28, 2016. www.russianships.info/eng/warships/project_122bis.htm.
4. Newton. 55.
5. The USS *Pueblo*.org web site states that the torpedo boats were DPRK P-4 torpedo boats, modeled after a Chinese design. Although facts on the specific boats that attacked the *Pueblo* are not known for certain, characteristically they were roughly 63 feet long and carried torpedoes and 2 heavy machine guns. Web. July 28, 2016., www.warboats.org/StonerFiles/Tonkin Combatants/GulfofTonkinCombatants.htm and https://en.wikipedia.org/wiki/P_4-class_torpedo_boat.
6. Bucher. 171–181. The term, MIG is commonly used to describe Soviet-made jet fighter planes manufactured by the now-defunct Mikoyan-Gurevich (hence MIG) Aircraft Company.
7. Mobley. "Lessons from the Capture of the USS *Pueblo* and the Shootdown of a U.S. Navy EC-121–1968 and 1969." 7.
8. Newton. 59.
9. Schumacher/Wilson. 88–101.
10. Newton. 65 and 68.
11. Bucher. 202.
12. Newton. 69.
13. Newton 71.
14. Bucher. 187.
15. Lerner. *The Pueblo Incident.* 169–171.
16. Schumacher/Wilson. 7–8.
17. Clark was succeeded by Robert Bishop in 1967.
18. Armbrister. 206.
19. Armbrister. 242–243.
20. *Ibid.*
21. North Korean Announcement: "Captain of Captured Armed Spy Ship Confesses." 25 January 1968. Folder 12, Box 09, Larry Berman Collection (Presidential Archives Research), The Vietnam Center and Archive, Texas Tech University. Web. 2 Nov. 2015. http://www.vietnam.ttu.edu/virtualarchive/items.php?item=0240912001.
22. Bucher. Appendix IV. Bucher and other members of the *Pueblo* crew were forced to write confessions which were then edited by the DPRK interrogators, who forced Bucher and the others to rewrite the confessions several times. Failure to comply would result in more beatings.
23. Bucher. Appendix V. Reading Bucher's confessions reveals the strange phraseology and tongue-in-cheek wording indicating Bucher's attempt at defiance and to show the world that he was being forced to write the confessions.
24. Newton. 128.
25. Newton. 114.
26. Baldwin, Hanson W. "U.S. Military Weaknesses Are Underlined by *Pueblo* Incident." Mar. 24, 1968. *New York Times* Web. May 11, 2016. UTA Library. Retrieved from https://login.ezproxy.uta.edu/login?url=http://search.proquest.com.ezproxy.uta.edu/docview/118159195?accountid=7117.
27. Cheevers. 125–126.
28. Author unknown. "Chronology of events." Original source NSA document. Web. 4 APR. 2016. nsarchive.gwu.edu/NSAEBB453/docs/doc23.pdf. From the George Washington University NSA collection. This is a chronology of events of the Pueblo incident. A copy is also held in

178

Notes—Chapter Three

the LBJ Library in Austin, TX. Hereafter referred to as Chronology.

29. Armbrister. 236–239.

30. Newton. 94.

31. United States Cong. House. Committee on Armed Services, Hearings before the Special Subcommittee on the USS Pueblo. *Inquiry Into the U.S.S. Pueblo and EC-121 Plane Incidents*. 91st Congress, First Session. Washington: GPO, 1969. 637. Print. Hereinafter referred to in citations as Hearings.

32. Blau and Meyer. 94.

33. Hearings. 644.

34. Mobley, Richard A. "Lessons from the Capture of the USS *Pueblo* and the Shootdown of a U.S. Navy EC-121—1968 and 1969." *Studies in Intelligence*. Vol 59, No. 1 (Extracts, March 2015) 4. Web. 16 Mar. 2016. https://www.cia.gov/library/center-for-the-study-of-intelligence/csi-publications/csi-studies/vol-59-no-1/pdfs/Revisiting-Pueblo-and-EC121.pdf.

35. Mobley, Richard. "*Pueblo*, A Retrospective." *Naval War College Review*. Spring 2001, vol. 54, no. 2. 98–117. Mobley's source is CIA *Pueblo* Sitrep 14.

36. Lerner, Mitchell. "Acts of War: North Korea's 1968 Hijacking of USS *Pueblo* Was Part of a Long-Standing Pattern of Risky Military Adventurism." *Military History* (Herndon, VA) (0889–7328), 26 (6), 24–32. March 2010.

37. Newton. 9.

38. United States. Central Intelligence Agency, Defense Intelligence Agency, U.S. Navy (NIC), U.S. Air Force (AFNIN), U.S. Army (ACSI). *Damage Assessment of the Compromise of Operational Intelligence Broadcast Messages On Board USS Pueblo (AGER-2)*. 17 March 1969. Web. 20 July 2015. nsarchive.gwu.edu/NSAEBB/NSAEBB453/docs/doc24.pdf.

39. Bolger. 10–11.

40. Bolger. 12.

41. Bolger. 65.

42. Bonesteel, Charles, General. Military message to U.S. JCS regarding his meeting with South Korean JCS. Date Time Group 27 Jan 66, 1025. Web. 4 August 2015. www.nsarchive.gwu.edu/NSAEBB/NSAEBB453/docs/doc05.pdf.

43. Chronology. 3. Note—time difference between N. Korea and Washington is 13 hours.

44. Brandt, Ed. *The Last Voyage of USS Pueblo*. New York: W.W. Norton, 1969. 9. Print.

45. The Military Armistice Commission was set up in July 1953 as part of the armistice agreement that closed the Korean War. The duties of the commission were to oversee the compliance of the North Koreans and the U.N. forces. Issues between the parties were to be resolved in meetings held at a facility that straddled the 38th parallel in Panmunjong. Admiral Smith was the first of the U.S. negotiators. After six months of talks, he was replaced by U.S. Army Major General Gilbert H. Woodward, who subsequently signed the actual agreement letters demanded by North Korea.

46. Absher, Kenneth Michael, and Michael C. Desch, and Roman Popadiuk, and the 2006 Bush School Master in Public and International Affairs Capstone Team. *Privileged and Confidential: The Secret History of the President's Intelligence Advisory Board*. Lexington: University Press of Kentucky, 2012. Introduction and Chap. 2. Print.

47. Armbrister. 258–259.

48. *Ibid*. It should also be noted that early in the White House discussions of the *Pueblo* incident, President Johnson also formed an ad hoc committee. That group was headed by former Undersecretary of State George Ball, and included retired Army General Mark Clark, retired Air Force General Laurence Kuter, and retired Navy Admiral David McDonald. They were tasked with analyzing the necessity of *Pueblo*–type missions, the design of those missions, and the operation of the [specific *Pueblo*] mission. Hereinafter, that group will be referred to as the Ad Hoc Committee.

49. Wheeler, Earle G. "For Admiral Sharp from General Wheeler." Top Secret Naval Message 25 January 1968, time 1610. Web. 22 September 2015. www.nsarchive.gwu.edu/NSAEBB453/docs/doc02.pdf.

50. Cohen and Tucker. 18.

Notes—Chapter Three

51. Tucker, Nancy Bernkopf. "Threats, Opportunities, and Frustrations in East Asia." in *Lyndon Johnson Confronts the World: American Foreign Policy, 1963–1968.* eds. Warren I. Cohen and Nancy Bernkopf Tucker, New York: Cambridge University Press, 1994. 132. Print.

52. History.com Staff. "Vietnam War Protests." Web. June 27, 2016. www.history.com/topics/vietnam-war/viet-nam-war-protests.

53. *Ibid.*

54. Cheevers. 224.

55. Rosenbaum, David E. "Mike Mansfield, Longtime Leader of Senate Democrats, Dies at 98." *New York Times,* October 6, 2001. Web. June 29, 2016. www.nytimes.com/2001/10/06/us/mike-mansfield-longtime-leader-of-the-senate-democrats-dies-at-98.html?pagewanted=all.

56. LaFeber, Walter. "Johnson, Vietnam, and Tocqueville." *Lyndon Johns Confronts the World.* 43.

57. Dallek. 520.

58. McMahon, Robert J. "Disillusionment and Disengagement in South Asia." *Lyndon Johnson Confronts the World.* 153.

59. History.com Staff. "Vietnam War Protests." Web. June 27, 2016. www.history.com/topics/vietnam-war/viet-nam-war-protests.

60. Dallek. 462.

61. Cohen and Tucker. 65–76.

62. Immerman, Richard H. "Lyndon Johnson and Vietnam." *Lyndon Johnson Confronts the World.* 64–65.

63. *Ibid.* 76.

64. Lyndon Baines Johnson Library and Museum. Tom Johnson's notes, *Pueblo* Box 2, Jan. 23–24. Mr. Tom Johnson recorded the official notes in most of the meetings held with President Johnson and his closest advisors. Those written notes are held in the Lyndon Baines Johnson Library and Museum in Austin, Texas. They reveal a great deal about the thinking of the president and his advisors. They also serve as a window to the hand-wringing, the attempts to develop response plans, the attempts to attribute the blame, the disconnection from the incident itself caused by multilayers of bureaucracy, and the flaws in leadership at the pinnacle of the U.S. Government in time of crisis. His notes will hereinafter be referred to as Tom Johnson's meeting notes, LBJL. Also Tucker, "Threats, Opportunities, and Frustrations in East Asia." *Lyndon Johnson Confronts the World.* 101.

65. Dallek. 452–453.

66. Califano, Joseph A. *The Triumph & Tragedy of Lyndon Johnson: The White House Years.* New York: Touchstone, 1991. 258. Print.

67. Cheevers. 196–205.

68. Dallek. 519.

69. Dallek. 281.

70. Tucker, Nancy Bernkopf, "Lyndon Johnson: A Final Reckoning." *Lyndon Johnson Confronts the World.* 311.

71. *Ibid.* 314. And Lerner, *The Pueblo Incident.* 100–102, 141–142, 167.

72. Tom Johnson's Meeting Notes, LBJL. Box 2, Pueblo 1. National Security Lunch, January 23, 1968, 12:58 p.m. Print. Wheeler's statement was later proven to be false. Good leadership would not make such a statement without conclusive proof.

73. Newton. 95–96.

74. Christian, George. "Meeting at the State Department on the Pueblo." Notes dated January 24, 1968, Folder 11, Box 09, Larry Berman Collection (Presidential Archives Research), The Vietnam Center and Archive, Texas Tech University. Web. 2 Nov. 2015. http://www.vietnam.ttu.edu/virtualarchive/items.php?item=0240911018. Also in Tom Johnson's meeting notes, LBJL. Box 2, Pueblo 3. Print.

75. *Ibid.*

76. Meeting Notes, National Security Lunch, January 24, 1968, 1:00 p.m. LBJL. Tom Johnson's meeting notes. Box 2, Pueblo 2. Print. Bucher's alleged confession is appendix A to this document. It should also be noted that while Dean Rusk voiced an opinion that the incident was pre-planned, two years later in an interview for Rusk's oral history for the LBJ Library, he stated that he would "never fully understand just why the North Koreans seized the *Pueblo.* Apparently he still did not understand Kim Il-sung's reasoning. Rusk's interview is documented in Tran-

Notes—Chapter Three

script, Dean Rusk Oral History Interview III, January 2, 1970, by Paige E. Muhhollen, Internet Copy, LBJ Library. Web. May 28, 2015. www.lbjlib.utexas.edu/johnson/archives.hom/oralhistory.hom/rusk03.pdf.

77. *Ibid.*
78. Lerner, Mitchell. "A Failure of Perception: Lyndon Johnson, North Korean Ideology, and the *Pueblo* Incident." *Diplomatic History* Vol. 25 No. 4 (2001): 649. Web. 8 Apr. 2016. UTA Library.
79. Newton. 96.
80. Bucher. Appendix IV.
81. Tom Johnson's meeting notes. January 24, 1968, 7:50 p.m. LBJL. Box 2, Pueblo 3. Print.
82. Tom Johnson's meeting notes. January 25, 1968. 8:30 a.m. LBJL. Box 2, Pueblo 4. Print.
83. *Ibid.*
84. Tom Johnson's meeting notes. January 25, 1968. 8:30 a.m. LBJL. Box 2, Pueblo 5. Print.
85. "Mar 1968—North Korean Seizure of U.S.S. Pueblo." *Keesing's Record of World Events.* Vol. 14. Mar. 1968. 22585. Print.
86. *Ibid.*
87. Brandt. 114–115.
88. Tom Johnson's meeting notes. January 26, 1968. 11 a.m. LBJL. Box 2, Pueblo 7. Print.
89. Tom Johnson's meeting notes. January 29, 1968. LBJL. Box 2, Pueblo 9. Print.
90. U.S. Government, Department of State. "U.S. Involvement in the Vietnam War: The Tet Offensive, 1968." Web. Aug. 1, 2016. https://history.state.gov/milestones/1961–1968/tet.
91. Wilbanks, James H. "Shock and Awe of Tet Offensive Shattered U.S. Illusions." *U.S. News.* Jan. 29, 2009. Web. Sept. 9, 2016. www.usnews.com/opinion/articles/2009/01/29/shock-and-awe-of-tet-offensive-shattered-us-illusions.
92. History.com staff. "Tet Offensive." 2009. Web Sept. 9, 2016. www.history.com/topics/vietnam-war/tet-offensive.
93. *Ibid.*
94. National Archives. "Statistical Information About Fatal Casualties of the Vietnam War." Web. Sept. 9, 2016. www.archives.gov/research/military/vietnam-war/casualty-statistics.html#date.
95. "Mar 1968—North Korean Seizure of U.S.S. Pueblo." *Keesing's Record of World Events.* Vol. 14. Mar. 1968. 22585. Web. stanford.edu/group/tomz/group/pmwiki/uploads/1379–1968–03-ks-c-EYJ.pdf Accessed 12/28/17.
96. Dallek. 515.
97. Newton. 100–102.
98. Newton 117.
99. Chronology. 17; Mobley. 103.
100. Author unknown. Undated. "Index of Possible Actions." Web. 24 Sept. 2015. www.nsarchive.gwu.edu/NSAEBB/NSAEBB453/docs/doc04.pdf. According to political reporter and author Jack Cheevers, at his NSA briefing book web site, www.nsarchive.gwu.edu/NSAEBB/NSAEBB453, the original document is held in the National Archives, Records Group, Records of General Earle Wheeler, Box 29, Tab 449.
101. Lerner, Mitchell. "A Dangerous Miscalculation: New Evidence from Communist-Bloc Archives about North Korea and the Crisis of 1968." *Journal of Cold War Studies*, 6.1 (2004): pg. 6. UTA Library. *Military and Government Collection.* Web. 13 Apr. 2016. http://ns6rl9th2k.search.serialssolutions.com/?ctx_ver=Z39.88–2004&ctx_enc=info%3Aofi%2Fenc%3AUTF-8&rfr_id=info:sid/summon.serialssolutions.com&rft_val_fmt=info:ofi/fmt:kev:mtx:journal&rft.genre=article&rft.atitle=A+dangerous+miscalculation&rft.jtitle=Journal+of+Cold+War+Studies&rft.au=Mitchell+Lerner&rft.date=2004–01-01&rft.pub=MIT+Press+Journals&rft.issn=1520–3972&rft.eissn=1531–3298&rft.volume=6&rft.issue=1&rft.spage=3&rft.externalDocID=629954071&paramdict=en-U.S. Also at Armbrister. 261.
102. Cheevers. 116–117.
103. Rusk, Dean. Interview for Lyndon Baines Johnson Library (hereinafter referred to as LBJL) Oral History Collection, Dean Rusk, Secretary of State—Interview III, Tape 1–19, "Indonesian Policy." Web. 28 May 2015. www.usspueblo.org/Pueblo_

Notes—Chapter Three

Incident/U.S._Reactions/LBJ%20Library%20Dean%20Rusk.htm.
104. McGarvey. 31–32.
105. United States. Central Intelligence Agency. "The President's Daily Brief." 23 January 1968. Web. 19 Sept. 2015. http://www.foia.cia.gov/sites/default/files/document_conversions/1827265/DOC_0005974348.pdf.
106. United States. Central Intelligence Agency. "The President's Daily Brief." 24 January 1968. Web. 19 Sept. 2015. http://www.foia.cia.gov/sites/default/files/document_conversions/1827265/DOC_0005974240.pdf.
107. United States. Central Intelligence Agency. "The President's Daily Brief." 24 January 1968. Web. 19 Sept. 2015. http://www.foia.cia.gov/sites/default/files/document_conversions/1827265/DOC_000597424.pdf.
108. Central Intelligence Agency. Intelligence Memorandum. 27 January 1968. "Pueblo Sitrep No. 13." Papers of LBJ. LBJL. National Security File. Country File, Asia and Pacific. Box 257. Print. Note also that the killing of another American soldier along the DMZ corroborates Daniel Bolger's previously cited work on the continuing low-intensity conflict in Korea.
109. Central Intelligence Agency. Intelligence Memorandum. 28 January 1968. "Pueblo Sitrep No. 14." Papers of LBJ. LBJL. National Security File. Country File, Asia and Pacific. Box 257. Print.
110. Central Intelligence Agency. Intelligence Memorandum. 29 January 1968. "Pueblo Sitrep No. 19." Papers of LBJ. LBJL. National Security File. Country File, Asia and Pacific. Box 257. Print.
111. United States. Central Intelligence Agency. "A Psychological and Political Analysis of Commander Bucher's Statements." 29 January 1968. Web. 19 March 2016. www.foia.cia.gov/sites/default/files/document_conversions/89801/DOC_0000866045.pdf.
112. *Ibid.*
113. *Ibid.*
114. *Ibid.*
115. Tom Johnson's meeting notes. January 30, 1968. LBJL. Box 2, Pueblo 11. Print.
116. Tom Johnson's meeting notes. January 31, 1968. LBJL. Box 2, *Pueblo* 12. Print. This meeting in the evening of January 30 lasted nearly two hours. Not once during the meeting did the president acknowledge U.S. government leadership responsibility for the capture of the *Pueblo*.
117. Gerald Ford Library and Museum. Web. Aug. 1, 2016. https://www.fordlibrarymuseum.gov/library/document/0054/1213075/pdf.
118. Gerald Ford Library and Museum. Web. Aug. 1, 2016. https://www.fordlibrarymuseum.gov/library/document/0054/4525475.pdf.
119. Bolger. 69. Author's source is quote on pgs. 533–534 in *The Vantage Point* authored by President Johnson. Also Lerner. *The Pueblo Incident.* 126.
120. Lerner. *The Pueblo Incident.* 131–133.
121. Cohen and Tucker. 101.
122. George Ball ad hoc committee. "Pueblo Committee Report to the President." Sixth Draft, February 7, 1968. 2–5. Web. July 17, 2015. nsarchive.gwu.edu/NSAEBB/NSAEBB453/docs/doc09.pdf Also in LBJL, National Security File, Intelligence File, Pueblo (January 1968), Box 11, Doc. 2. Print.
123. Lerner. *The Pueblo Incident.* 102.
124. Brandt. 111.
125. Letter to William Fulbright from President Lyndon B. Johnson, February 8, 1968. Folder 08, Box 10, Larry Berman Collection (Presidential Archives Research). The Vietnam Center and Archive, Texas Tech University. Web. October 29, 2015. http://vietnam.ttu.edu/virtualarchive/items.php?item=0241008005. Interestingly this letter has a typed memo from LBJ attached as a cover, advising Fulbright to tear up the letter and flush it away, and that LBJ did not want a record of it. Fulbright was an outspoken critic of the Vietnam War, even publishing a book in 1966, *The Arrogance of Power*, which was highly critical of the United States intervention in Vietnam.
126. Cong. Rec. January 23, 1968. 679. Print.

Notes—Chapter Three

127. Cong. Rec. "The Pueblo Affair." January 29, 1968. 1231–1232. Print.
128. Cong. Rec. January 23, 1968. 685–686. Print.
129. *Ibid.* 727. Wilson was a strong advocate for the release of the *Pueblo*. A native of the San Diego, California area, his voice was heard many times over the course of the eleven month imprisonment of the *Pueblo* crew. Another reference is Armbruster, 86.
130. Cong. Rec. "The Seizure of American Vessel an Overt Act of War." January 23, 1968. 816. Print.
131. Cong. Rec. "Pirating of the *Pueblo*." Jan. 23, 1968. 818. Print.
132. Cong. Rec. "Let the United Nations Settle U.S.S. *Pueblo* Incident." January 23, 1968. 783. Print.
133. Cong. Rec. "Administration Refuses to Tell American People Truth About *Pueblo* Because—." February 8, 1968. 2792–2793. Print. and Lerner, *The Pueblo Incident.* 166.
134. Lerner, *The Pueblo Incident.* 166–167.
135. Tom Johnson's meeting notes. January 30, 1968. LBJL. Box 2, Pueblo 10. Print.
136. Chronology. 7. and Newton. 80–81.
137. Brandt. 111.
138. Tom Johnson's meeting notes. January 24, 1968. LBJL. Box 2, Pueblo 3. Print.
139. Cheevers. 112.
140. Lawrence, David. "*Pueblo* Seizure Threatens Crisis." This document was not dated, although it is annotated "24th" assumed to be January 24, 1968. The publication name was also not noted, but it is assumed that Lawrence was writing for U.S. News. Accessed at Tom Johnson's meeting notes, LBJL. Box 2, Pueblo 3. Print.
141. Armbruster. 87.
142. Author unknown. "The *Pueblo* Incident." *The Evening Star*, (Washington, D.C.), January 24, 1968. Accessed at Tom Johnson's meeting notes. January 24, 1968. LBJL. Box 2, Pueblo 3. Print.
143. Armbrister. 249.
144. Tom Johnson's meeting notes, LBJL. January 27, 1968. Box 2, Pueblo 7. Print
145. Tom Johnson's meeting notes. January 27, 1968. LBJL. Box 2, Pueblo 8. Print.
146. Transcript of February 4, 1968 *Meet the Press.* Web. 22 Feb. 2016 http://www.virtual.vietnam.ttu.edu/cgi-bin/starfetch.exe?5AA1zLyNd9fDLt81aXKfFmEnnsH7TjnlsGCpjOco.USxTZruFsIbB5FZOpntXrY045vOFkVkDh9pIU@9rwPBwy8KGIhBxrOLQ7ApLdpUnR4/2131102022.pdf.
147. Newton. 119. (Emphasis added.)
148. *Ibid.*
149. Armbrister. 275.
150. Newton. 119.
151. Armbrister. 26.
152. Memo to President Lyndon B. Johnson from Whitney Shoemaker: "Weekly Summary of Presidential Mail for the Week Ending February 8, 1968." February 9, 1968. Folder 06, Box 11, Larry Berman Collection (Presidential Archives Research), The Vietnam Center and Archive, Texas Tech University. Web. 29 October 2015. www.vietnam.ttu.edu/virtualarchive/items.php?item=0240922023.
153. Memo to President Lyndon B. Johnson from Whitney Shoemaker: "Weekly Summary of Presidential Mail for the Week Ending March 21, 1968. March 22, 1968. Folder 06, Box 11, Larry Berman Collection (Presidential Archives Research), The Vietnam Center and Archive, Texas Tech University. 29 October 2015. www.vietnam.ttu.edu/virtualarchive/items.php?item=0241106019.
154. Armbruster. 89.
155. *Ibid.* 89.
156. *Ibid.* 105.
157. *Ibid.* 85.
158. Armbruster. 257–258.
159. Paterson, Pat, LCDR, USN. "The Truth About Tonkin." *Naval History Magazine* February 2008, Vol. 22. No. 1. Anapolis. Web. 13 July 2016. www.usni.org/magazines/navalhistory/2000-02/truth-about-tonkin.
160. Armbruster. 92.
161. *Ibid.* 97.
162. *Ibid.* 95.

Chapter Four

1. Lerner, Mitchell. "A Failure of Perception: Lyndon Johnson, North Korean Ideology, and the *Pueblo* Incident." 647.
2. Christian, George. "Meeting at the State Department on the Pueblo." Notes dated January 24, 1968, Folder 11, Box 09, Larry Berman Collection (Presidential Archives Research), The Vietnam Center and Archive, Texas Tech University. Web. 2 Nov. 2015. http://www.vietnam.ttu.edu/virtualarchive/items.php?item=0240911018. Also in Tom Johnson's notes, LBJL. Box 2, Pueblo 3.
3. Cumings, Bruce. *Korea's Place in the Sun: A Modern History.* New York: W.W. Norton, 2005. Print. 22–40.
4. Lee. 108.
5. *Ibid.* 135–137.
6. Cumings, Bruce. *Korea's Place in the Sun: A Modern History.* New York: W.W. Norton, 2005. Print. 86–87. Also see the Taft/Katsura agreement of 1905, a telegram sent from Tokyo to President Theodore Roosevelt describes a verbal understanding between Japan and the United States in relation to American interests in the Philippines and Japanese interests in Korea. A copy and an explanation can be seen at www.dokdo-research.com/temp25.html.
7. Byung-joon, Ahn. "North Korean Foreign Policy: An Overview," in *The Foreign Relations of North Korea: New Perspectives.* Ed. Jae Kyu Park and Byung Chul Koh and Tae-Hwan Kwak. Seoul, Korea: Kyungnam University Press, 1987. 29. Print. Byung-joon also wrote that it was Stalin's intent to dominate Korea and make the country another communist satellite nation.
8. Fry, Michael. "National Geographic, Korea, and the 38th Parallel." *National Geographic,* August 4, 2013. Web. June 4, 2016. http://news.nationalgeographic.com/news/2013/08/130805-korean-war-dmz-armistice-38-parallel-html.
9. Cumings. 189.
10. Cumings, Bruce. *North Korea, Another Country.* New York: The New Press, 2004. 123. Print.
11. *Ibid.* 125.
12. Byung-joon, Ahn. 15–38.
13. Cumings. *North Korea, Another Country.* 159.
14. Feherenbach, T.R. *The Fight for Korea: From the War of 1950 to the* Pueblo *Incident.* New York: Grosset & Dunlap, 1969. 154. Print.
15. Koh, B.C. "The *Pueblo* Incident in Perspective." *Asian Survey,* vol. 9, no. 4, April 1969. 264–280. UTA Library. Web. Apr. 28, 2016. http://www.jstor.org/stable/2642545.
16. *Ibid.* However, Kim did not isolate North Korea from the Soviets or the Chinese. He traded with both, and in fact, played off of each of them in order to gain favor from both governments, even during periods when there were disagreements between the two major powers.
17. Kiyosaki, Wayne S. *North Korea's Foreign Relations: The Politics of Accommodation, 1945–75.* New York: Praeger, 1976. 24. Print.
18. Lerner. *The* Pueblo *Incident.* 103.
19. Author unknown. Global Security Organization. "Juche: Self-Reliance or Self-Dependence." Web. April 13, 2016. www.globalsecurity.org/military/world/dprk/juche.htm.
20. Park, Han S. "Juche as a Constraint." in *The Foreign Relations of North Korea: New Perspectives.* Ed. Jae Kyu Park and Byung Chul Koh and Tae-Hwan Kwak. Seoul, Korea: Kyungnam University Press, 1987. 74. Print.
21. French, Paul. *North Korea, the Paranoid Peninsula.* New York: ZED Books, 2005. 30–32. Print.
22. Lee, Grace. "The Political Philosophy of Juche." *Stanford Journal of East Asian Affairs.* vol. 3, no. 1, Spring 2003. 112. Web. June 6, 2016. https://stanford.edu/group/sjeaa/journal3/korea1.pdf.
23. Koh, B.C. 274.
24. Many sources also write "*Chuche*" for the word *Juche*. I have used the *Juche* spelling throughout this document.
25. Cumings. *Korea's Place in the Sun.* 196.
26. Some scholars also define *Juche* as "take charge-ism." Economist author Nicholas Eberstadt uses that term in his book, *Korea Approaches Reunification.*

Notes—Chapter Four

27. Downs, Chuck. *Over the Line: North Korea's Negotiating Strategy.* Washington: The AEI Press, 1999. 13. Print.
28. Lee. 111.
29. Lee. 106.
30. Lee. 106.
31. French. 30–32.
32. Cumings. 1.
33. French. 30–32.
34. Lee. 107.
35. French. 33–35.
36. Rummel, R.J. *Statistics of Democide: Genocide and Mass Murder Since 1900.* Center for National Security Law, School of Law, University of Virginia. Charlottesville, Virginia. 1997. Chap. 10. Web. June 8, 2016. https://www.hawaii.edu/powerkills/SOD.CHAP10.HTM.
37. *Ibid.*
38. Park, Han S. 77.
39. French. Chap. 10.
40. Norman, Greg. "Hungry North Korean Soldiers Are Being Given Leave to Find Food, Report Says." *Fox News.* January 2, 2018. Web. http://www.foxnews.com/world/2018/01/02/hungry-north-korean-soldiers-are-being-given-leave-to-find-food-report-says.html.
41. Koh, Byung Chul. "Foreign Policymaking Process" in *The Foreign Relations of North Korea: New Perspectives.* Ed. Jae Kyu Park and Byung Chul Koh and Tae-Hwan Kwak. Seoul, Korea: Kyungnam University Press, 1987. 45. Print.
42. French. 34.
43. Koh. 270–271.
44. Interestingly, those North Korean threats continue today, probably with the same intent as that of Kim Il-sung nearly fifty years ago.
45. Armbrister. 27.
46. Kiyosaki. 19–21.
47. Kiyosaki. 19–21.
48. Baek, Jong-Chun. 91.
49. Schindler, John R. "Cold War Disaster: The Loss of USS Pueblo." Web. Sept. 13, 2016. https://20committee.com/2012/11/30/cold-war-disaster-the-loss-of-uss-pueblo/. Schindler was a former professor of national security affairs at the U.S. Naval War College and spent a decade with the NSA as an intelligence analyst, and a senior fellow of the International History Institute at Boston University.
50. Lerner. "A Dangerous Miscalculation." 8. It is believed that the classified material and code machinery was given to the Soviet Union.
51. All referenced sources in my reading reveal that the *Pueblo* was well outside the North Korean territorial waters. North Korea claims 12 miles from their coast as their territorial waters. The *Pueblo*'s radar revealed that the ship was 15.8 miles from the nearest North Korean land. (For example, see *Bucher*, page 174.)
52. Koh, B.C. "The *Pueblo* Incident in Perspective." *Asian Survey*, vol. 9, no. 4 (Apr. 1969) 264–280. University of California Press. UTA Library. Web. Apr. 28, 2016. http://www.jstor.org/stable/2642545.
53. Lerner. "A Dangerous Miscalculation." 9.
54. Harris, Stephen R LCDR. *My Anchor Held.* Old Tappan, New Jersey: Fleming H. Revell, 1970. 10. Print.
55. Bucher, Lloyd M, CDR, USN, and Mark Rascovich. Pueblo *and* Bucher. London: Michael Joseph Publishing, 1970. 218. Print.
56. *Ibid.* 218–219.
57. Harris. 14.
58. Cheevers. 226.
59. Lerner. "A Dangerous Miscalculation." 9.
60. Bucher/Rascovitch. 231.
61. Harris. 20.
62. Harris. 32.
63. Harris. 33.
64. Armbrister. 251–254.
65. Armbrister. 256.
66. Cheevers. 135–136.
67. Armbrister. 269.
68. Armbrister. 269–272.
69. *Ibid.*
70. Harris. 28.
71. Bucher/Rascovitch. 257.
72. Lerner. "A Dangerous Miscalculation." 9.
73. *Ibid.* 258.
74. Schumacher/Wilson. 123.
75. Brandt. 119–121, and USS *Pueblo* organization at http://www.usspueblo.org/

Notes—Chapter Five

Pueblo_Incident/U.S._Reactions/U.S._Reactions.html.
76. Harris. 48.
77. Schumacher/Wilson. 17
78. Harris. 37.
79. Bucher/Rascovitch. 301.
80. Bucher/Rascovitch. 270.
81. Newton. 127.
82. Armbrister. 286–287.
83. *Ibid.*
84. Armbrister. 288.
85. Cheevers. 205–211.
86. Armbrister. 295.
87. Armbrister. 295.
88. Cheevers. 215.
89. Bucher/Rascovitch. 332.
90. Bucher/Rascovitch. 324.
91. Harris. 85.
92. Harris. 83.
93. Harris. 89.
94. Harris. 81–89.
95. Harris. 89.
96. Spaulding, Raymond C., Capt. U.S. Navy Medical Corps. "Some Experiences Reported by the Crew of the USS *Pueblo* and American Prisoners of War from Vietnam." *Proceedings* of the International Conference on Psychological Stress and Adjustment in Time of War and Peace. Presented in Tel Aviv, Israel, 6–10 January 1975. Print. 7.
97. *Ibid.* 8.
98. Schumacher/Wilson. 25.
99. Bucher/Rascovitch. 235.
100. Bucher/Rascovitch. 307–309.
101. *Ibid.* 309.
102. Bucher/Rascovitch. 263–264.
103. Harris. 79. Harris relates that these lines were in one or more of the many propaganda ideology films they were forced to watch.
104. Harris. 77.
105. Harris. 167–169.
106. Schumacher/Wilson. 170–171.
107. Harris. 33.

Chapter Five

1. Downs. ix–x.
2. Armbrister. 245–247.
3. Lerner. *The Pueblo Incident.*123–125; Armbrister. 246.
4. Armbrister. 245–246.
5. *Ibid.*
6. Staff. "Mar 1968—North Korean Seizure of U.S.S. *Pueblo*. Panmunjom Meetings of U.S. and North Korean Military Representatives. Increase in North Korean Attacks in Demilitarized Zone. North Korean Commando Raid on Seoul." *Keesings Record of World Events.* Vol. 14, March 1968. pg. 22585. Web. stanford.edu/group/tomzgroup/pmwiki/uploads/1379–1968–03-ks-c-Eyj.pdf.
7. Cheevers. 166.
8. Lerner. *The Pueblo Incident.* 123–125.
9. Kiyosaki. 83.
10. Downs. 13.
11. Downs. 3.
12. Griffiths, John C. *Hostage: The History, Facts & Reasoning Behind Hostage Taking.* London: Andre Deutsch Ltd. 2003. 7. Print.
13. Moments in U.S. Diplomatic History Staff. *The USS Pueblo Incident—Assassins in Seoul, A Spy Ship Captured.* Association for Diplomatic Studies and Training. Web. adst.org/2013/01/the-uss-pueblo-incident-assassins-in-seoul-a-spy-ship-captured/#.WjLp1_CnGM8>
14. Downs. 112–113.
15. Armbrister. 299.
16. Cheevers. 255.
17. Downs. 137.
18. Kriebel. 98.
19. *Ibid.* 99.
20. Armbrister. 328.
21. Armbrister. 333.
22. Cheevers. 254–255.
23. Armbrister. 335.
24. Lerner. "A Dangerous Miscalculation." 19.
25. Lerner. "A Dangerous Miscalculation." 20.
26. Downs. 142–146.
27. Schumacher/Wilson. 215–216.
28. Lerner. *The Pueblo Incident.* 219–220.
29. Cheevers. 273.
30. Kiyosaki. 83.
31. Downs. 145.
32. DPRK's KCNA: "Spy Ship Pueblo." News Release from Korean Central News

Agency. January 20, 2003. Web. Aug. 27, 2015. http://fas.org/irp/news/2003/01/dprk012003.html. Federation of American Scientists web site.

33. Lerner. "Acts of War: North Korea's 1968 Hijacking of USS *Pueblo* Was Part of a Long-Standing Pattern of Risky Military Adventurism." 32.

34. Mobley. "Lessons from the Capture of the USS *Pueblo* and the Shootdown of a U.S. Navy EC-121–1968 and 1969." 3. *Studies in Intelligence*. Vol 59, No. 1 (Extracts, March 2015) Web. accessed 3/9/16. www.cia.gov/library/center-for-the-study-intelligence/csi-studies/studies/vol-59-no-1/pdfs/Revisting-Pueblo-and-EC121.pdf.

35. Bolger. 90–91.

36. Kwak, Tae-Hwan. "North Korea and South Korea," in *The Foreign Relations of North Korea: New Perspectives*. Ed. Jae Kyu Park and Byung Chul Koh and Tae-Hwan Kwak. Seoul, Korea: Kyungnam University Press, 1987. 325. Print.

37. CIA Intelligence Information Cable dated May 8, 1968. LBJL. National Security Files, Country File, Asia and the Pacific. Box 256, Korean Memos and Cables.

38. Lerner. "A Dangerous Miscalculation." 16.

39. Lerner, Mitchell. "A Failure of Perception: Lyndon Johnson, North Korean Ideology, and the *Pueblo* Incident." 647–675.

40. Lerner. "A Dangerous Miscalculation." 7.

41. *Ibid.*

42. Kiyosaki. 87–88.

43. Staff author. "Kim Il-sung's New Military Adventurism." Directorate of Intelligence, Central Intelligence Agency. Intelligence Report dated November 26, 1968. pgs. 41–45. Web. Mar. 20, 2016. www.foia.cia.gov/sites/default/files/document_conversions/14/esau-39.pdf.

44. Kiyosaki. 25.

45. Clough, Ralph N. "The United States," in *The Foreign Relations of North Korea: New Perspectives*. Ed. Jae Kyu Park and Byung Chul Koh and Tae-Hwan Kwak. Seoul, Korea: Kyungnam University Press, 1987. 256. Print.

46. Koh, B.C. "The *Pueblo* Incident in Perspective." 275.

Chapter Six

1. "Executive Orders, Executive Order 10631—Code of Conduct for members of the Armed Forces of the United States." Accessed 9/18/17 at National Archives website. https://www.archives.gov/federal-register/codification/executive-order/10631.html.

2. Schumacher/Wilson. 102.

3. Armbrister. 352.

4. Cheevers. 294.

5. Bucher. *Bucher, My Story*. 377.

6. Armbruster. 98.

7. *Ibid.* 102.

8. *Ibid.* 105.

9. Armbrister. 358–364.

10. Stockdale. 14.

11. Stockdale. 15.

12. Armbrister. 370.

13. Armbrister. 372.

14. Cheevers. 302–306.

15. "The Pueblo Inquiry." March 17, 1969. *Wall Street Journal (1923–Current File)* Accessed at UTA Library. Sept. 9, 2016. Web. https://login.ezproxy.uta.edu/login?url=http://search.proquest.com.ezproxy.uta.edu/docview/133453556?accountif=7117.

16. Cheevers. 332–333.

17. Armbrister. 383–385.

18. Cheevers. 333.

19. Statement of John H. Chafee, Secretary of the Navy. May 6, 1969. Web. Accessed Aug. 19,2016 at www.usspueblo.org/Court_of_Inquiry/SecNav_chafee.html and Armbrister. 388.

20. Staff writer. "Navy's Anguish Over *Pueblo* Case Described in a Long-Secret Report." *The New York Times*. January 12, 1982. Web. www.nytimes.com/1982/01/12/us/no-headline-168651.html?pagewanted-print accessed Dec. 27, 2017.

21. Cheevers. 333.

Epilogue

1. Lerner. *The Pueblo Incident*. 233.

2. United States Assistant to the Pres-

ident for National, Security Affairs. 1969. "Retaliatory measures for downed reconnaissance plane and pueblo incident." UTA Library. Web. Jan. 17, 2016. https://login.ezproxy.uta.edu/login?url=http://search.proquest.com.exproxy.uta.edu/docview/1679096562?accountid=7117. This document records a telephone conversation between President Nixon and Henry Kissinger on April 15, 1969, at 6:30 p.m. discussing the possibility of capturing a North Korean fishing ship.

3. Bucher. 65, and Chap. IV.

4. Baek, Jong-Chun. "Military Capabilities" in *The Foreign Relations of North Korea: New Perspectives*. Ed. Jae Kyu Park and Byung Chul Koh and Tae-Hwan Kwak. Seoul, Korea: Kyungnam University Press, 1987. 94. Print.

5. "North Korea to Create Its Own Time Zone." *Fort Worth Star Telegram*. Aug. 8, 2015. Print.

6. "Video from N. Korea Simulates Nuclear Strike on Washington." *Star Telegram* (Fort Worth), 27 March 2016. A. Print.

7. Armbruster. 94.

8. "Crewman Duane Hodges Brought for Rites." *Eugene Register-Guard*. Friday, December 29, 1968. Web. Sept. 6, 2016. news.google.com/newspapers?nid=1310&dat=19681227&id=1QpWAAAAIBAJ&sjid=TeEDAAAAIBAJ&pg=2486,7059343.

9. Armbruster. 94.

10. Veteran Tributes organization. Web. Sept. 6, 2016. http://veterantributes.org/TributeDetail.php?recordID=1221.

11. Armbrister. 393.

12. Armbruster. 96.

13. Armbrister. 396.

14. The news of the capture of the two U.S. gunboats by Iran on Tuesday, January 12, 2016, was widely disseminated. Two articles concerning the incident are:

Allam, Hannah. "Iran Frees 10 U.S. Sailors After 16 Hours in Custody." *Star-Telegram* (Fort Worth) Washington Bureau 14 January 2016: A1. Print.

Baldor, Lolita C., and Robert Burns. *Associated Press*, "Defense Chief: U.S. Sailors Made an Error." *Star-Telegram* (Fort Worth), 15 January 2016: A11. Print.

15. "Navy Officer Fired Over Iran Incident." Associated Press. *Star Telegram* (Fort Worth), 13 May 2016. A11. Print.

Sources Consulted

Unpublished (Archival) Print Sources

Lyndon Baines Johnson Presidential Library, Austin, Texas.
National Security Files, Country Files, Asia and the Pacific, and Korea (Boxes 256–258).
National Security Files, Memos to the President (Volume 35, Box 19).
National Security Files, National Security Council Histories, *Pueblo* Crisis, 1968 (Boxes 27–30).
National Security Files, Intelligence File (*Pueblo*, Box 11).
Tom Johnson's Meeting Notes (Boxes 2–4 Conversations Regarding the USS *Pueblo*).

Unpublished (Archival) Digital Sources

The George Washington University Archives. The National Security Archive—Archive of Declassified U.S. Documents. National Security Agency Documents (USS *Pueblo* Documents, North Korea Documents, South Korea Documents; Copies of U.S. Navy Message Traffic re. USS *Pueblo*).
The George Washington University Archives. The National Security Archive—Archive of Declassified U.S. Documents. United States Cryptologic History, Special Series Crisis Collection (Volume 1. USS *Liberty* Documents).
Gerald R. Ford Presidential Library and Museum, Ann Arbor, Michigan (Documents regarding the USS *Pueblo*).
Larry Berman Collection, Box 9 Folder 11–12, and box 10 Folder 8; Box 11 Folder 6, and other *Pueblo* documents from the Texas Tech virtual archives.
Lyndon Baines Johnson Presidential Library (Oral Histories—E. Ross Adair Interviews; Oral History of Dean Rusk, Interview III, Tapes 1–19).
Texas Tech University Vietnam War Archives.
University of Rhode Island Special Collections (John H. Chafee Papers, Subgroup III).

Government Documents and Publications (Print)

Bolger, Daniel P., Major. "Scenes From an Unfinished War: Low-Intensity Conflict in Korea, 1966–1969." *Leavenworth Papers*. Combat Studies Institute Press. No. 19, July 1991.
Congressional Record. Washington, D.C. U.S. Government Printing Office. Various months and years of issue. University of Texas at Arlington Library.
Inquiry into the USS *Pueblo* and EC-121 Plane Incidents. *Hearings Before the Special Subcommittee on the U.S.S. Pueblo of the Committee on Armed Services, House of Representatives Ninety-First Congress*, First Session, 1969. Washington, D.C.: U.S. Government Printing Office, 1969.

Sources Consulted

Inquiry into the USS *Pueblo* and EC-121 Plane Incidents. *Report of the Special Subcommittee on the U.S.S.* Pueblo *of the Committee on Armed Services, House of Representatives Ninety-First Congress*, First Session, 1969. Washington, D.C.: U.S. Government Printing Office, 1969.

Strauch, Ralph E. "The Operational Assessment of Risk: A Case Study of the *Pueblo* Mission." Santa Monica, CA: Rand Corporation, March 1971. Prepared for United States Air Force Project Rand.

Government Documents and Publications (Digital)

Central Intelligence Agency, "Kim Il-sung's New Military Adventurism." Intelligence Report. November 26, 1968. CIA, Freedom of Information Act document web site.

Department of Defense Manpower Center. American War Library. (Troop strength data.) American War Library web site.

Central Intelligence Agency, "The President's Daily Brief." Various dates. CIA, Freedom of Information Act document web site.

Department of State. *Foreign Relations of the United States, 1964–1968.* Vol. XXIX, Part 1, Korea, document 133, 138, and others. State Department History web site.

Department of State. "U.S. Involvement in the Vietnam War: The Tet Offensive, 1968." State Department History web site.

Foster, John S. Memorandum from the Director of Defense Research and Engineering to Secretary of Defense McNamara, Dec. 7, 1967. State Department History web site.

Gerhard, William D. and Henry W. Millington. "Attack on a Sigint Collector, the U.S.S. *Liberty*," NSA Central Security Service. United States Cryptologic History, Special Series Crisis Collection, Vol. 1, 1981.

Goldberg, Arthur J. *Report of the United Nations Command to the United Nations on the Increase in Violations by North Korea of the Military Armistice Agreement in Korea.* Nov. 2, 1967. United Nations repository at un.org.

Meyer, J.A. "Comint—Hard Facts in the Cold War." date unknown. NSA document, NSA web site archives (Public Information Files).

National Archives. "Executive Orders, Executive Order 10631—Code of Conduct for Members of the Armed Forces of the United States."

National Archives. Various Pueblo related documents accessed at https://www.archives.gov Search "USS *Pueblo*."

National Security Agency Archives. Various *Pueblo* related documents accessed at University of Texas at Arlington Library online, ezproxy data base. and NSA archives at nsarchive.gwu.edu Search "USS *Pueblo*."

Newton, Robert E. "The Capture of the USS *Pueblo* and its Effect on SIGINT Operations." 1992. Center for Cryptologic History, NSA.

Sarantakes, Nicholas Evan. "The Quiet War: Combat Operations Along the Korean Demilitarized Zone, 1966–1969." *The Journal of Military History*, 64, April 2000. Written for the U.S. Naval War College. U.S. Naval War College web site.

Primary Published Sources

Bucher, Lloyd. *Bucher, My Story.* Garden City, NY: Doubleday, 1970.

Bucher, Lloyd M., Commander, USN, and Rascovitch, Mark. *Pueblo & Bucher.* London: Michael Joseph Ltd., 1971.

Harris, Stephen R., Lieutenant Commander, USN. *My Anchor Held.* Old Tappan, New Jersey: Fleming H. Revell, 1970.

Schumacher, Carl F., and George C. Wilson. *Bridge of No Return: The Ordeal of the U.S.S. Pueblo.* New York: Harcourt Brace Jovanovich, 1971.

Sources Consulted

Secondary Published Sources (Print)

Absher, Kenneth Michael, Michael C. Desch, Roman Popadiuk and the 2006 Bush School Master in Public and International Affairs Capstone Team. *Privileged and Confidential: The Secret History of the President's Intelligence Advisory Board.* Lexington: University Press of Kentucky, 2012.

Allam, Hannah. "Iran Frees 10 U.S. Sailors After 16 Hours in Custody." *Star Telegram* (Fort Worth), January 14, 2016.

Armbrister, Trevor. *A Matter of Accountability: The True Story of the Pueblo Affair.* Guilford, CT: The Lyons Press, 2004.

Baldor, Lolita C., and Robert Burns. "Defense Chief: U.S. Sailors Made an Error." *Star Telegram* (Fort Worth), January 15, 2016.

Bamford, James. *Body of Secrets; Anatomy of the Ultra-Secret National Security Agency.* New York: Anchor Books, 2002.

Blau, Peter M. *The Dynamics of Bureaucracy.* Chicago: University of Chicago Press, 1963.

Blau, Peter M., and Marshall W. Meyer. *Bureaucracy in Modern Society.* New York: McGraw-Hill, 1987.

Boston, Ward. "Time for the Truth About the *Liberty*." *San Diego Union Tribune,* June 8, 2007. *San Diego Union Tribune* archives.

Brandt, Ed. *The Last Voyage of USS* Pueblo. New York: W.W. Norton, 1969.

Califano, Joseph A. *The Triumph & Tragedy of Lyndon Johnson: The White House Years.* New York: Touchstone, 1991.

Cheevers, Jack. *Act of War: Lyndon Johnson, North Korea, and the Capture of the Spy Ship* Pueblo. New York: NAL Caliber, 2013.

Cohen, Warren I., and Nancy Bernkopf Tucker, eds. *Lyndon Johnson Confronts the World: American Foreign Policy 1963–1968.* New York: Press Syndicate of the University of Cambridge, 1994. (Nancy Bernkopf Tucker, "Lyndon Johnson: A Final Reckoning." Nancy Bernkopf Tucker, "Threats Opportunities, and Frustration in East Asia." Richard H. Immerman, "Lyndon Johnson and Vietnam." Walter LeFeber, "Johnson, Vietnam, and Tocqueville." Robert J. McMahon, "Disillusionment and Disengagement in South Asia.")

Cristol, A. Jay. *The Liberty Incident: The 1967 Israeli Attack on the U.S. Navy Spy Ship.* Washington: Brassey's, 2002.

Cumings, Bruce. *Korea's Place in the Sun: A Modern History.* New York: W.W. Norton, 2005.

Cumings, Bruce. *North Korea, Another Country.* New York: The New Press, 2004.

Dallek, Robert. *Flawed Giant: Lyndon Johnson and His Times, 1961–1973.* New York: Oxford University Press, 1998.

Downs, Chuck. *Over the Line: North Korea's Negotiating Strategy.* Washington: The AEI Press, 1999.

Fehrenbach, T.R. *The Fight for Korea: From the War of 1950 to the* Pueblo *Incident.* New York: Grosset & Dunlap, 1969.

French, Paul. *North Korea: The Paranoid Peninsula—A Modern History.* New York: ZED, 2007.

Gallery, Daniel V., Rear Admiral Ret. *The* Pueblo *Incident.* New York: Doubleday, 1970.

Griffiths, John C. *Hostage: The History, Facts & Reasoning Behind Hostage Taking.* London: Andre Deutsch, 2003.

Jacobson, Harold, and William Zimmerman, eds. *The Shaping of Foreign Policy.* New York: Atherton, 1969.

Kernell, Samuel, and Samuel L. Popkin, eds. *Chief of Staff: Twenty-Five Years of Managing the Presidency.* Berkeley: University of California Press, 1986.

Kiyosaki, Wayne S. *North Korea's Foreign Relations: The Politics of Accommodation, 1945–75.* New York: Praeger, 1976.

Sources Consulted

Lerner, Mitchell B. *The* Pueblo *Incident: A Spy Ship and the Failure of American Foreign Policy.* Lawrence: University of Kansas Press, 2002.
Liston, Robert A. *The* Pueblo *Surrender: A Covert Action by the National Security Agency.* New York: Bantam, 1991.
McGarvey, Patrick J. *C.I.A.: The Myth and the Madness.* New York: Saturday Review Press, 1972.
"Navy Officer Fired Over Iran Incident." Associated Press. *Star Telegram* (Fort Worth), May 13, 2016.
Owen, David. *The Politics of Defence.* New York: Taplinger, 1972.
Park, Jae Kyu, Byung Chul Koh and Tae-Hwan Kwak, eds. *The Foreign Relations of North Korea: New Perspectives.* Seoul, Korea: Kyungnam University Press, 1987. (Johg-Chun Baek, "Military Capabilities." Ahn Byung-joon, "North Korean Foreign Policy: An Overview." Ralph N. Clough, "North Korea and the United States." Byung Chul Koh, "Foreign Policymaking Process." Tae-Hwan Kwak, "North Korea and South Korea." Han S. Park, "Juche as a Constraint.")
Powers, Thomas. *Intelligence Wars: American Secret History from Hitler to Al-Qaeda.* New York: New York Review of Books, 2002.
"Video from N. Korea Simulates Nuclear Strike on Washington." *Star Telegram* (Fort Worth). March 27, 2016.

Secondary Published Sources (Digital)

Aldrich, George H. "Questions of International Law Raised by the Seizure of the U.S.S. Pueblo." *Proceedings of the American Society of International Law at Its Annual Meeting (1921–1969).* Vol. 63 (1969). University of Texas at Arlington Library—JSTOR data base.
Armbruster, William A. "The *Pueblo* Crisis and Public Opinion." *Naval War College Review.* Naval War College, Newport, RI. Vol. XXIII, No. 7, Mar. 1971.
Baldwin, Hanson W. "U.S. Military Weaknesses Are Underlined by *Pueblo* Incident." *New York Times.* March 24, 1968. University of Texas at Arlington Library. ezproxy data base.
Boston, Ward. "Time for the Truth About the *Liberty*." *San Diego Union Tribune*, June 8, 2007.
Butler, William E., Oliver J. Lissitzyn and Jerome Alan Cohen. "*Pueblo* Crisis: Some Critical Reflections." *Proceedings of the American Society of International Law at Its Annual Meeting (1921–1969)*, Vol. 63, Perspectives for International Legal Development. University of Texas at Arlington Library data bases, JSTOR.
Fry, Michael. "National Geographic, Korea, and the 38th Parallel." *National Geographic*, August 4, 2013. *National Geographic* web site.
Global Security Organization web site. "AGER 2 *Pueblo* (ex-FP 344, ex-FS 344, ex-AKL 44)." Other various *Pueblo* documents.
Grimes, William. "Antonio Prohias, 77, Drew 'Spy vs. Spy' Cartoon." *New York Times*, March 3, 1998.
History.com staff. "Vietnam War Protests." At History.com. Various articles regarding the student war protests during the 1960s and public opinion during the Vietnam war.
Hutchison, Phillip J. "Leadership as an Ideograph: A Rhetorical Analysis of Military Leadership Training Material." *Journal of Leadership Studies.* vol. 7. no. 3. 2013 Wiley Online Library. onlinelibrary.wiley.com/doi/10.1002/jls.21293/full.
Koh, B.C. "The *Pueblo* Incident in Perspective." *Asian Survey*, vol. 9, no. 4. April 1969. University of Texas at Arlington Library, JSTOR data base.
Kriebel, Wesley P. "Korea: The Military Armistice Commission 1965–1970." *Military*

Sources Consulted

Affairs, Vol. 36, no. 3 (Oct. 1972). University of Texas at Arlington Library, JSTOR data base.
Lee, Grace. "The Political Philosophy of Juche." *Stanford Journal of East Asian Affairs.* Vol. 3 No. 1. Spring 2003. Stanford University web site.
Lerner, Mitchell. "Acts of War: North Korea's 1968 Hijacking of USS *Pueblo* Was Part of a Long-Standing Pattern of Risky Military Adventurism." *Military History.* March 2010.
Lerner, Mitchell. "A Dangerous Miscalculation: New Evidence from Communist-Bloc Archives about North Korea and the Crisis of 1968." *Journal of Cold War Studies,* 6.1, 2004. University of Texas at Arlington Library online, Military and Government Collection.
Lerner, Mitchell. "A Failure of Perception: Lyndon Johnson, North Korean Ideology, and the *Pueblo* Incident." *Diplomatic History,* Vol. 25, No. 4, 2001. University of Texas at Arlington Library online, Military and Government Collection.
The *Liberty* Incident Web Site. Sponsored by A. Jay Cristol. A supplement to his book regarding the attack on the *Liberty.* Miami, FL. Several documents used, including copies of original Navy radio messages.
"Meet the Press" transcript of Secretaries Rusk and McNamara on Feb. 4, 1968. University of Texas at Arlington Library, serial solutions data base.
Mobley, Richard A. "Lessons from the Capture of the USS *Pueblo* and the Shootdown of a U.S. Navy EC-121, 1968 and 1969." *Studies in Intelligence,* Vol. 59, No. 1, (Extracts, March 2015) CIA web site.
Mobley, Richard A. *"Pueblo,* a Retrospective*." Naval War College Review.* Spring 2001, Vol. 54, No. 2.
"Navy's Anguish Over *Pueblo* Case Described in a Long-Secret Report." *New York Times.* Jan. 12, 1982. www.nytimes.com/1982/01/12/us/no-headline-168651.html?.
"North Korean Seizure of U.S.S. *Pueblo.* Panmunjom Meetings of U.S. and North Korean Military Representatives. Increase in North Korean Attacks in Demilitarized Zone. North Korean Commando Raid on Seoul." *Keesing's Record of World Events.* Vol. 14, March 1968. Pg. 22585. stanford.edu/group/tomzgroup/pmwiki/uploads/1379–1968–030ks-c-EyJ.pdf.
"Operational Orders," Dec. 18, 1967 0752Z, at USS *Pueblo* organization web site (usspueblo.org).
Paterson, Pat., LCDR. "The Truth About Tonkin." *Naval History Magazine.* Feb. 2008, Vol. 22, No. 1. U.S. Naval Institute web site.
Rummel, R.J. *Statistics of Democide: Genocide and Mass Murder Since 1900.* Center for National Security Law, School of Law, University of Virginia. Charlottesville, VA, 1997. At University of Hawaii web site.
Russian ships information at Russian-ships.info Information regarding types and roles of Russian war ships. Sponsored by Russian military enthusiasts.
"Sailing Orders," Dec. 18, 1967 0752Z, at USS *Pueblo* organization web site (usspueblo.org).
Smith, Richard K. "The Violation of the *Liberty." United States Naval Institute Proceedings.* June 1978.
Spaulding, Raymond C., Captain, U.S. Navy Medical Corps. "Some Experiences Reported by the Crew of the USS *Pueblo* and American Prisoners of War from Vietnam." Presented at and published by the *Proceedings of the International Conference on Psychological Stress and Adjustment in Time of War and Peace.* Tel Aviv, Israel. 6–10 January 1975. Print.
"Spy Ship *Pueblo*." News release from Korean Central News Agency. Jan. 20, 2003. Federation of American Scientists web site.
Stockdale, James Bond. "The Principles of Leadership." *American Educator.* date unknown. libguides.usna.edu/ld/0hp?content_id=17258864.

Sources Consulted

"3 G.I.'s Are Hurt by Seoul Raiders." *The New York Times.* (1923-current) Several other articles from *The New York Times* are referenced in footnotes. University of Texas at Arlington Library, ezproxy data base, JSTOR data base, and *New York Times* archives.

"Two Sent Back to North as Moles." *Korea Joongang Daily.* Feb. 6, 2012. Online daily Korean news feed at mengnews.joins.com.

USS *Pueblo* organization accessed at www.usspueblo.org. Web site sponsored by USS *Pueblo* veterans association. Many original and secondary documents related to the *Pueblo* capture, as well as many photographs.

Index

Numbers in **_bold italics_** indicate pages with illustrations

Abel, Elie 94
Albert, Carl 90
anti-war activities **_68_**, 69
Armbruster, William 2
Armistice Agreement 38, 101, 117, 136
Armistice Commission 37, 47, 66, 82, 94–95, 144–145
Auxiliary General Environmental Research (AGER) **_17_**–19, **_21_**
Auxiliary General Technical Research (AGTR) 8–**_9_**
Ayling, Charles 116

Balboa Naval Hospital 170
Baldridge, Herman 59, 122
Ball, George 86
Bamford, James 13, 41
USS *Banner* (AGER 1) 17–19, 31–33, 49, 51, 79, 163–164, 167
barn, North Korean prison **_56_**–57
Barron, James 60
Batrayev, Boris 82
Berens, Ronald **_120_**
Berger, Samuel 38, 66
Bergner, Allen A. 153, **_154_**–**_155_**
Bibee, David L. 37
Bishop, Robert 18
Bland, Howard 113, **_120_**
Blansett, Rushel **_145_**
Blau, Peter 8
Blue House 39, 42–**_43_**, 44–47, 63–64, 86, 108, 132, 137
Bonesteel, Charles 43, **_45_**–46, 63–65, 102, **_143_**
Boston, Ward 13
Bowen, Harold G. 153–**_154_**, 156, 159, 161

Bramford, James 41
Bray, William 89
Bremerton, Washington 19, 83
Bridge of No Return 139, 141–143
Bringle, William 61
Bucher, Lloyd: capture 50–54, 56; coerced confession 58, 74–75, 114; court of inquiry 153–154, **_155_**, 156, **_157_**, 159–162; imprisonment 56–59, 81, 113–114; viewed from the White House 74–75, 83–85, 95
Bucher, Rose 75
Bundy, McGeorge 14
bureaucratic inertia 48

USS *Canberra* 79
Carter, Jimmy 152
Carter, Marshall 41–42, 65
Cassell, George L. 23–24, 34, 60, 159
Center for Prisoner of War Studies, Naval Health Research Center 126
Central Communist Committee 125
Central Intelligence Agency (CIA) 62, 73–75, 81–84, 110–111, 129, 148, 166
Chafee, John 160–**_162_**
Chancellor, John 91
Cheevers, John "Jack" 35, 162
USS *Chesapeake* 60
Chicca, Robert **_145_**
Chief of Naval Operations (CNO) 15, 40–41, 61–62, 153
Choe Kyu-ha 38
Christian, George 74, 90
Christian Science Monitor 171
Ciccolella, Richard G. 37, 136
Clark, Charles 56
Clickbeetle 16–19

Index

Clifford, Clark 12, 66, 70, 77, 94
Clough, Ralph N. 150
Code of Conduct for U.S. Armed Forces 151–152
Cohen, Warren 1
Cold War 47, 72, 99, 108
Commander in Chief Pacific (CINCPAC) 23, 40–41
Commander in Chief Pacific Fleet (CINCPACFLT) 23, 41, 59–60, 62, 159
Commander Naval Forces Japan (CNFJ) 24, 41, 50, 53, 59–61, 163
Congressional Record 15, 36
coping skills of the Pueblo crew 126–127
Cronkite, Walter 70, 78
Cuba 4

Dallek, Robert 12, 69
Defense Intelligence Agency (DIA) 41, 63
Defense Research and Engineering 177
Demilitarized Zone (DMZ) 36–37, 42, 45–46, 48, 65, 71, 80, 82, 117, 132, 137, 139, 142, 166
Democratic Party 68–69
Democratic People's Republic of Korea (DPRK) 36, 77, 95, 108–109, 113, 118, 121, 128, 146, 166
Denham, John 80
Dirkson, Everett 84–85
Downs, Chuck 132

EC-121, U.S. spy plane 108, 147, 163
Edwards, Jack 89
Engels, Friedrich 103
Eisenhower, Dwight D. 77–78, 99
USS *Enterprise* 60, 67, 79–80
Epes, Horace 60
Eshleman, Edwin 160
Evening Star 92–93

farm, North Korean prison *57*, 121–122, 127
Father Flanagan's Boys Town 160
Fleming, Bob 90–91
Ford, Gerald 84–86
Fort Meade, Maryland 5
Fort Rosecrans National Cemetery 171
Foster, John S., Jr. 39
French, Paul 107

Fubini, Eugene 17
Fulbright, J. William 87

Gallup Poll 96
Geneva Convention of the High Seas 1958 26–27, 128
Gidrolog (Soviet ship) 80
Gladding, Everett 161
Goldberg, Arthur J. 38, 66, 75–77, 95
Goldman, Monroe *120*
Goodpaster, Andrew 77
Goodwin, Richard 72
Grimm, Edward E. 153–*154*, 161
Gromyko, Andrei 77
Gulf of Tonkin Incident 92, 97

Hall, Durward 88
Halpern, Seymour 15
Hammond, Robert 58–59
Hangul Bridge 142
Harris, Stephen 58, 115–116, 118–119, 125, 130, *144*, *157*, 161
Harris, Tim 154
Harvey, Miles 153–*155*, 158, 160
Hawaiian good luck sign 120
Helms, Richard 32, 66, 70, 73–74, 76–77
USS *Higbee* 79
Hodges, Duane 73, *141*–142, *146*, 168
House Armed Services Committee 32
Howze, Hamilton H. 136
Hutchinson, Phillip J. 28
Hyland, John 59, 60–62, 67, 153

Ideograph 28
Iredale, Harry *120*
Israeli Air Force 11–13
Israeli Navy 11–13

Japanese oppression 100–101
Jenerette, Vandon 39
Johnson, Frank L. 24–26, 31–35, 47, 60–61, 161
Johnson, Lyndon 12, 36, 44–46, 65–68, 70, 74, 77, 79, 81, 84–87, 90, 96, 99–100, 118, 128, 129, 135, 137, 142, 149, 150; Presidential Library 81
Johnson, Tom 79, 180–183
Joint Chiefs of Staff (JCS) 7, 41, 49, 65, 67, 87, 153, 164
Joint Reconnaissance Center (JRC) 8, 41
Juche (self-reliance) ideology of North

Index

Korea 3, 99, 100, 103–111, 113, 116, 123–126, 128–130, 132, 136, 137–138, 144, 147, 149, 167; *chaju* (political independence) 104, 132; *charip* (economic self-sustenance) 104; *chawi* (self-defense) 104–105, 107, 109, 116, 144

Kaiser, Henry 71
Kalugin, Olig 148
Kang Ban Sock 125
Katzenbach, Nicholas 32, 66, 74, 77, 100
Kempton, Murray 97
Kennedy, John F. 67, 81, 99
Kennedy, Robert 71, 124
Keys, James E. 154–*155*
Kidd, Isaac, Jr. 14
Kim Il-sung *101*; actions 42, 47, 95, 135, 147–150; history 100–105, 125; propaganda 106–109, 111, 113, 130, 140, 142, 144; warnings 36
Kim Jong-il 167
Kim Jong-un 167
Kim Kwang-hyop 78–79
King, Martin Luther, Jr. 70–72, 123–124
Kissinger, Henry 163
USS *Kittyhawk* 67
Kiyosaki, Wayne S. 108
Koh, B.C. 150
Korean Communist (KORCOM) 24–25, 129–130
Korean People's Army (KPA) 58, 102
Korean Workers Party (KWP) 36, 79, 103, 105, 167
Kosygin, Alexi 76, 82
Kuykendall, Daniel 89

Lacy, Gene 52, 127, *144*
Law, Charlie *120*, 122
Lawrence, David 92
Layton, James *120*
Leonard, Eleanor 138, 139
Leonard, James F. 138
Lerner, Mitchell 62, 75, 100, 148
USS *Liberty (AGTR 5)* 7–16, 163–165
Los Angeles Times 156
low intensity conflict (LIC) 38, 44, 47, 65

Mack, Lawrence 95
MAD Magazine 4
USS *Maddox* 97

Mansfield, Mike 69, 88
Mao Tse-tung 103
Maritime Commission, War Shipping Administration 8
Marxism-Leninism 103
Matsunaga, Spark 89
McCain, John S., Jr. 15–16
McCarthy, Joseph R. 99
McGarvey, Patrick 5, 48
McGonagle, William 11
McKee, Seth 59–60
McNamara, Robert S. 39–40, 47, 65–66, 70, 74–76, 84, 94–95
Medal of Honor 29
Meet the Press 94
Meyer, Marshall 8
Military Sea Transportation Service 9
Milwaukee Sentinel 93
Ministry of National Defense (MND), North Korea 52
Mitchell, John 163
Mobley, Richard A. 62
Moorer, Thomas 34–35, 47, 61–62
El Mundo 4
Murphy, Edward 58, 95, 98, 114–115, 159, 161

National Geographic 102
National Military Command Center 41
National Security Agency (NSA) 1, 9, 40–41, 47–48, 52, 61, 63, 65, 74–75, 84, 87, 114, 164–167; NSA Center for Cryptologic History 63
National Security Council (NSC) 74
Naval Air Station Miramar 168–169
Naval Investigative Support Office (NISO) 30
Naval Post-Graduate School, Monterrey, California 171
Naval Security Group, Pacific 161, 165
Naval War College Review 2
Navy Court of Inquiry (USS *Pueblo*) 2, 97, 153–154, 156, 159–161, 170
Nedzi, Lucien 33
New York Daily News 91
New York Post 97
New York Times 44, 92, 94, 98, 156, 161
Newsome, William *158*, 161
Newsweek 111–*112*
Newton, Robert E. 63
Nitze, Paul 32, 49, 66, 70, 74
Nixon, Richard M. 163

Index

Nodong Sinmun 135
North Korean Foreign Ministry 144
North Korean Ministry of National Defense (MND) 52
North Korean Navy (NKN) and Air Force 40, 52, 54, 58
North Korean prison "Rules for Life" 122
North Korean Propaganda 73, 92, 107, 109, 111–112, 117–118, 123–124, 129–131, 140, 142, *147*, 167

Office of Naval Intelligence (ONI) 5, 165
Office of Naval Intelligence Publications (ONIP) 165
Owen, David 48
USS *Oxford* 7
USS *Ozbourn* 79–80

Pacific Air Force Command Hawaii 60
Pak Chung-kuk 5, 127, *133*–139
Pak In-ho 146
USS *Palm Beach* 18, 22, 154–155
Panmunjom, Korea 82, 123, 144
Park, Han S. 106
Park Chung-hee 39, 42, *44*–46, 71–72, 148
Pearl Harbor, Hawaii 23
Pentagon East Asia Policy Office 132
People's Liberation Army (PLA) 86
Peppard, Donald *120*
Pike, Otis 34–35, 41
Porter, William 45, 65–66, 135
Pratt, Richard R. 153–*154*
Pravda 13
President's Foreign Intelligence Advisory Board 66
Prohias, Antonio 4
Protraktor (Soviet ship) 79
public sentiment 68–69, 71, 78, 96–98
Pyongyang, North Korea 48, 56, 66, 81–82, 89, 94, 121, 131, 139, 142, 146, 148–149
Pyongyang Times 58, 149

Radio Pyongyang 40, 42
Rand Corporation 32, 35
Rand Report 48
Rather, Dan 91
Ray, James Earl 70
Razvedka 6
Reader's Digest 156

Reagan, Ronald 87, 168, *169*
religious activities of *Pueblo* crew 125–126
Republic of Korea (ROK) 36, 38–39, 48, 64–65, 80, 102, 134, 148
Reynolds, Frank 91
Rhee, Syngman 102
Rhodes, John Jacob 15
Rivers, L. Mendel 87, 160
Rogers, Paul 89
Rogers, William 163
Rostow, Walt W. 32, 65–66, 74–76, 80–81, 84, 90
Rowan, Carl 91
Rule of the Sea 26, 34–35
Rummel, R.J. 105
Rusk, Dean 36, 38, 45, 65–66, 70, 74–76, 81, 84, 90, 92, 94–95, 102, 135, 139

San Diego, California 167–168, 170
San Diego Union Tribune 13, 68
Sankei Shimbun 42
Sarantakes, Nicholas 39
Scarborough, William *120*
Schumacher, Carl Frederick (Skip) 19, 22, 50, 53, 55, 58–59, 115, 117, 121, 127, 130, *144*
Sea of Japan 50, 71, 79, 164
Second Korean Conflict 36
Seoul, South Korea 42, 142
Sharp, Ulysses S. Grant 34, 66–67
Sidney, Hugh 93
Sikes, Robert Lee Fulton 15, 48–49
Simmons Victory 8–9
Sinchon Museum of American Atrocities 130
Sirhan, Sirhan 71
Slatinshek, Frank 34–35
Smith, Bromley 66
Smith, John V. 66, 95, 132–135, 137
Smith, Margaret Chase 168
Smith, Richard K. 11
SO-1 (Soviet ship) 50
South Korean Joint Chiefs of Staff 64
Soviet Committee for State Security (KGB) 82
Spaulding, Raymond C. 126–127
Spivak, Lawarence 95
Stalin, Joseph 103
Stennis, John 87
Stimson, Henry L. 4–5
Stockdale, James B. 29–31, 158

198

Index

Strauch, Ralph 32–33, 35, 48
Students for a Democratic Society (SDS) 68
Suryong 102

Taedong River, Pyongyang, North Korea 146; USS *Pueblo* Museum (North Korea) *147*
Taylor, Maxwell 66, 84
Tet Offensive 70–71, 78–79
three A's 137–140
303 Committee 31
Thurmond, Strom 87–88
Time Magazine 93
Tooma, Sam 18
Truman, Harry 99
Tsushima Strait 25, 79
Tuck, Dunnie, Jr. 58, 118
Tucker, Nancy Bernkopf 1, 72
USS *Turner Joy* 97

Ulchin, South Korea 137
United Nations (UN) 84, 89
United Nations Command (UNC) 136–137
UN General Assembly 78

UN Security Council 38, 75–76, 78, 82, 94
U.S. Department of Defense (DOD) 5, 90, 96
U.S. Embassy, Seoul, Korea 42
United States News 92
University of Nebraska 160

Vance, Cyrus 45–46
Vandenburg Air Force Base 6

Walker spy ring 62
Wall Street Journal 160
Washington Evening Star 92
Washington Post 156
Westmoreland, William C. 46
Wheeler, Earl 44, 49, 66–67, 73, 77, 84
White, Marshall W. 153–*154*
Wilson, Bob 69, 88
Wonsan, North Korea 51–52, 54–55, 60–61, 66, 76–77, 80, 110–111, 134
Woodward, Gilbert 38, *133*–135, 137–*140*

Yellow Sea 18
Yokosuka, Japan 79
Young, Stephen 123

199